First published in 1994
by Bellevue Books.

Bellevue Books,
Unit E4, Sunbury International Business Centre
Brooklands Close, Sunbury On Thames, Middlesex TW16 7DX.
England.

© David R. Wood & Ian Campbell 1994.

British Library Cataloguing in Publication Data.

A CIP record of this book is available from the British Library.

ISBN 1 873335 03 2

Printed in England.

CONTENTS

PREFACE.

Despite its territorial conquests and aspirations, the Roman Empire was not only tolerant, but even respectful of the cultures of those who succumbed to its military prowess. Rome became a centre of learning where science and philosophy could flourish.

Regrettably with the transformation of the Roman Empire into the Holy Roman Empire, this intellectual freedom was lost. It was replaced by a period of ecclesiastical despotism which stifled Man's progress for hundreds of years and in general terms is referred to as the Dark Ages.

The wisdom and records of thousands of years of classical civilization were either destroyed, suppressed or rewritten to conform to the teachings of the Roman Church. Thus progressive Man died until the Renaissance which some historians date from the invention of printing in 1440 AD. The beginning of the Renaissance was, however, initially confined to architecture and the arts; science, particularly astronomy and anthropology, was still required to conform.

A typical example of this, as late as 1616, was the persecution of Galileo. The church had decided that the findings of the Greek astronomer Hipparchus were acceptable. Simply,this stated that God's Earth was the centre of the universe and that every celestial body rotated round the planet upon which he had created Man. This theory was developed and published by Claudius Ptolemaus in "The Great Astronomer". With the support of the Church, 'geocentricity' lasted over one thousand years and none would dare to contest it.

Nevertheless, a Polish astronomer, Nicolaus Copernicus published in 1543 the heretical *De Revolutionibus Orbium Coelestium*, in which he had the audacity to state that the Sun was the centre of the Solar System. It is not difficult to imagine what would have happened to that learned gentleman if he had lived in Rome.

Knowing that Galileo was supportive of the 'heliocentric' theory, Cardinal Bellarmine warned him neither to "hold nor defend" the heretical doctrine and henceforth he issued a decree stating it to be "false and erroneous". Knowing better than to argue the point, Galileo retired gracefully to continue his studies privately.

Several years later, with a new Pope in office, Galileo pleaded with the Church to withdraw the ridiculous decree of 1616. They naturally refused, but gave him permission to write a comparison of the geocentric and heliocentric systems on the condition that his work did not favour the latter.

Eventually, Galileo produced the "Dialogue of the Two Chief World Systems", which was universally acclaimed as a masterpiece. The Jesuits were infuriated, claiming that the work supported the Copernican theory and was more damaging than "Luther and Calvin put together". By a clever piece of fraudulent rewriting of the original license, it was possible to prosecute Galileo for "vehement suspicion of heresy" and place him under house arrest for the rest of his life.

Equally heretical was the suggestion that their omnipotent God would hurl missiles at the planet upon which he had established his Church. In fact, it requires very little imagination to see that the publication of such a threat would be considerably more damaging to the established doctrine than the heliocentric theory. Furthermore, the threat would be realised to be continuous, with each 'safe' century only bringing Mankind nearer to his inevitable demise. Obviously here was something which must continue to be 'overlooked' at any cost and which could never be rationalized. Even more ominous is the fact that here we are dealing with something which governments would also prefer to remain unpublicized. So apparently random are the movements of asteroids and comets that it is comparatively simple to ignore them as items unworthy of research, until they are literally on our doorstep. If on the other hand, a method existed of accurately determining an impact years ahead, would this knowledge be divulged to the general public? The authorities could justifiably consider that it would result in a break-down of law and order.

Any number of examples of covert action by governments have come to light in recent years and they have been of far less importance than the possibility of the wholesale destruction which would result from a large cometary impact.

It would certainly appear that the general public are once again being subjected to another 'Dark Age', but this time by a totally different agency.

Over the past 50 years the major part of Man's ingenuity has been directed towards the scientific development of surveillance techniques, weapons of destruction and the means by which to deliver them to our fellow creatures. As inevitable as that scenario seemed at the time, in hindsight it could now be considered to have been largely wasted effort. Could we not now direct that expertise to ensuring the survival of our species?

Certain informed and outspoken scientists have already pointed out the danger of ignoring the existence of the threat. Furthermore, some have examined information recorded in so-called 'legendary' encounters with those 'serpents of the sky' which date back to pre-Dark Age times. There now appears to be overwhelming evidence of cataclysmic events in the remote past and this book examines one such fragment which has not only been ingeniously designed to survive suppression, but has also been preserved by comparatively recent custodians.

Here you will see the self-evident proof that the danger has always been known and how that information was concealed in cipher to prevent its destruction by those who would prefer it to remain unknown. Nevertheless, by the time this book goes to press the largest astronomical explosion in the solar system since the origin of man will be imminent. On or about the 20th of July 1994 Comet Shoemaker-Levy will impact the planet Jupiter and in the preceding months the public will be 'fed' a variety of scenarios of information and disinformation as to whether Earth itself could ever suffer such an impact. Rest assured it could!

INTRODUCTION.

IN recent years, the story of Rennes-le-Château has received sufficient exposure to attract and retain a large number of readers, who have kept themselves informed of the findings of the numerous investigators of the mystery.

Any number of books on the subject have been written in a manner which presumes the reader already has a working knowledge of the subject. The authors of those books and the thousands who have taken a deep or even passing interest, are inclined to overlook the fact that they make references to items with which they are familiar, but of which the new reader has no knowledge.

Indeed, to produce a comprehensive work containing all the related material in one volume would result in something akin to an encyclopedia. For this reason we have given our readers a bibliography of books written in English and French, which embrace all the known ingredients of the story of Rennes-le-Château. Much that is contained in them has subsequently been found to be in error, but the reader may still find value in following the trails which the authors have followed with such tenacity.

One could even learn a good deal by classifying not only the material, but also the motives of the authors. Some present a considerable amount of historical fact, others have laced certain of these together with their own imaginative interpretations. With few exceptions, however, very little of the history referred to can be confirmed. Certain authors have followed what appeared to be genuine leads and published their research, only to find they had been intentionally misled by those who would prefer the mysteries of Rennes-le-Château to remain unsolved.

Only one book, *GENISIS, The First Book of Revelations*, looked beyond the historical facade in an attempt to discover why the valley of Rennes-le-Château had attracted so much attention in the past. Using a totally different approach, the author discovered something quite remarkable which had totally escaped the notice of the other investigators. Furthermore, what he found could and still can be confirmed. All that was needed was an absolute proof of his findings and after years of intensive analysis that proof is now available in this book.

For the sake of new readers, let us now give a brief outline of where and what is Rennes-le-Château. Having lived with the mystery for fifteen years, it is difficult to revert to the position of being totally unaware and then introduce a newcomer to the complexities of all that is involved. We must, however, attempt to assume that position and would ask the readers who are more

LOCATION MAP OF RENNES LE CHATEAU

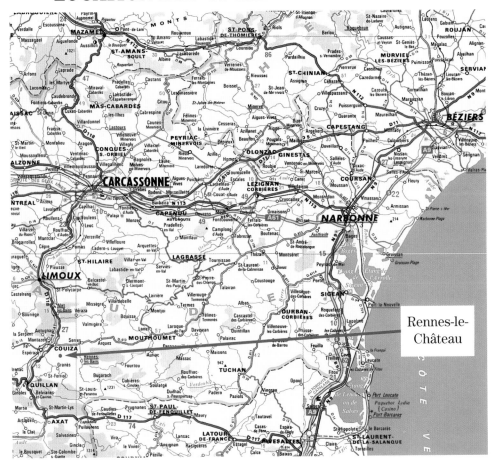

informed to pass by this introduction.

The small mountain-top village of Rennes-le-Château was, until quite recently, so unimportant as to seldom, if ever, be marked on road maps. Initially, therefore, reference to the map (see illustration), will serve to put you in the right place in France. Once there you may refine your whereabouts by using the two 1:25,000 I.G.N. maps of the area (ARQUES 2347 est and QUILLAN 2347 ouest). Even a cursory browse over the place names will serve to arouse your curiosity. The Valley of God, The Dead Man, The Seat of the Devil, The Circle, The White Fort, The Black Rock, The Serpent, Arques (Ark); already the imagination begins the task of conjuring up scenarios which would accommodate such extremes.

Inevitably, you feel there is more to this area than meets the eye and you are right! As we have said, the bibliography of this book will serve to show there is any amount of associated material which has been gathered under the conglomerate banner of Rennes-le-Château.

At first it seems impossible that an insignificant village could attract so much attention through the ages. The tentacles of the mystery spread not only worldwide, but back in time to encompass countless other events which are also shrouded in mystery. Druids, Celts, Romans, Visigoths, Merovingians, Knights Templar and Cathars parade through the history of the valley until the year 1209. In that year, Pope Innocent III sent an army to exterminate the majority of the population in the whole of the Languedoc. This once thriving region became a sparsely populated wasteland and has remained so ever since.

Nothing was then heard of the area until 1885 when a priest, Bérenger Saunière, was appointed to the derelict church at Rennes-le-Château. In the process of renovating it, he discovered 'something' - supposedly coded documents. He then, apparently, became wealthy enough to adopt an extravagant life style and complete the renovation of the church in a lavish, but strange manner. Statues and decoration hinting at Pagan and alchemical doctrine remain there to this day.

It is the investigations into the life of this priest and his associates which have dominated a considerable amount of the current literature. Hand in hand with those enquiries, is the speculation as to whether he unearthed a vast treasure and if so, what it was. Treasure hunting has always been a subject which can be guaranteed to attract a vast number of people. It did, and the history of the valley provided any number of possible treasures. These ranged from the material, in the form of gold and jewels, to secrets of the occult and esoteric.

The treasures of the Temple of Solomon, including the Ark of the Covenant, the Holy Grail, the gold of the Visigoths, the lost hoards of the Knights Templar and the secrets of the gnostic Cathars can all be speculatively traced to the region, and sometimes with good reason.

Following in the footsteps of the enigmatic priest of Rennes-le-Château and fourteen years after his mysterious death, one Otto Rahn began to search the Cathar fortress of Montségur and the surrounding area for the Treasure of Solomon and the Holy Grail. He was apparently operating under the direct instructions of those infamous founders of the Third Reich, Himmler and Rosenberg. His mission, echoed by Spielberg's film "Raiders of the Lost Ark", was to secure and steal these treasures for Germany.

This, of course, brings our mystery into very recent times and also adds considerable weight to the treasure theories. We would certainly not dismiss

12

the story, and being duty bound to present the whole picture, we will deal with it in more detail later.

Even more tenuous, but certainly worthy of examination, is the possibility of Time being one of the factors involved in the mystery. Elizabeth van Buren goes as far as to refer to it as the 'Temple of Time' and many authors have hinted at the Comte de St. Germain being a time traveller of sorts. Electro-gravitics and 'Time-Slips', accidental or otherwise, have permeated through the curtain of electromagnetic hyperspace. Bruce Cathie's *Bridge to Infinity* exposes to the layman, relationships between Time and force-fields which would previously have remained in a realm of mathematics beyond the conceptual.

Once again, to be sure we leave no stone unturned, we have referred to one of the greatest Time mystery stories which has a considerable scientific grounding - The Philadelphia Experiment. With all these apparently unrelated items we begin to see the possibility of Rennes-le-Château being, not only the drawing board of the gods, but possibly a geometric receiving station.

Sceptics will immediately ignore these possibilities as groundless, but they could never lightly dismiss what this book will reveal. Here, the reader will see irrefutable evidence of the famous French author, Jules Verne, covertly displaying that he was in possession of at least some of the salient features of the secret of Rennes-le-Château. A secret which we can now conclusively prove was also known to Nicolas Poussin, the artist who it is universally agreed, was deeply involved in the whole affair.

Modern scientific discoveries, particularly in the field of astronomy, now begin to produce the evidence which validates the concern of those who would have been ridiculed in their time for disclosing such a secret. It is also doubtful that even in comparatively recent times, the trigonometrical analysis of the Temple of Rennes-le-Château could have been achieved without computers or accurate mapping. Nevertheless, despite its accuracy and ingenuity, the design is extremely old. It probably has its roots in ancient Egypt or even earlier, but the evidence presented in this book can still be seen and confirmed to this very day. Simply join the two 1:25,000 maps referred to earlier and mount them on to a firm support. With simple drawing instruments, the reader may then plot the geometric Temple of Rennes-le-Château (see appendices 1,2 and 3). For those who prefer to work with computers, the plot may be transferred to a CAD system such as 'Generic-3', which is ideally suited to delve deeper into the mystery than we have space to convey in this book. So informed, the reader may now enter the arena of the mystery of Rennes-le-Château.

CHAPTER 1.
THE ONGOING MYSTERY (David Wood)

*An outline of the investigation. Some thoughts on what the
geometry means. How old could it be? A variation by mistake
or intention?*

T HE word universally applied to Rennes-le-Château is mystery, which can
be defined in various ways. It can mean 'only known to those who have
been initiated', or 'hidden from human knowledge and inspiring awe', or
'intentionally hidden' and finally it can mean a trade, craft or calling.
Dependent upon one's viewpoint, Rennes-le-Château most certainly qualifies in
one or other of these categories. Considering the quantity of material
published about it, even the last definition is valid, for Rennes-le-Château has
literally become an industry. In this respect the industry encompasses a host of
subordinate interests. None of these taken individually could be the 'raison
d'être', but when one considers the degree of fascination generated by several
authors and their diverse interpretation of events, one wonders whether it is in
their interests to ensure that the mysteries are never solved.

In the pot-pourri of Rennes-le-Château we find history, politics, religion,
masonry, mythology, geometry and a good deal more, all interwoven in an
inextricable web of cipher and disinformation which still seems to prevail.

My particular agent provocateur was Henry Lincoln and the BBC Chronicle
programme 'The Priest, the Painter and the Devil'. Here I found a facet of the
mystery to which I could apply my particular talents of trigonometrical and
aerial surveying.

Lincoln had demonstrated the possible existence of a loosely pentagonal
shape as a ground feature in the vicinity of Rennes-le-Château. He posed the
question of the Pentacle (Pentagram) to Monsieur Plantard* who replied:-

"I cannot answer that".

This answer coupled with other pentagonal clues caused Lincoln to ponder
on the well-known possibility of geometric shapes possessing power. He
closed by saying :-

"I do not know. Perhaps in some ways I do not want to know". Contrary to
Lincoln I did, and there began my geometric analysis of Rennes-le-Château.

Armed with a theodolite and the best mapping available, I set off for the
South of France. On my return, I converted a bedroom into a drawing office
and started plotting. I reproduced stable monochromes of the mapping and
created a temperature controlled area to obviate any paper stretch of the maps
which I had mounted on a non-shrink base. Then back to Rennes-le-Château

---

* *Supposedly Secretary General of the 'Prieuré de Sion'.*

THE CIRCLE OF CHURCHES: PENTAGRAM: MERIDIAN

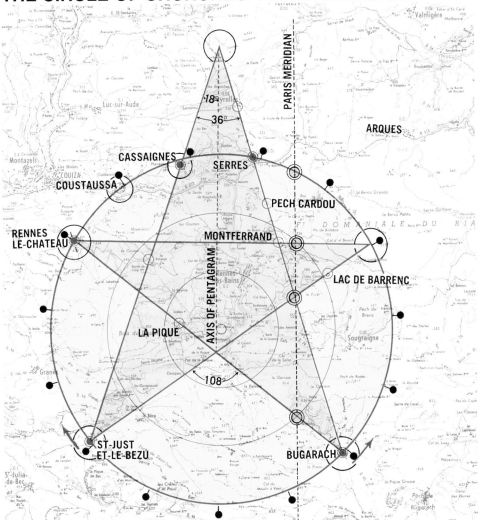

FIG. 1 This figure shows churches and other important features connected to the mystery superimposed on a 1:25,000 map. Note how these have been used to generate the extended pentagram. Note also the remarkable correspondences which occur between the Paris Meridian, the pentagram and the intermediate radii of the Circle of Churches. The black markers are the **15** mathematical divisions of the circumference required to produce a perfect theoretical pentagram, but one which lacks the remarkable Phi controls of the figure on the ground.

for more measurements. The breakthrough occurred when I identified a circle of features which formed a perfect circle. These were châteaux, churches and outstanding rock features, most of which had already been closely associated with the mystery. I then discovered that the positions of these features also disclosed something far more profound; a unique form of pentagram (see Fig. 1), the description of which is explained in *GENISIS, The First Book of Revelations*. The publisher, who was fully aware of my investigations decided it was ready to go to print, even though he considered a good deal of the mathematical material was too involved to present to the general public. When *GENISIS* finally took shape, much of what I considered essential had been removed. Nevertheless, I considered I had made a valuable contribution to the solution of the mystery and I continued with confirming and refining my calculations; a lonely and frustrating process.

As I was already working 'inside' map measure, the calculations were becoming lengthy and tedious. The only solution was to transfer the work to a computer and have the advantage of using some recently developed CAD (Computer Aided Design), software with mapping capability.

In the years that followed, various interested parties visited my home to observe my progress and I presented some of my findings in R.I.L.K.O (Research into Lost Knowledge Organisation) lectures. My audience at these lectures were informed people with a far greater understanding of the fringe information associated with the mystery than the average public and their response encouraged me to continue.

Then one day, one of my early sceptics, Ian Campbell, arrived with a large smile and said:- "You are right, aren't you?" That was the beginning of the close association between my co-author and myself. He had acquired the necessary maps and with a CAD computer program had been quietly checking my geometry himself, and that is the only way to fully appreciate the ingenuity involved in its design.

At last I had someone who fully appreciated the mathematics and was equally disciplined in his calculations. 'Near enough', the password of previous investigators, was not good enough for us. We sought mathematical perfection and we found it! Together we probed deeper and deeper into the complexities of the mystery.

As the readers of *GENISIS* will know, the identification of the geometry of Rennes-le-Château was initially achieved by the analysis of the relative positions of churches, ancient châteaux and outstanding rock features. How, one may ask, can pin-point accuracy be achieved when measuring from church to church, or château to mountain peak? Where in the church or on the mountain peak, is the position to measure to ?

To understand this, the reader must appreciate scale. Given sufficient magnification, the human hair or even microscopic detail, can be precisely measured. The reverse is also true. A diagram sufficiently magnified and marked on the ground can then be reduced to workable proportions and exhibit incredible accuracy. In the case of Rennes-le-Château, we have a diagram with a diagonal measure of some nine and a half miles being reduced to twenty four inches of map measure and the small church of some forty feet in length would be reproduced on the 1:25,000 map as no more than one fiftieth of an inch. Smaller than normal ruler measurements on paper cannot be reasonably expected to hold true, particularly when one considers the vagaries involved in map printing from the cylinder of a lithographic printing machine and the possibility of paper movement by the absorption of water vapour in the air.

In the case of a mountain top we are more fortunate, as thanks to surveying practice, it is usual to mark the highest location on a mountain with a spot-height. In certain cases they may be trig-points, which are found at the apices of trigonometrically calculated triangles. These form the basic matrix of large scale land surveying referred to as triangulation. The advantage of these points is that they can be guaranteed to replicate on a map the precise ground position, and they thereby obviate some of the inaccuracies inherent in representing other features at a reduced scale. The trig-points are, of course, chosen as positions from which observations can be taken with a theodolite and they are, as a consequence, either at, or close to the apex of the mountain. These trig positions are chosen as the most favourable sighting points and may well have been the same, or close to, those which an ancient intelligence may have decided to use for alignments and intersections or something more significant.

These positions and the permanence of other natural (or manipulated) rock features would have restricted the choice of sites upon which the 'constructed' markers could be built in order to conform to the required geometric pattern being achieved. These buildings were, nevertheless, necessarily so positioned as to be considered reasonable for the purpose for which they were designed. Furthermore, as will be seen, they were not placed so obviously that all and sundry would have recognised the ground pattern they were meant to preserve.

It would also appear that the minimum number of markers were selected to be able not only to preserve the main geometric figure, but in many cases also to indicate a secondary level of geometry and the nature of its interaction with the first. To achieve this, a rapidly undulating terrain was necessary and this possibly explains, amongst other reasons, why this particular area was chosen.

The claims that the arrangement of the sites could have been coincidental may be immediately dismissed by two important factors:-

1. A number of the markers control the size and position of a perfect Circle of Churches and outstanding rock features.

2. Their positions on the circumference determine a special pentagonal figure which, to date, appears to have never been previously identified, but displays mathematical properties closely associated with the mystery (see Fig. 1).

This unique pentagonal figure varies only in minute detail from one that is geometrically symmetrical and it also exhibits special features which mark it as having equally significant doctrinal implications.

These features together with their historical and geometric connections may well explain the disproportionate attention the area received in bygone ages.

A vast amount has been written, speculating as to what might be buried in the area sufficient to have attracted such organisations as the Cathars, the Knights Templar and the Roman Catholic Church. Ignoring this wealth of speculation, examination of the geometry described in this book will prove an intentional design, spectacularly impossible to have occurred by chance.

Having convinced ourselves of this, it was our objective to establish its purpose and to do that, we would be well served to know when it was constructed.

I had attempted to date the design, and the results of my enquiries to this end may be found in *GENISIS - The First Book of Revelations*. There can be little doubt that it is of great antiquity and one must, therefore, consider whether its purpose was contemporary to those times, or whether it was intended to be discovered at a later period. Certainly the subtlety of the markers strongly indicates the latter. So contrived is the method of determining the geometric shapes that one is forced to consider an implied secrecy - information which should not be easily discernible to a casual observer. In fact, it is a design which would never have become obvious before the perfection of sophisticated mapping techniques and even then, only with prior knowledge of the figures and ratios associated with the doctrine of the Ancients.

Considering the ingenuity and intelligence of the designers, it is reasonable to assume that they would have anticipated changes in units of measure and therefore, if they required to convey actual numerical data, they would also have to acquaint the discoverer with the unit of measure they required him to use.

Alternatively, or in conjunction with this, they could guarantee perpetuity of understanding by the interaction of axiomatics such as Pi, Phi and the trigonometrical ratios.

Again - with the premise of the great antiquity and with the anticipation of the durability of the 360 degree circle - they could demonstrate geometric figures where angular and linear relationships exist which would alert an observer to the existence of a pattern so repetitive as to deny that it could have occurred by chance.

All this would by necessity assume a certain threshold of intelligence prior to any recognition whatsoever on the part of the discoverer. The question then arises as to what the intention of the designers might have been. It is extremely unlikely that it is an 'exhibition piece' to demonstrate their mathematical prowess and that it is not so, will become more obvious as the solution proceeds. On the other hand, the figure and the complexity of its variations obviate the possibility of it having been designed to introduce a primitive mind to the subjects of geometry and mathematics. In fact, it could be argued that this 'missile from the past' is aimed specifically at a moment in time when the intended recipients would be prepared to recognise it, and moreover this recognition would cause it to home in on to a precise chronological target. Examination of the extent of our sciences may well hold the key as to why our time is the target time.

Here we seem to be presuming the existence of a superior intelligence having lived in remote times, or even that a civilisation was passing down information from remoter times, without necessarily having a full understanding of the content of the material they were preserving.

If this is indeed the case, the diagram must contain information which is identifiable with that on the very fringe of modern technology and furthermore should demonstrate relationships which are, at this time, unrecognisable but also undeniably of importance to future technology. They would also probably be found to occur with sufficient emphasis for the discoverer to be alerted to their possible function, despite his ignorance of their exactitude.

Here, too, it could be considered that this logic is suspect, by virtue of its Ptolemaic attitude in a chronological sense, but when one remembers that 'any time' could have been the 'target time', the objection dissolves. The time was always to be determined by the progress of the species, and its failure to progress sufficiently would be the measure of whether it deserved to be rewarded with the inherent message.

It could be a far more potent question, to ask why the designers thought there would be a specific point in the progression of Mankind where they anticipated that their assistance would be required to advance our species or even help it to survive.

Why, for example, was the diagram not indicative of the use of electricity - demonstrating formulae of inductance, resistance and the like? The answer is possibly because this force manifests in nature and would, therefore, be bound to have been investigated and harnessed.

The vast majority of our progress stems from related scientific discovery, but is there a point at which the very laws by which we quantify our results cease to function? Could it be that unless this point is passed, this barrier broken and this cage opened, that scientific progress would stagnate?

Not stagnate by virtue of Man losing the pioneering spirit, but because he would not by sophistication of his related sciences ever stumble, by chance or endeavour, or even desire, across a bridge so frail and tenuous as to appear incapable of supporting his tediously acquired tool-kit of scientific data.

Would this not be the abyss, which Man would need assistance to cross over and would it not be obvious to place a signpost on the edge of that abyss, to be read only when one reached it - regardless of when?

Another possibility which we would be foolhardy to ignore, is that the designers were adept in calculating the orbits of celestial bodies. By this, we do not refer to the planetary movements which are presently understood, but to those far beyond the range of our telescopes or sufficiently random as to be beyond our ability to predict scientifically. These were the celestial bodies which they knew would return and could terminate the growth of the only intelligent species remaining in our system. This factor was hinted at in *GENISIS* and as we continued our investigation, we knew we would need to be alert to this and the many other possibilities which may present themselves. As we will discuss later, one of these could also concern 'the final frontier' - Time.

Returning to the geometry of Rennes-le-Château, we are at first sight confronted with what appears to be a symmetrical pentagonal shape so arranged as to cause one point to penetrate the circle which forms the cradle for the remaining four.

The points which generate and control this figure are with one exception outstanding features in the topography of the area, ancient châteaux and churches built on Druid sites. At the time, this 'over- building' was considered to be a method of purifying Pagan sites, but ironically this process has actually perpetuated the locations which we now know were so placed as to establish a geometric message. This figure, extending over some forty square miles of mountainous terrain with difficult intervisibility, could never have been recognised - much less constructed - prior to the development of air survey techniques and triangulation methods.

Initially, the pentagonal figure appears to be perfectly symmetrical, but on close examination the pentagram has been caused to rotate slightly. The measure of this rotation can be seen in the variation between the axis of the pentagram and a line constructed from the centre of the circle to the apex of the pentagram which breaks the circle. The feet and hands have been confined within the circle (see Fig. 1).

My first assumption was that the designers had attempted to create a perfectly symmetrical figure. The apparent inaccuracies were, I believed, due to poor instruments and the difficult terrain. If this had been the case, there would be good reason to assume a Middle Ages dating for the figure. In view of the Pagan, Cathar and Templar history associated with the area, it could then easily be dismissed as a grandiose centre of Gnosticism, defiantly, but occultly displaying that emblem most reviled by the Christians - the Pentagram.

More research, however, provided earlier dating of the markers which caused us to pay more attention to the 'purifying' theory. With the additional knowledge that this was an area of Druid worship, together with the Paris Meridian conundrum, which will be discussed in detail later, we were forced to reconsider the date of origin. If the construction was of such great antiquity - who were the designers and was the rotation an inaccuracy or a refinement?

We began to investigate the ground figure with more respect and soon realised that far from being inaccurate, we were witnessing an intentional movement or vibration of the theoretical figure. Furthermore, it was apparent that it was essential to have a good understanding of the theoretical figure and its implied position on the ground, before we could study the ground figure itself with any confidence and determine the reason for its subtle movement.

To achieve this we developed a computer plot, and in return it rewarded us by revealing other parameters which could have only been discovered after months of calculations.

What had started as lines between ground markers was now an intricate self-confirming web of geometry and trigonometry which could be examined as a 'stand alone' structure. It was something which was so mathematically rigid that it could be constructed without any further reference to a map. The ground positions had served their purpose. As was obviously intended, they had signalled the presence of the Temple and invited us to enter.

CHAPTER 2.
INTO THE VALLEY OF MYSTERY

The people and organisations involved. The scene is set.
A visit to the church at Rennes-le-Château.
The discovery of some parchments. A case of Simony.
The strange death of the priest.

O date, the story of 'l'affaire de Rennes-le-Château' has concentrated on the machinations of Bérenger Saunière, who was appointed priest to the village of Rennes-le-Château, Aude, France in the year 1885. This chapter is for the benefit of the reader who is, as yet, unfamiliar with this part of what must surely be considered as one of the most profound mysteries on Earth.

In the beginning was the CIRCLE. And the CIRCLE was TIME. And TIME was the CYCLE. And Man looked from TIME to CIRCLE ; from CIRCLE to CYCLE and CYCLE to TIME again, and could not tell the difference. Had George Orwell been born in a different era, he might well have summed up a treatise on the examination of the affair of Rennes-le-Château like this, for it is like trying to trace the genealogy of a family whose cupboards are full of illegitimate skeletons. You know the bloodline exists, but you are never sure who has it.

Any journalist, when confronted by the story of Rennes, would ask simply what were the the five 'w's' of the affair - the who, what, why, when and where? Using these basic building blocks, a story can usually be pieced together as layer upon layer registers to give a full picture of an event or a sequence of events. Unfortunately, with Rennes-le-Château and its attendant mysteries, this approach does not easily work. There are far too many choices for each category. Even the 'who' is enough to negate this approach. It certainly concerned Abbé Bérenger Saunière and his housekeeper Marie Denarnaud in the latter part of the last century, but it also involved his mentor, Abbé Boudet, curate of the twin village of Rennes-les-Bains. It could also be said to have involved the entire village of Rennes-le-Château, for they all supposedly benefited from the large scale spending of their priest through his good works on behalf of the village. But more than this, the mystery over the years has pulled in whole races of people if we are to believe certain experts - Druids, Visigoths, Merovingian princes, Carolingians and Cathar heretics, Knights Templar and German mining engineers. Indeed, today, we also have strong evidence that the Egyptians played their part.

Additionally, the mystery involved other characters upon the world stage of the arts, from Nicolas Poussin to Teniers, from Voltaire to Jules Verne and Jean

Rennes-le-Château - village of mystery and the domain of the priest Bérenger Saunière (inset).

Cocteau, from Richard Wagner to Claude Debussy and Emma Calvé. In other words, what became known as 'l'affaire de Rennes' encompassed a large part of the club which formed 'Tout Paris' in the latter part of the last century. Everybody who was somebody seems to have had a finger in the pie. The Church was involved at the highest level as were the French and Austrian Royal families, and later, even today, the mystery has drawn the attentions of governments and secret services from around the world. So what possibly could have happened in this lost corner of almost medieval France that would set light to the world? Let us first visit the area with the eyes of a tourist who has a passing interest in the local history.

Imagine it is a late afternoon of a fine autumn day in the Languedoc region of southern France. A fine scent of wild mint hangs in the air. You are travelling the narrow road which runs from the Mediterranean coast at Perpignan

La Tour Magdala built by Saunière. Its position marks one of the points of the Pentagram on the Circle of Churches.

towards Couiza in the west. The road climbs and descends through the harsh, craggy, barren landscape of limestone country. You pass countless deep ravines. Many of them are now no more than dried-up stream beds, giving a desert feel to the region. The air is heavy, the heat oppressive. The valley is, after all, further south than the Côte d'Azur! The broom-covered hillsides to the north contrast strongly with the pine-clad mountains to the south. Overhead, a lone buzzard circles vigilantly on a warm thermal awaiting a glimpse of its prey. In most directions lies barren desolation. It is a hard, hot, hostile country.

To the north, an escarpment rises gently to 700 feet or more in one final gasp, before levelling out around Carcassonne which lies nearly 30 miles away. But to the south and west, a series of ridges rise, each higher than the other, as the hills of the Corbières transform into the foothills of the Pyrenees. The valley of the Rialsesse which you are following is one of the last easily accessible routes from east to west before the Pyrenees, which, for nearly two

The small mountain village of Coustaussa showing the ruined château. In the distance can be seen Rennes-le-Château.

thousand years has been a major crossing point of the southern Languedoc, part of the trans-Pyrenean Pilgrim route to Santiago de Compostela in northern Spain.

The modern road passes right through the ancient village of Arques before encountering its huge cube-shaped château, with rocket shaped round towers at each corner. The huge, blood-red fireball of the setting sun is nudging the first of the ridges to the west as we leave the village, the road twisting and turning along the valley floor. Ahead lie the last ridges of the Corbières, each, in the diminishing light, a different shade of grey. All that is missing is the music of the Valkyries to understand exactly where you are - in the land of the gods and the giants. You are near one of the locations where the 'psychically aware' claim to feel a 'presence', and as our investigation proceeds, the reasons for these overpowering feelings, in comparatively unrelated positions, will emerge.

Suddenly the road jinks right, then left as it crosses yet another dried-up

Villa Bethania built by Saunière and named after the castle of Bethany owned by Lazarus, brother of Mary Magdalen.

river bed. Immediately to the left, a dome of limestone rock juts proudly from the valley floor. On this craggy dome, now veiled on three sides by trees, once stood a tomb, or a reconstruction of it, immortalised by Poussin in his painting, 'Les Bergers d'Arcadie'. The tomb, alas, no longer exists, having been recently demolished by its owner in a belated effort to dissuade the thousands of tourists who invaded his privacy every year.

Past the tiny hamlet of Les Pontils the road straightens briefly before the junction to Rennes-les-Bains, where people have taken the spring waters for millennia past. An odd farmhouse is visible on the valley floor as the road sheds its height, but the hills to the left grow evermore menacing as the immense Pech Cardou, the highest hill in the area at over 2,500 feet, comes into sight. The ridges start to separate and take on individual characteristics. A thin plume of smoke issues from the top of the next to highest ridge, smudging lazily into the greying sky. With binoculars, you can make out a motley collection of ancient adobe-type houses atop this indifferent hill. The last of the sun's fiery disk dips below the far horizon leaving only a golden twilight. As you approach Couiza, where the river Rialsesse couples with the Aude, the hilltop village disappears from view. Suddenly, you are in the midst of a typical Languedoc village. There is traffic to worry about and people crossing your path. You take sanctuary in an overnight hostelry.

Next morning, after feasting on fresh French bread , jam and strong coffee, you seek directions to Rennes-le-Château. Strangely, the community of Couiza does not shout about its mysterious neighbour and there are few signposts to guide you. You take the D118 road to Quillan, and just where the village of Couiza thins out, a half-obscured sign points left up an undistinguished track to 'Rennes-le-Château. 4.5 km'. The first visit should be made on foot as nothing else will ever quite give you the same feeling of the utter remoteness of the village. Certainly, having attained your goal on foot, you would not readily make the trip again unless your life either depended on it or you are blessed with an unhealthy affinity for masochism. Without the luxury of transport, a century ago, you also begin to realise just how fit the inhabitants of the village must have been.

The road winds ever upwards, following the contours of the hillside, zigzagging to cope with the steepness of the slope. There in the distance, you look up to the ruins of ancient Coustaussa castle which stands across the valley of the Rialsesse, 200 feet above the valley floor. You look upward to the top of your own hill hoping to catch a glimpse of the secret village, but it remains hidden from view. After an hour's steady climb, the heat has taken its toll and now, as the track reaches a hairpin bend before turning south, the ruins of Coustaussa stand nearly 1,000 feet below you and still the track climbs steadily.

The scrub hillside now shows signs of cultivation as the first of several vineyards come into view. The grapes are luscious, black and bursting, but beware, for weathered sign boards tell that they are poisonous! Now and again a sheep track issues onto the road from the upper part of the hill, only to disappear down the hillside to your left. In such wasteland, at least the mountain sheep and goats must be in their element. Suddenly the landscape changes again. You climb past a plateau to your left where the rock is rich ochre in colour and no longer limestone. A final hairpin and the gate to the village stands before you.

It has taken nearly two hours to make the climb from Couiza. You are exhausted, and stagger into the village, vainly seeking bar or inn for restoration, past the infamous church and on up to the village square and a glorious view of the Pyrenees. You have reached your journey's end. Welcome to Rennes-le-Château, but remember that whatever you see is only the tip of an extremely ancient iceberg. In selecting your resting place and looking to the south, you are rewarded with an impressive view. A matrix of summits present themselves and freed from the confusion of the twisting valleys, you have an awareness that at this altitude, one is 'entering' the arena of the mystery.

Refreshed by the view of the distant Pyrenees, you appreciate why the inhabitants of the village first chose to live on such a site. The views are magnificent, the site a naturally defensive one and should anyone be imprudent enough to want to attack, they would probably have lacked the energy to do so after such an exhausting climb. Thus, Rennes-le-Château has probably remained relatively hidden and unimportant for hundreds of years. So what has brought you to this lost village in the Corbières? Will it prove to be as mysterious as you have been led to believe? A glance to your right at the improbable chess-styled crenellated tower which was Saunière's library, perched precariously on the edge of the cliff is certainly incongruous. It is an audacious structure for the village to possess. Why was it built there? Who paid for it? A simple walk on the path which passes beneath the tower and the wall of Saunière's garden impresses the complexity of the necessary engineering for the project and therefore the relatively high cost. Did the village priest pay for it himself, as has been rumoured? Next, climb back up the path and head down the road past the Villa Bethania, (the priest's house which he also had built at his own expense). Take the little turning to the left and on the right is a small churchyard. On the left a statue of the Virgin stands atop an ancient Visigothic pillar. In front of you is a most remarkable church doorway. Close inspection reveals carvings, symbols and a strange inscription incised over the tympanum of the doorway - "Terribilis est locus iste" - "This is a terrible place". You push the heavy wooden door which belies its weight as it swings open fairly easily.

Suddenly you are startled by a hideous figure which lies in wait, just inside. You see a little box on the wall to the right of the door asking you to put money in. You do so and the church becomes illuminated by a few electric light bulbs. You cross the threshold into another world. The decoration seems too much for such a lowly village, the statuary too ornate, the lily too gilded. You are seeing Christian imagery veneered over alchemical doctrine. What on earth is going on? A visual exploration of the church takes only minutes to see, but a lifetime to understand. Why do the stations of the cross run anti-clockwise? Why does the floor exhibit the chequer board of masonic temples, laid askew? Is somebody trying to tell you something? Outside, the surreal experience continues. As is the custom in this part of France, tombs are often adorned with plastic flowers which do not wither and die, giving a deceptive freshness to the casual glance. Many tombs are more substantial than you might expect in such a poor village. Several are constructed of quality marble, expensively engraved. Who paid for them ? Where did the money come from ? Rennes, after all, has never had any industry to generate such wealth. Pictures of the dear departed adorn many of the tombs - faces to put to the names of the mystery that will later unfold. Before leaving the churchyard, a last glance at the exterior of the church shows that the windows were not pierced straight through the walls, but were offset. Why? Rennes-le-Château has a habit of posing such questions. From a wealth of contradictory evidence, an 'authorised version' has emerged for the benefit of the casually interested visitor.

According to the accepted story, in 1885 a new priest, Bérenger Saunière was appointed to the church of St. Mary Magdalen at Rennes-le-Château. Saunière was born on the 11th April 1852 in Montazels and came from a local family. He has been described as a strong outdoor type. His yearly stipend for the parish was about 400 francs per year, which even at 19th century values did not amount to very much. The church Saunière found himself in charge of was dilapidated, roofless and gradually falling into ruin. Parts of its structure dated from the era of the Visigoths who left the area in the 7th century and its construction utilised simple local materials of stone, mortar and plaster which were at the mercy of the elements once they were exposed. For a time, Bérenger Saunière had to make the best of a bad job, coping as best he could against the elements, but he soon realised that he had to do something to save the church, otherwise the village would have nothing.

One day in 1887, with the help of a couple of workmen, he started work on the interior of the church and prised up a flagstone near the altar. The underside of this stone had an engraving upon it showing two people on horseback. This is now known as the "Dalle des Chevaliers - Knights' Stone", which is on display in the Rennes-le-Château museum. Saunière had the workmen excavate the cavity beneath the stone but stopped them when they found what has been vaguely described as some form of treasure. Understandably, Saunière continued the work alone. Sometime later, obviously with more money at his disposal, the priest started dismantling the altar. There, inside one of the altar pillars, he discovered some hollow wooden tubes, whose ends had been sealed with wax . Inside were parchments written in what seemed to be Latin or Greek, but in code. In the next three years, Saunière spent 700 francs on a new altar and a further 1,350 francs on stained glass windows. Shortly after the discovery of the parchments and after contacting the church authorities in Carcassonne, Saunière allegedly headed for St. Sulpice in Paris with the parchments. St. Sulpice was and is the centre of occult studies for the Catholic Church in France, with experts in medieval writings. Whilst waiting in Paris for the codes to be broken, Saunière met several influential people including the leading diva of the day, Emma Calvé. The collision between these two people coming from backgrounds worlds apart, must have been fascinating - the poor village priest and the opera star, but it would appear they had something in common.

When St. Sulpice finished its work, Saunière returned to Rennes-le-Château, but not before he had purchased copies of three paintings including works by Poussin and Teniers.

Although these two famous artists specialised in biblical scenes, it is thought that the priest did not acquire them solely for their biblical content. Upon his return to the village, Saunière set about his task in earnest. Attended by his teenage 'housekeeper' from Couiza, Marie Denarnaud, the priest started working day and night on the restoration of the church. Over the next four years, several strange things happened in Rennes-le-Château. Tombstones were defaced in the churchyard and the priest was seen walking the hills of the region, often at night, returning with bags of stones, ostensibly to decorate a grotto in his garden.

Saunière continued to spend money on the church, and in 1891 he paid 150 francs for a statue of St. Mary Magdalen to be placed above the church entrance. A new pulpit was added inside, for a further 750 francs. Between 1886 and 1888, the church's income rose from 239 francs to 1,914 francs. In 1897, Saunière spent another 2,824 francs on fitting out the church with statuary, paintings and a new font. Elaborate statues were installed including one which some believe is meant to represent Asmodeus. This is the hideous figure which greets you as you enter the church. Religious works were ordered from local factories and from Toulouse. Much of the detailed painting was apparently executed by Saunière himself. What was he trying to say? Where was the money coming from? Some believe the priest later paid for a new tarmacadam road to be built from Couiza all the way to Rennes-le-Château and for a water tower to be constructed so that the villagers could have water on tap - an unheard of luxury for a medieval village in those days.

Eventually, in 1905, Saunière's masters in the Church heard of the large amounts of money he was spending and called him to account. They grew even more suspicious of his conspicuous wealth and accused him of simony - the selling of pardons. In 1909, Saunière, having refrained from giving a satisfactory explanation to the charges was transferred to Coustouges, but refused to accept the appointment and was subsequently suspended. Instead, he installed an altar in the Villa Bethania and continued to celebrate mass. In 1911, Billard, the Bishop of Carcassonne, as a result of three 'trials' warned Saunière not to celebrate mass. The priest appealed unsuccessfully to Rome, and was never again priest of Rennes-le-Château. On January 17th 1917, despite the fact that Saunière was in rude health, Marie Denarnaud ordered a coffin for him. He conveniently died five days later, on January 22nd.

His funeral was a curious event with complete strangers mixing with the villagers to pay their respects. Each person, as they passed the seated body of Bérenger Saunière, plucked a red pompom from the gown which he was wearing, in some kind of esoteric ceremony. At the reading of the priest's will it was clear that Marie Denarnaud, Saunière's simple housekeeper already possessed everything, including the Villa Bethania and the library tower. The last history saw of her was as an old lady, prowling in the grounds of the Villa Bethania, burning huge bundles of bank-notes, after the government had announced a reissue of the currency, which made the old notes valueless.

Marie Denarnaud, apparently not wishing to have to explain the huge sum of money, chose to destroy it rather than account for it. She died, aged 85, in 1953, crippled by a stroke which paralysed her vocal chords and hands, thus conveniently preventing her from passing on her master's secrets. But was Bérenger Saunière really her master! It would seem that Marie Denarnaud had had control over the monies and properties in which Saunière had an interest, for a long, long time. Had the dog wagged its tail or was the tail wagging the dog? Whatever the true position between the incongruous couple, one fact remains clear. As yet, the world has seen nothing of Saunière's secret, which seemingly died with him in 1917, but as you will see in this book, the real core of the mystery is far older and more intriguing than anything written about it so far, and certainly of much greater importance. Before we can get our story under way, however, we must take account of other factors which are undeniably associated with the valley of mystery.

CHAPTER 3.
THE CONNECTIONS

The possible treasures. The Priest's strange hobby.
Other connections. A coded document. The Egyptian connection.
The Priory of Sion. The Temple of Solomon.
Cathar treasure. King Arthur. The Circle of
Churches. Saunière accused.

THE area surrounding Rennes-le-Château has always been rich in stories of lost treasure, whether they be Celtic, Biblical, Roman, Visigothic, Merovingian, Carolingian, Cathar or Knights Templar. All of these races and groups of people have a history of settling in the Rennes area. All have stories of treasure which has disappeared without trace. Did Saunière find one of these? Would that account for his wealth? We are studying an enigma which started its life at the dawn of recorded history. In this we are lucky, for had Saunière lived 100 years earlier, the tracks would have been impossible to follow. Now, however, we have records of his expenditure on the church. We know from whom he bought his statuary. We know who did the work. Indeed, we could until recently, still speak to people who knew the priest and his housekeeper. We also have photographs of the priest and Marie Denarnaud, the villagers and the village. We have accurate maps of the area and many of the ancient structures are extant. In this sense, the mystery of Rennes-le-Château is also a mystery of our time. This is the first time that enough pieces of the jigsaw can be put together to recognise the picture they portray. We can visit the Louvre in Paris and purchase copies of the paintings Saunière acquired. We can access electronic databases to check the facts of the story. It is possibly the first time a misty outline of the whole picture can be seen.

If we delve beneath the surface of the mystery, we soon come across different explanations for Saunière's actions and the treasure. Some have accused him of sorcery, of dabbling in the black arts, of re-enacting ancient rites or even of making a pact with the devil. Certainly the area is steeped in folklore, myth and legend. In a work of doubtful origin called *Le Serpent Rouge* which surfaced in the late 1960's, a series of verses, relating to a monthly horoscope, recalled salient features in the Rennes landscape. It told a version of the story of 'Sleeping Beauty', the princess condemned to eternal sleep until awakened by a courageous prince. Simply a fairy story? Perhaps not, when, in *Le Serpent Rouge*, we are led to a succession of secret places in the landscape. The same theme has already been used by others. Richard

Wagner in his epic work 'The Ring of the Nibelungen' retells the old Norse saga of the fall of the gods. In 'The Valkyrie', Brünhilde having tried to save Sigmund from being killed by Hunding against the wishes of her father Wotan, suffers the same fate; condemned to eternal sleep in the ruins of an enchanted castle. This connection is reinforced later in the enigmatic works of Jules Verne. Although one connection with Rennes-le-Château is that Richard Wagner allegedly visited Saunière at the Villa Bethania, we have not been able to find any trace of the visit.

What is indisputable though, is the theme of the work and the borrowing of unusual names from the Rennes valley for some of the places and things in the operas. The first opera of the Ring Cycle, 'The Rheingold' speaks of a hidden hoard of gold at the bottom of the Rhine, guarded by the Rhine maidens. It could easily have been written around the Rennes valley. The location fits perfectly. Not only is Brünhilde's horse named after the village of Granès which lies a couple of miles south-west of Rennes-le-Château, but the castle of Valhalla lies astride the Paris Meridian, a few miles to the south. Coincidentally, the concealment of treasure with an interred king or chief under a river bed was the method chosen by the Visigoths who inhabited the valley during the 5th and 6th centuries. In *The Holy Blood and the Holy Grail*, constant reference is made to the Priory of Sion and the underground stream. Underground streams are also a feature of the idyllic land of Arcadia, the word which occurs on the tomb illustrated in Poussin's 'Les Bergers d'Arcadie' and which will form an integral part of the solution of the mystery.

Alchemy, the transmutation of base metal into gold is another theme which crops up in the legends of the area. Was Jules Verne hinting at magical ceremonies of this nature in his book, *Château of the Carpathians* which mentions several names which can be found only in the Rennes area? What of captain Bugarach in one of Jules Verne's other famous adventures, *Clovis d'Ardentor*? Was he not named after the mountain peak which looks over Rennes with ever watchful eye? Is this just another coincidence? Was the character of the guide, Jouanne not named after the hillside farm near Rennes-les-Bains?

Another legend which touched the village is that of the Rosicrucians' quest for the Elixir of Life, a potion rumoured to grant eternal life to whoever drank it. Just wild legends concerning alchemy, except perhaps that the ancient Visigothic Château d'Hautpoul which lies adjacent to the church at Rennes-le-Château boasts an Alchemist's tower. In these connections we may have stumbled across the reason for the priest Saunière's strange hobby of collecting pebbles for his grotto. There is evidence that at some time, a gold statue had been melted down to enable the gold to be more easily concealed.

The Alchemist's Tower of the Château d'Hautpoul in the village of Rennes-le-Château. The Hautpoul family were supposedly one-time custodians of the secrets.

To understand this, we must refer to the function of the old shot-towers.

Grape shot, which was needed for cannons, was produced by dropping molten lead inside a tower and interrupting its fall into a water tank by a wire mesh. The height and gauge of the mesh could be used to determine the size of the lead shot which was then removed from the water tank at ground level. The Alchemist's tower may well have been used for the purpose of producing gold pebbles. These could then have been covered with a suitable clay and baked. It would only remain for them to be scattered in the bed of streams to ensure they would never be found, other than by those who could recognise them.

The passage of time would discolour them and perfect the concealment. If Saunière had become aware of this secret, he would have collected likely looking 'pebbles' from the streams, taken them back to the church and tapped them with a hammer.

If they cracked, he found gold; if not, his strange behaviour was concealed by utilising the 'duds' in the construction of his grotto. It is ironic to consider that using an alchemist's tower in this way could be seen as transforming gold into base clay - the perfect antithesis of all that is alchemical. It is indeed coincidental that in the thirteenth house of the zodiac of *Le Serpent Rouge* - Ophiuchus, we find "the base lead of my words may contain the purest gold".

Les Bergers d'Arcadie (The Shepherds of Arcadia) by Nicolas Poussin, featuring the famous Poussin tomb which provided not only geometric and numerical clues, but ultimately the identity of SET.

Alchemy, amongst other things, is the legend of the Elixir of Life and is supposed by some to have been the secret held by the Man in the Iron Mask. The link here with Rennes-le-Château, is through the auspices of Nicolas Fouquet, Superintendent of Finances for Louis XIV, his brother the Abbé Louis Fouquet and the celebrated artist Nicolas Poussin. Coincidentally, a third Fouquet brother happened to be the Archbishop of Narbonne which controlled the area of Rennes-le-Château. The legend has it that when Louis XIV learned of the existence of the secret passed on to his Superintendent of Finances, he exerted tremendous pressure to gain its details. When Fouquet refused to divulge it, Louis had him incarcerated in prison with an iron mask to hide his identity. Perhaps the secret that Nicolas Fouquet took to his grave was that of the Elixir of Life or the Philosopher's Stone. Either way, the king went to great lengths to secure the Poussin painting, 'Les Bergers d'Arcadie'. What was the secret, if any, contained in its enigmatic inscription:- 'ET IN ARCADIA EGO'?

This strange inscription has never been satisfactorily translated, but as the reader will eventually see, we have undoubtedly decoded the message contained in it.

A monument at Shugborough Hall in England, displays a mirror-image relief engraving of 'Les Bergers d'Arcadie'. Shugborough also holds a key to another secret of Rennes-le-Château inasmuch that it used also to house a painting by Teniers, 'The Temptations of St. Anthony'. Both the names Poussin and Teniers feature in one of the deciphered parchments found by Saunière at Rennes-le-Château as well as the word 'Temptation', and in this book we expose the 'key' that the painters possessed.

"BERGERE PAS DE TENTATION QUE POUSSIN TENIERS GARDENT LA CLEF PAX DCLXXXI PAR LA CROIX ET CE CHEVAL DE DIEU J'ACHEVE CE DAEMON DE GARDIEN A MIDI POMMES BLEUES"

"SHEPHERDESS NO TEMPTATION THAT POUSSIN TENIERS HOLD THE KEY PEACE 681 BY THE CROSS AND THIS HORSE OF GOD I COMPLETE (OR DESTROY) THIS DEMON OF THE GUARDIAN AT NOON BLUE APPLES"

There is one final, curious detail about the Poussin connection. If you visit any reasonably sized library and research the work of Nicolas Poussin, you will discover that one of the world's leading experts over the years has been Anthony Blunt, keeper of the Queen's pictures and spy for the Russian K.G.B. One can only speculate on how much the Russians knew about the Poussin secret!

Return to the church. Study the statues, paintings and decorations in the church. Are the colours symbolic or do they convey esoteric meanings through their alchemical colour scheme? Where does the word alchemy come from? Is it not the ancient name of Egypt - Al Khemia? What if it is? Normally, it would be hard to make a connection except that a statue of the Egyptian goddess Isis was found in the valley at Rennes-les-Bains in the last century, and there are mentions of a temple to the same goddess in old records of the area. Other writers see a connection between the river SALS which runs through Rennes-les-Bains and SAIS in Egypt. Nor do the connections finish there. In *GENISIS*, it was postulated that the twin villages of Rennes-le-Château and Rennes-les-Bains translate as "Queen of the House" and "Queen of the Waters" and that these two appellations were identical to those that the Egyptians gave to their two goddesses Nephthys and Isis.

Above. The entrance to the church carrying the dedication to the Magdalene and the famous inscription, 'Terribilis Est Locus Iste.'

Left. The demonic statue erected by Saunière which stands in the doorway of the church at Rennes-le-Château.

In *The Holy Blood and the Holy Grail*, the authors Michael Baigent, Richard Leigh and Henry Lincoln, reveal a shadowy organisation called the Priory of Sion which has secretly existed since the twelfth century. They state that it has the power to create kings. Whether it existed or not, perhaps remains to be seen, but what can be seen straight away is that the weather vane outside the church of St. Mary Magdalen at Rennes-le-Château does not move - it is fixed in the lee of the church, the last place where a weather vane would be of any use and, if the directions NORTH, SOUTH, EAST and WEST are translated into their French equivalents, NORD, SUD, EST and OUEST, then their initial letters,(with the 'E' seen end on) spell SION ! Another of Saunière's little clues, perhaps. And, if we're playing with acronyms - SION could be said to represent the Egyptian tetrarch Set, Isis, Osiris and Nepthys.

In a publication known as *Les Dossiers Secrets* by Henry Lobineau, deposited secretly at the Bibliothèque Nationale in Paris is a list of the Grand Masters of the Priory of Sion.

Jean de Gisors 1128-1220	Marie de Saint-Clair 1220-1266
Guillaume de Gisors 1266-1307	Edouard de Bar 1307-1336
Jeanne de Bar 1336-1351	Jean de Saint-Clair 1351-1366
Blanche d'Evreux 1366-1398	Nicolas Flamel 1398-1418
René d'Anjou 1418-1480	Iolande de Bar 1480-1483
Sandro Filipepi 1483-1510	Leonardo da Vinci 1510-1519
Connétable de Bourbon 1519-1527	Ferdinand de Gonzague 1527-1575
Louis de Nevers 1575-1595	Robert Fludd 1595-1637
J. Valentin Andrea 1637-1654	Robert Boyle 1654-1691
Isaac Newton 1691-1727	Charles Radclyffe 1727-1746
Charles de Lorraine 1746-1780	Maximilian de Lorraine 1780-1801
Charles Nodier 1801-1844	Victor Hugo 1844-1885
Claude Debussy 1885-1918	Jean Cocteau 1918-1963

The list is certainly a powerful one, including many who could best be described as the frontier breakers of their own ages. Lobineau is thought to have been the pen name of Leo Schidlof, an Austrian who died in 1966, so the veracity of the list is difficult to check. As we live in an age which published the famous Hitler Diaries, we can never be too careful as to what we believe. Although Henry Lincoln, in his meeting with the former founder member of the Priory of Sion, Pierre Plantard de St.Clair, seems to accept the Priory of Sion as fact, we should bear in mind that others postulate that the organisation is simply an invention by a couple of students, a theory which has accumulated much weight over the years! Indeed, a reading of Umberto Eco's *Foucault's Pendulum* describes an imaginary body which fits the modern organisation of the Priory of Sion like a glove.

The Catholic Church would certainly seem to be heavily involved. The Abbés Gélis and Boudet both play leading parts in the orthodox mystery, as does Billard, the Bishop of Carcassonne. What did the priests at St. Sulpice accomplish? There are now translations of the codes which appeared in the alleged parchments - which themselves seem too sophisticated for the time in which they were supposedly written. Could the writers of the parchments have been that clever? Could Saunière have correctly interpreted the importance of the codes? Would he have had the intellect and/or the education to do so? What was the connection with Rome? Did Saunière really have the temerity to write to the Pope with reference to the simony charge and possibly question the reply he received? Other organisations supposedly connected with the mystery include the Rosicrucians, Rose Croix, Masons, Knights Templar and the Cathars. Of these, we know certainly that the Templars kept two or three preceptories in the area, of which the one at Le Bézu is probably the most famous. Why, when the order was given by Philippe le Bel to have all the Knights Templar in France rounded up at dawn on October 13th 1307, were the Templars at Le Bézu, le Valdieu and Blanchefort allowed to remain free?

There are certainly Templars buried in the countryside surrounding Rennes, with or without their treasure and remember, it was the Knights Templar who fought their way to Jerusalem in the crusades and whilst there, allegedly excavated the stables underneath the Temple of Solomon. What did they unearth and did any of it find its way to Rennes-le-Château? After all, even in modern times, treasure was discovered in another of their bases, Gisors, not far from Paris. Gisors is linked to the Priory of Sion through Guillaume de Gisors, 1266-1307, the very year the Knights Templar were extirpated by Philippe le Bel. Also, it is well known that the Templars were well versed in the use of codes. Could some at least of the coded documents have been encrypted by the Knights Templar? If treasure is to be one of the underlying themes of Rennes, then we must also consider other treasures which reputedly have meandered into the story. The gold mines at Blanchefort and other sites in the Rennes valley were known and exploited by the Celts and the Romans. The Visigoths, who under Alaric, sacked Rome in 410 A.D., allegedly made off with the treasure of the Temple of Solomon which had been previously looted by the Romans at the fall of Jerusalem. This much is recorded by history, and the treasure included the sacred seven branched menorah of the Jews together with the Ark of the Covenant. The Visigoths then settled in the area of the Haut Razès (Rennes) and even built their capital there (Rhédae), below the existing village of Rennes-le-Château. The treasure has since disappeared from view, but it is known that when the Visigoths buried their leaders, they did so by damming and diverting a river or stream, excavating a chamber in the riverbed, burying their chief and treasure and then removing the dam. Thus were all vestiges of the concealment destroyed. The men who had carried out the work were then executed so that no one knew where the burial had taken place. As we have stated previously, much is made in the extant literature on Rennes-le-Château and its connection with the Priory of Sion and of the 'underground stream'.

The next treasure that possibly vanished in the area was that of the Merovingians, whose genealogy ran from Clodion (the Long haired) in 428 A.D. through to Sigebert in 678 A.D. This connection to Rennes-le-Château is twofold. Dagobert II is mentioned in the coded parchments found in the Visigothic altar :-

A DAGOBERT ET A SION EST LE TRESOR ET IL EST LA MORT

TO DAGOBERT AND TO SION IS THE TREASURE AND IT IS THERE DEATH (or HE IS THERE DEAD)

History tells us that when Dagobert II was murdered, his son Sigebert was taken to Rennes-le-Château and furthermore, that this event is the one depicted on the 'Dalle des Chevaliers' stone found in the church of the Magdalene at Rennes-le-Château. Could the Merovingian treasure have been concealed beneath the ancient Visigothic foundations of the church, only to be rediscovered by Abbé Saunière some 1200 years later?

Perhaps the treasure was not just of one type, for there is a powerful legend that the Merovingians were descendants of a bloodline issuing from a union between Mary Magdalen and Jesus Christ. Mary Magdalen accompanied by Joseph of Arimathea and others is said to have landed in southern France some time after the alleged crucifixion of Christ, and there are some who say that they may well have settled in the Rennes area. A written genealogy proving such a union could be even more valuable than any gold or jewels which could be found, if it fell into the right hands.

The Merovingians were succeeded by the Carolingians who attained the throne of France through Charlemagne and added the title of Holy Roman Emperor in 800 A.D. to their collection of noble titles. Carcassonne became one of Charlemagne's most important cities, and Rhédae (Rennes), one of its most important outposts.

During the next few centuries, Rennes-le-Château became the property of the House of Barcelona, then the Lords of Béziers. By this time in the 12th

Montségur - last bastion of the Cathars which fell in 1244. It was in this area that Otto Rahn and Skorzeny searched for the Treasures of the Temple of Solomon, under the instruction of Himmler.

century, the crusades had already begun and the Cathar heresy was spreading throughout the Languedoc. Many of the surviving Cathars were finally rounded up in the mountain fortress of Montségur, less than thirty miles due west of Rennes-le-Château. There in 1244, after a siege of many months, the Cathars finally were starved into submission and burned to death, but not before four Cathars reportedly slipped over the walls and down the cliff face, an extremely difficult operation if the treasure was gold.

Between 1118 and 1307 the Knights Templar, a shadowy, powerful and secret organisation became arguably the most powerful group in the world. They controlled vast tracts of land and possessed immense wealth. Anyone who entered the institution had to assign his worldly goods to the Templars and as these 'warrior' monks were often the second sons of lords, the organisation swiftly inherited vast fortunes and titles to land. In addition, their military strength often gave them more power than that of their contemporary kings. The Grand Master of the Templars from 1156 until 1169 was Bertrand de Blanchefort and the Château de Blanchefort is a fortification which lies only a couple of miles from Rennes-le-Château, across the high plateau. Templar preceptories were established at Blanchefort, Le Bézu and le Valdieu, all within shouting distance of Rennes-le-Château. Although no specific Templar treasure has ever been reported lost in the area, there is evidence of extraordinary Templar burials in mountainside caves, cleverly concealed and almost impossible to enter. One can only wonder at the riches these might contain.

Finally, after years of almost open war against the community of Rennes-le-Château by the Count of Trestamarre, the Voisin Lords, protectors of Rennes-le-Château for several years, married into the noble family of the Hautpouls, which in turn laid claim to the ancient title of Blanchefort. The last of the line of the Hautpouls of Blanchefort was Marie de Négri d'Ables, the lady whose strangely coded tombstone, Bérenger Saunière is known to have defaced in the churchyard at Rennes-le-Château. Legend tells us that Marie de Négri d'Ables was the last custodian of a great secret which had been handed down through her family. When she knew that her death was imminent and having no-one to pass the secret on to, she is thought to have entrusted it to the then curate of Rennes-le-Château and chaplain to the Hautpoul family, the Abbé Bigou. Marie de Négri d'Ables died on January 17th 1781, a date which features strongly in the enigma of Rennes-le-Château. Whether the secret of the Hautpoul family concerned treasure or evidence of a genealogy linking a modern family by blood to the old Merovingian dynasty and even earlier to Christ, remains a mystery. It is, after all, uncertain whether the carriers of the secret would necessarily have known all the details or even the nature of it. If the royal bloodline did and does exist, as is the case claimed in *The Holy Blood and the*

The tomb featured in Poussin's 'Les Bergers d'Arcadie' recently destroyed by the present owners (inset).

Holy Grail, then there is the possibility that there exists, even now, someone who could trace his ancestry back to the royal house of David through Christ - a claimant to most of the thrones in the western world. If this were true, then there would probably be many people in positions of great power who would prefer such a claim not to be made.

The Holy Grail, which we briefly touched on, is another of those enduring legends which permeate the mists of time. Did it ever exist and is there a connection with Rennes-le-Château? In *The Emerald Cup*, Col. Howard Buechner claims that the Holy Grail, in the form of an artefact, was part of the cache of Temple Treasures found by the Third Reich; another strange facet of the mystery with which we will deal later. Of course, there is no hard evidence for the existence of such an object and scholars are still debating the interpretation of the words "Holy Grail". In the French language it is known as the "Saint Graal" which can easily sound like "Sang Réal" or Blood Royal.

If it is the latter, there is a strong possibility that this is the genealogy implied at Rennes-le-Château. If, however, we think of the Holy Grail as a chalice then you have to explore from whence this image came. The Grail story can be traced back to a medieval 'minnesinger' or troubadour, Chrétien de Troyes, who sang his story about the knights who guarded the sacred chalice.

The story was written down by Wolfram von Eschenbach some time after 1190 and has passed into legend. It is featured strongly in the story of King Arthur and the Knights of the Round Table and has since been adapted by writers such as Mallory and composers like Wagner in his opera 'Parzifal'.

Although Arthur is commonly thought of as an English king, his kingdom of Camelot has never been located. Even the historical existence of Arthur has never been satisfactorily proved, but there are strong indications that his kingdom lay somewhere in the Pyrenees, which themselves are close to Rennes-le-Château.If this link is somewhat tenuous,there is another, more direct.

On the tomb in Poussin's painting of 'Les Bergers d'Arcadie', a shepherd is pointing at the legend inscribed on the tomb :- 'ET IN ARCADIA EGO'. Where is Arcadia? What does the name mean? Simply the land of the bear. The beginning of the word is etymologically derived from ARCTUS, the bear and is echoed in the name Arthur. In other words, Arthur was the bear king or king of the land of the bear and the bear country could well have been the Pyrenees which in medieval times included the area around Rennes-le-Château. Was Poussin therefore telling us that the great secret lay in the land of the bear? The last subject to be connected with the Rennes valley is that of landscape geometry. Henry Lincoln, in his Chronicle TV programme, 'The Priest, the Painter and the Devil', had the Poussin painting analysed by the art historian, Christopher Cornford, who found that the painting was constructed on a pentagram and that this design secretly controlled the picture. In the Chronicle series of programmes concerning the mystery at Rennes-le-Château, the camera team took a copy of the painting to the tomb on the limestone dome near Les Pontils and set up two cameras - one on the painting, the other on the local countryside to try to match the background of the painting to that of real life. Unfortunately, the background camera became misaligned, and the shot seen by the public never matched the actual background in the painting.

However, my co-author David Wood spotted the error, and was intrigued by the mistake in the television film. It seems it had gone unnoticed and was a genuine error. It was also one of the reasons which set David Wood wondering whether there was any geometry overlaying the Rennes valley. Wood found that there was indeed a geometric structure at Rennes - a Circle of Churches comprising those at Rennes-le-Château, St. Just-et-le-Bézu, Bugarach, Coustaussa and Serres, all situated on the circumference of a gigantic circle overlaying the area.

This circle was nearly six miles in diameter and encompassed an area which was truly mountainous. More than this, if the churches and one or two other salient features were linked up on the map, an extraordinary unique

44

pentagram appeared.

Wood felt that this was too good to be true and visited the Rennes valley with two colleagues to survey the area, using skills acquired in the Survey Section of the Royal Engineers. His work on the map checked out and he published the results in his book *GENISIS*.

Unfortunately, the very existence of the Circle of Churches in the Rennes valley poses more questions than it answers. Some of the churches in the circle have been proven to date back to Visigothic times and are almost certainly located on sites of earlier temples or shrines, built there by the Romans and Celts. The necessary mathematics needed to be able to survey such a vast area in tremendously difficult country accurately, was not developed until the 7th century A.D.! If the Visigoths, Romans and Celts had lacked the ability to put down the geometry at Rennes, then who did? Certainly some people involved in the Rennes enigma knew something about the geometry of the landscape of the Rennes valley. That much is amply illustrated by the placing of the Poussin tomb which is exactly located by geometric discipline, although not forming part of the ancient design. Was this geometry part of the attraction to the area for the alchemists?

One of the allegations against Saunière was that he regularly took part in a ritual known as the Convocation of Venus, a way of telling the future, and that he charged wealthy clients vast sums for doing so. He was probably helped in this by the fact that the pentagram formed in the valley echoes the celestial pentagram traced in the heavens every eight years by the planet Venus (see *GENISIS p*108) - "As above, so below" as the adepts are fond of saying! Whether we want to believe in such esoteric components of the Rennes-le-Château mystery or not, we should be aware that many strong alignments do occur in the valley, and that such alignments could well have been used to locate hoards of treasure or secret burials. We should also note that Leonardo da Vinci might also be connected to the mystery as the background to his masterpiece the 'Virgin on the Rocks' has been identified as existing on the heights of Pech Cardou (see *GENISIS pp*225-228). Whatever the outcome of the mystery, certainly no area on earth has ever attracted so many illustrious names. Intriguingly, Leonardo is named as a Grand Master of the shadowy Priory of Sion from 1510 to 1519 - another link with Rennes, perhaps !

Imagine the times in which part of the enigma was being enacted. It is the latter part of the eighteenth century. Revolution is coming to France, and the priesthood provided only slightly less popular candidates for the guillotine than the aristocracy. Abbé Bigou had possibly been entrusted with a great secret by Marie de Négri d'Ables, Dame d'Hautpoul de Blanchefort. When Bigou, seeing the writing on the wall, decided to escape to Spain he could have created the coded parchments and concealed them inside the hollow altar pillar.

We now learn that he died some time later in Spain. And so, for a hundred years, the secret would have died with him, concealed in the Visigothic altar pillar in the church of St. Mary Magdalen in Rennes-le-Château. This then is the underlying background of the story of Rennes-le-Château. The major difficulty is, how much of it is true? The problem with trying to get to grips with a subject as complex as that of Rennes-le-Château is made far more complicated by the dearth of source material which is available. Baigent, Leigh and Lincoln have done a fine job in bringing such a fascinating subject to the attention of the public, and could be regarded as the catalysts who started the whole affair fermenting in England so many years ago. Even so, there have been any number of French authors who have predated *The Holy Blood and the Holy Grail*, so that while it has become an international best-seller, there are other prominent authors, most of whom are French, who also deserve much credit. The problem we have found in reading many volumes on the subject is it always raises the nagging question :- "From what source did the material come?" Already, we have discovered that much of the popular story of Bérenger Saunière is at best a 'faction' and at worst, pure fabrication. We know now that the huge sum of money which he is supposed to have acquired from the finding of treasure or information and evidenced by the lavish spending of money on charitable projects, just isn't true. The Church accused Saunière of simony (the selling of pardons), and asked him to account for his wealth. His defence, couched in his own hand, is on the lines of "I didn't do it. It wasn't me. It's not like me. I wouldn't ever do it, but if I did do it, then its probably only because everyone else was doing it and I needed the money." In other words, he defended himself like some young teenager caught with his hand in the money box. We also have had sight of books of accounts, kept, once more by Abbé Saunière, which show income from the sale of pardons by mail order, amounting to several thousands of francs per year.

On the practical side, the building of the road from Couiza to Rennes-le-Château for which some authors give credit to Saunière, was not completed until after the priest had died. Similarly with the story of the mains water system, which was not even started until six years after Saunière's death. In simple terms, the finding of treasure has been used to explain how the priest came by such huge sums, whereas in fact, his mail-order simony was more than enough with which to re-build the church, the Villa Bethania and the Tour Magdala. Therefore, an argument could be made for explaining that Saunière may not have found a treasure of any sort, but was letting people think that he had in order to explain his wealth, rather than admit the simony charge. So, did

Saunière actually find anything? It would be nice to think he did. After all, several authors have staked their reputations on it by publishing works to that effect. After more than a decade of studying the enigma, all we can say about the story of Abbé Bérenger Saunière is that we just do not know. We do not even know whether he found coded parchments in the Visigothic altar pillar. Some authorities state that the altar pillar was a fake. Others, that there is evidence to show the documents were fabricated by Philippe de Chérisey at the behest of Pierre Plantard de St.Clair, the self-appointed 'Nautonnier' of the resurrected Priory of Sion, which was, as we have said, not an institution of antiquity but only reformed in modern times. Indeed it is also said that Plantard employed sixty-five people at various times to fabricate documents and to rearrange tombstones in the churchyard. In other words, as far as the Rennes-le-Château/Bérenger Saunière/Priory of Sion mystery goes, who knows what is the truth and what is pure speculation or fabrication?

What we do know, is that we are not clever enough to draw the line between truth and libel suits in this matter, and have decided to approach the enigma from the basis of what we can corroborate and prove - this is the geometry, and the geometry can be backed up by mathematical certainty and historical doctrine. Therefore, with this book, we have no intention of winning many friends and hope only to influence people with thinking minds. Indeed, if we can make any reader stop and check something for themselves so that they can accept or reject our argument by using their own intellect, we will have achieved our purpose. We seek nobody's lip-service and we are sure that we are bound to upset various sections of the community. But, if that is the price of disclosing the truth, then that too will be worth it. We are certain, nevertheless, that if you follow our arguments and examine them rigorously, this book will have a profound effect on your thinking and on the various subjects discussed.

From our point of view we know what we have proved, and it suggests something of great antiquity. That a great secret exists in the area may have been the factor which attracted diverse forces through the ages, and they in turn are each accompanied by their attendant mysteries and secrets. The area of Rennes-le-Château is a magnet - possibly known to be a safe haven from natural disaster and that would be sufficient reason for the kaleidoscope of treasure stories. We will shortly examine the keys to the secret of the enigma, but before doing so, we will deal briefly with what we consider to be unfair and misconceived criticisms by the debunkers of *GENISIS*.

CHAPTER 4.
THE RIGHT TO REPLY. (David Wood)

The vindication of GENISIS. Are we alone? Geometry is important.
Henry Lincoln's attack. Gérard de Sède's attack. The Reverend's attack.
The Albigensian Campaign.

WHEN Henry Lincoln presented the BBC Chronicle programmes outlining the mystery of Rennes-le-Château, I was particularly interested in his suggestion of the possibility of a large scale pentagonal ground plan. Having been trained in trigonometrical and aerial surveying methods, I wondered if I could make a useful contribution to the solution. At the time I had moved into the reproduction side of the printing trade, which was an additional asset, allowing me to create accurate monochrome separations of the existing mapping of the area.

Among my hobbies, I had become interested in the interpretation of myth and legend, which in turn led me to study astronomy and the occult sciences.

With this bag of tools I set off for Rennes-le-Château to give what help I could. What I found shocked me, but I felt impelled to make my findings known. I discovered an incredible geometric figure which was self-evident to anyone with an elementary knowledge of mathematics, but the response to my discovery was something I could never have foreseen. I was inundated with correspondence which suggested everything from having me burned at the stake to being canonised.

Could geometry really be so controversial? With hindsight I can now accept that it can. After all, geometric figures do have certain properties and it can be very embarrassing to one's fellow investigators, when having denied something they find it mathematically provable.

I recall the Headmaster of a Grammar School who, in open forum, told me that the extended pentagram I had found, which we will explain later, could not possibly have angles of 36 degrees at its star points. It can, of course, be easily proved that it has and I should have felt victorious, but in truth I was embarrassed for him. Certain other 'mathematicians' have denied the geometric properties outlined in *GENISIS*, but to date none have accepted my invitation for a round table discussion.

However, as the letters poured in I knew I had been too presumptuous in assuming that everyone knew there were three sides to a triangle. Next came the problem of dealing with the meanings which have been attributed to various geometric figures, since the dawn of civilisation. Despite the fact that there are countless scholarly references which confirm it, I was considered sexually obsessed for relating the circle and pentagram to the female.

And so it went on! Egyptian connections in the valley of Rennes-le-Château - rubbish they said! Earth destruction by a comet - nonsense, it is only a 'dirty snowball'! homo sapiens no more than 200,000 years old - impossible! Now, less than ten years later, all those fantastic findings of *GENISIS* are accepted by dozens of authorities in both the scientific and artistic spheres.

In the pages which follow, the reader will find not only supporting evidence and mathematical proof of the geometry of *GENISIS*, but a good deal more. I would beg those who feel emotionally opposed to our research to check carefully before they fly to their pens and publish something which may cause them embarrassment in the future.

Henry Lincoln, for whom I have the greatest respect, commented favourably on the accuracy of the initial geometry outlined in *GENISIS*. For that I am grateful, but I was surprised by a scathing remark in a book which he co-authored, *The Messianic Legacy*. Here I found:-

> "Finally, in an opulently produced work entitled Genisis (sic), David Wood combined some rigorous geometric calculation with numerology, Egyptian mythology, skeins of sundry esoteric traditions and Platonic references to Atlantis. Using these as if they were a Rorschach test, he proceeded to adduce evidence that Rennes-le-Château bore witness to the historical existence of Atlantis, as well as a species of 'super-race' - extra-terrestrial - from which mankind was descended."

Oddly enough this 'Ink Blot' insult rings true in a reverse fashion. We have found that *GENISIS* had the effect of exposing the dogmatic beliefs lurking in the so-called open minds of certain other investigators. They suddenly saw the geometric figures, their interactions and their ancient symbolic meanings, all harmonising with the previously unrelated tentacles of the mystery. This resulted in their displaying the psycho-pathological reactions for which the Swiss psychoanalyst Hermann Rorschach designed his 'Ink Blot' tests in the first place. There were others, however, on whom the figures had a totally different effect and their letters spoke of feelings of elation, relief, and of recognition from what appeared to them to be distant race memories.

Continuing with the attack on *GENISIS*, the authors of the *The Messianic Legacy* state:-

> "As organised religion and its dogmatic conceptions of God continue to lose credibility, individuals begin to seek a 'higher intelligence' elsewhere - across the galaxy, if need be. It is as if, feeling abandoned by the deities of the past, they were impelled

out of sheer panic to fabricate a new form of reassurance that 'we are not alone'.

It is precisely this kind of 're-channelling' of the religious impulse into science fiction that accounts for the popularity of such films as Star Wars, with its mystical, 'quasi-Taoist Force' , and Close Encounters of the Third Kind. Once again people look outwards for solutions, when they should be looking within themselves."

We can do no more than refer those informed gentlemen to the SETI (Search for Extra-Terrestrial Life) programme under the control of Carl Sagan. From time to time, some eight observatories have been involved in searching the skies for extraterrestrial signals and large sums of money are allocated in the attempt to "fabricate a new form of reassurance that 'we are not alone.'" Furthermore, surely those authors know the opinions of the well-informed.

"... we have additional evidence that the origin of life has a high probability, at least on planets with an abundant supply of hydrogen-rich gases, liquid water and sources of energy. Since those conditions are common throughout the universe, life may also be common. Our best guess is that there are a million civilisations in our galaxy at or beyond the earth's present level of technological development"
Scientific American May 1975 (The Search for Extra Terrestrial Intelligence by Carl Sagan and Frank Drake).

Note in particular "beyond the Earth's present level of technological development". The authors of the *The Messianic Legacy* have probably overlooked the fact that Man has already landed on the moon. The space age is here and without wishing to put a 'secret government cat' among the 'trusting population pigeons', many consider that extremely close encounters of the third kind may already be in progress. The final sentence in the 'Messianic' attack is particularly relevant:-

"Once again, people look outwards for solutions, when they should be looking within themselves".

We would warn these authors that by looking too deeply into themselves, they may find the biggest enigma of all - the inexplicable size of the human brain! This will be dealt with in more detail later.

We have no idea which one of the three authors initiated the attack, but eventually in 1989 Michael Baigent and Richard Leigh co-authored *The Temple and the Lodge* in which we find:-

"In other words, God was to be discerned in the principles of shape - determined ultimately, by the degrees in an angle - and by number".

And from Vitruvius, *De Architectura* 11.c.1:9 they quote:-

"Paramount among these laws was geometry, on which the architect was obliged to draw in order to construct temples by the help of proportion and symmetry ...."

Now this and a number of other references they make to the importance of geometry through the ages, at least shows that these two authors have fully appreciated its significance and they have, therefore, now probably recognised the advanced geometric techniques which were outlined in *GENISIS*.

Shortly after, in 1991, Henry Lincoln in *The Holy Place*, devoted considerable space to both praising and lampooning the contents of *GENISIS*. Although he overlooks the remarkable trigonometrical and doctrinal properties of the extended 'Wood Pentagram', he uses it as the centre-piece for his 'geometric' development of the area. His scaling does, however, leave something to be desired. Excusing himself with:-

"...... even on a large scale map exactitude of measure over small distance is impossible, ...".

He proceeds to state categorically that:-

"... (On the 1:25,000 scale map, a mile equals 64mm)"

Actually, this is not so. The figure is more like 64.37376mm and if you think that is splitting hairs, refer to Appendix Four in *The Holy Place* wherein he states:-

"Below are listed the EXACT (*his caps not mine*) distances of crucial sites in the construction of The Holy Place to the Meridian line....."

Now those 'EXACT distances' range up to 12 miles and even at 10 miles the error would be more than 100 yards! We began to wonder why we were bothering to compute to less than 50 inches on the ground.

We then turned our attention to some of Henry's angles:-

"I checked the angles to other churches. The result was breathtaking: a stunning regularity revealed itself."

We must admit we were also 'stunned', for the bunch of angles Henry shows as each being 18 degrees, varied from 15 degrees to 19 degrees on our map. Nevertheless, with a thick enough pen it is amazing how many points on a map, can be aligned.

Concerning Henry's alignments, one might summarise them in the timeworn joke:-

"Never mind the quality - feel the width".

I have often wondered why some investigators of this subject feel they have to 'snipe' at others, when it would be in everyone's interest to exchange information; albeit, while still respecting copyright. An example of this occurred when I was tipped off that Henry Lincoln had chosen to follow me on the geometric trail at Rennes-le-Château. Naturally, I contacted Henry, who immediately replied that he was on the point of contacting me.

He suggested we met and that he would show me the galley proofs of his references to my material. I, in turn, agreed to show Henry some of my latest findings. Inevitably, when we met, the galley proofs were not available and later when I received the printed book, I realised why. Nevertheless, I still have the greatest respect for Henry and have often said we would have made a good team.

We will comment briefly on the next attack which came from the French author Gérard de Sède in his book carrying the extremely original title *Rennes-le-Château*. The signed copy I received carried the remark "avec perplexité" which was really superfluous, for it was quite clear how puzzled de Sède was in the seven pages which he devoted to *GENISIS*. Being one of the early 'compilers' of fragments of Rennes-le-Château literary memorabilia, it was probably quite a shock to him to find a massive design of geometric excellence on his doorstep. He describes it as 'imaginary' and one supposes he will find some consolation in trying to imagine it is not there; but it is, and it always will be!

The next book which criticises us is a perfect gem. It comes from the pen of the Reverend Fanthorpe and once again sports a most original title, *Secrets of Rennes-le-Château*. Having more than a passing interest in the subject we read it eagerly. Had someone cracked it at last? The title certainly suggests there is something important contained in the 241 pages which are the result of 15 years of investigation and we spent a considerable time trying to find it. The last page of the book probably holds the secret as it portrays Fanthorpe and his wife, highly amused. Probably that is because the reader has had to plough through a mountain of unrelated tedious material looking for a non-existent secret. Personally, we found page 240 the most intriguing of all. (*Editor's note: Page 240 is blank*).

Anyway let us see what he has to say about *GENISIS*:-

"David Wood's ideas in Genisis are, to say the least, distasteful, sensational, highly controversial and totally opposed to what we ourselves would seek to defend as the simple, rational, central and inviolable facts at the heart of traditional Christian faith."

Now what would Rorschach have said about that highly emotional outburst, when here we are, carefully measuring, analysing and tracing the connections as honestly and accurately as we can. Eventually, our detective work begins to point quite clearly in the direction which Fanthorpe considers 'distasteful, sensational, highly controversial...', but why should it invoke such an emotional response? Could it be that we are closer to the truth than some would like us to be? He continues his attack with:

> "But let us always beware of falling into the trap which engulfed an obsessively enthusiastic pyramidologist a few years ago. Having spent half a lifetime working on his theories he finally reached the Great Pyramid and began taking measurements 'on the ground'. He was caught by a custodian in the act of removing a piece of ancient stone because it didn't fit in with his theories !"

Is this fellow seriously insinuating we have moved a church or even a mountain? Surely only faith can do that! Finally, he delivers his divine judgement:-

> "There is, however, little or no justification for the agglomeration of bizarre Freudian nightmares, grotesque pagan sexual myths and darker Jungian archetypes which Wood has superimposed on whatever geometrical patterns may (or may not!) subsist in the Languedoc landscape."

Had Fanthorpe said we were wrong to reveal what we had found, we could follow his reasoning, but we can only say that from our viewpoint the world deserves to know what we have discovered.

So much for the Fanthorpe attack, but although they do not appear to contribute anything to the mystery of Rennes-le-Château, we would refer to a couple of other points in his work. In replying to the suggestion that Saunière's wealth may have come from the Vatican's desire to silence him with a bribe. Fanthorpe replies:-

> "If the hypothetical powerful vested interests who wanted things kept quiet had been as immoral, as cynical and as pragmatic as that, they would have silenced Saunière far more cheaply, efficiently and permanently !"

My word, what an admission! We would remind the author of his own reference to the three dead bodies found in Saunière's garden in 1956. He tells us all three had been shot and then he poses the question as to whether it was the work of some organisation wishing to silence Saunière only to be outgunned by Saunière himself (*'Secrets of Rennes-le-Château' p141*).

A 'U-turn' indeed, but which organisation pray? Continuing in the same theme, we noticed another sentence in which the Reverend Fanthorpe refers to the Cathars:-

> "The Cathars led a charmed life for centuries in a world full of dangerous enemies"

We are well aware of who the enemies of the Cathars were and we feel impelled to respond on their behalf. These Cathars lived a pure and simple life, but as we said in *GENISIS*, their destruction was one of the most savage acts of butchery the Church of Rome ever committed and we make no apology for repeating it:-

> "From 1209 for forty years, on the express orders of Pope Innocent III, an 'extermination occurred on so vast, so terrible a scale, it may well constitute the first case of genocide in modern European history'. The agents of the massacre were an army of some 30,000 knights and foot-soldiers from Northern Europe. Their victims: almost the entire 'Cathari' or Albigensian population of the Languedoc region of what is today southern France. At that time it was a peaceful and cultivated population of independent people whose only crime seems to have been that it followed a religious way of life contrary to the one decreed by Rome.
>
> The Cathari, or Cathars as they are more popularly known, were Gnostics. To Rome they were infected, and therefore infectious. By the time the Crusade was over, the Languedoc had been utterly transformed, plunged back into the barbarity which characterised the rest of Europe. With that transformation came anonymity. And so it remained for 600 years - until the end of the nineteenth century."　　　　　(*GENISIS*, p13)

It was during this bloody campaign that Béziers was pillaged and in *The Albigensian Crusade*, Jonathan Sumption reports:-

> "A German monk repeated a story that Arnald-Amaury, when asked in the middle of the slaughter how the catholics (*sic*) could be distinguished from the heretics, replied 'Kill them all; God will recognise his own'; and this motto has passed into history as the epitome of the spirit which had brought the crusaders to the south. Whether Arnald-Amaury was consulted, or ever uttered any such sentiment, remains unclear. But it is not important. The legate

reported the massacre without comment to Innocent III, remarking only that 'neither age, nor sex, nor status had been spared". Neither he nor his clerical colleagues had any sympathy even for the catholic (*sic*) victims. They had, after all, been offered peace if they would surrender their heretical neighbours, and they had rejected it."

We, therefore, assume that one of the 'dangerous enemies' the Reverend refers to was none other than the Church of Rome. Little wonder he passes it by so lightly, but let us be fair, he was duty bound to admit that at Montségur the Catholics burnt alive 200 Cathars.

Now Lionel Fanthorpe is an ordained Anglican priest and with that authority says:-

"Judge not, that ye be not judged, is one of the most fundamental of all Christian ethics."

As he devotes four or five pages to criticising the authors of *The Messianic Legacy*, we can only assume this is one Christian fundamental he has chosen not to embrace. There are any number of 'perhaps' in *The Secrets of Rennes-le-Château*, but one in particular caught our attention:-

"If it needs a thief to catch a thief, perhaps a priest has some sort of psychological advantage when it comes to trying to get inside the heart and mind of another priest - even if their worlds are 1500 kilometres and 100 years apart."

These confessions are certainly refreshing, but apart from the fact that it is an unfortunate parallel in itself, we wondered why Fanthorpe would imply he had a psychological advantage over the rest of us in understanding the dubious behaviour pattern of Saunière, but maybe he has! However, if his psychology is valid over 1500 kilometres surely our computerised trigonometrical survey of only 15 kilometres warrants more than his dismissive remarks previously referred to.

We feel we should have been more attentive when we read on page one that Fanthorpe considers:-

"Exploring and researching the Rennes mystery can be compared to peeling a gigantic onion."

By the end of his book we must admit it had the same effect on us as if we had peeled that gigantic onion ourselves! We may find some consolation in that, subsequent to him having written his book, Lionel was willing to admit he had judged us too hastily, but his printed words remain and:-

§

"The Moving Finger writes; and, having writ,
Moves on: nor all thy Piety nor Wit
Shall lure it back to cancel half a Line,
Nor all thy Tears wash out a Word of it."

(The Rubáyát of Omar Khayyám)

The time has now come to face facts. Henry Lincoln admitted in his foreword of *GENISIS* that my geometric discovery was - "Amazing!" He continued by outlining the criteria he used in his judgement - "demonstrable and provable". Geometry is by its very nature demonstrable, but as remarkable as the alignments, which I found, were and as improbable as it was for them to have generated the extended pentagram by chance, some still had reservations; maybe, just maybe, they are coincidental.

As we all know, that which geometry 'demonstrates' can be tested and analysed by trigonometry, but the correct measure must be established before the 'demonstrable' becomes 'provable'. The angular measure in the proof is the Babylonian 360 degrees of the circle and this in turn disclosed the provably related linear measure of the construction, by a most ingenious method. With these, the geometric figure of *GENISIS* has been **'proved'** and as the reader will see, if I have misinterpreted the message contained in it, then so did Jules Verne and Nicolas Poussin. Nevertheless, even with the conviction that the solutions in this book are unassailable, it may be difficult for the reader to understand why they should have been shrouded in so much secrecy.

This factor certainly puzzled Henry Lincoln as he makes clear in his closing paragraphs of *The Holy Place*, where he says:-

"They spoke in riddles because they seemed to be gripped by some mysterious constraint. Why? It is a resonant question, and one which I cannot answer. I certainly feel no such constraint. Nor can I see any reason to conceal such a discovery. It may be, though, that my willingness to reveal it owes less to my knowledge of the discovery than it does to my ignorance of its implications for my predecessors."

Of course the simple answer is that in anything he has revealed, there is no need for it to be suppressed. But suppression there was and the resultant constraint persisted until comparatively recent times as the reader will see when we examine the works of Jules Verne.

It is in Henry Lincoln's last sentence that he shows considerable insight, when he states:-

> "I am aware of no necessity to speak in riddles as they have done.
> But in that necessity may lie the greatest mystery of all."

By the end of this book, the reader will realise how profound that statement is and how, in the opinion of many learned people, the 'establishment' has reason to ensure certain information does not become too easily accessed by the general public.

We would now refer to another book by Victor Clube, astrophysicist at Oxford University and Bill Napier of the Royal Observatory in Edinburgh who have gone to great lengths in *The Cosmic Serpent* to alert their readers to the ever present threat of 'celestial impact'. It was subsequent to writing the bulk of this book that we were fortunate enough to acquire a copy of another of their books *The Cosmic Winter*. This not only supported the validity of reviewing old writings for evidence of celestial hazards, but also referred to the suppression factor which we had felt duty bound to expose. Again it was in the closing paragraph of *The Cosmic Winter* that we find an ominous confirmation of our findings:-

> "There is considerable intellectual capital invested in the status quo, enough to ensure that those with an interest in preserving it, the 'enlightened' and the 'established', will continue to present the cosmos to us in a suitably non-violent form. The history of ideas reveals that some will even go further and act as a kind of thought police, whipping potential deviants into line. For them, temporal power takes precedence over the fate of the species.
> There is a need for this book."

Undoubtedly there is a need for that book as there is for this one.

CHAPTER 5.
THE KEYS TO THE SECRET

The Churches. The Golden Section. The ratios of Pi and Phi.
The Pythagorean School. The Pentagram. The Power of Shapes.
Do plants know? The Star Union. Pentagram and Hexagram unite.

FOR the geometry of the Rennes-le-Château valley to have a validity, certain difficulties have to be overcome. For there to be any pattern for us to examine, there must be a basis of continuity for us to interpret such a pattern - a continuity of number, scale, measure and base, (as in the different number systems of base 10 - decimal, base 12 - duodecimal or base 16 - hexadecimal). If there is not this link between the designers of the Rennes-le-Château geometry and ourselves, then anything we think we have found might be mere conjecture.

The problem is made doubly difficult by the age of the markers of the initial Circle of Churches. If we accept them at their face value, i.e. that the oldest of the buildings still extant are of the 12th and 13th centuries, then at least the skills required to calculate their geographical positions did exist. If, however we trace, as some archaeologists have done, the foundations of these buildings to Visigothic times, i.e. the 5th and 6th centuries A.D. then, so we are told, the necessary wherewithal which would have enabled the calculations to take place did not exist. This then, is the conundrum. If, as we suspect, the original markers of the Circle of Churches and relevant designs were standing stones, this would suggest that the geometry may be up to 4,000 years old, earlier than any known or admitted system of trigonometrical survey necessary to have placed them accurately in such a mountainous location.

If we believe the experts, and the geometry is of such great antiquity, the implication follows that it was not ancient Man who created the design. This poses a further problem. If an alien culture was responsible for the geometry of the Rennes-le-Château valley, then how did it know that Man would develop in such a way as to be able to recognise its significance. After all, not sharing their measure, number or scale, then in what language could they have left their message and be sure that in the millennia to come, Man would someday discover the geometry and understand it? As difficult as this conundrum may at first appear to solve, a solution does exist.

After considerable research, we found the method whereby an Intelligence could actually mark the Rennes-le-Château diagrams on the ground, conveying number, scale and measure, using only universal constants. There are many of these, but we began by looking at the simplest - the relationship between the

THE REGULAR PENTAGRAM

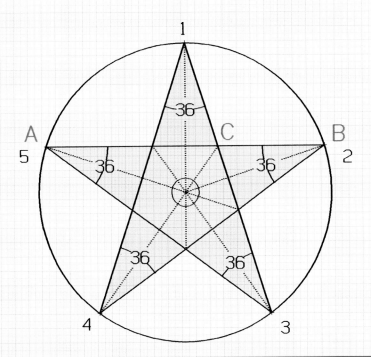

FIG 2. The regular pentagram is formed from a circle of 5 divisions of 72º **AB/AC = 1.618033989 = (Ø)**, which in the regular pentagram is true of all the pentagonal chords. The angles are of course 36 degrees at the star-points. Although considered 'Sacred', it pales to insignificance when measured against the 'Sacred properties of the extended pentagram.'

Right: The sign of the Microcosm said by Paracelsus to encompass all the occult forces of nature and to be the 'Quintessence of the Great Work'.

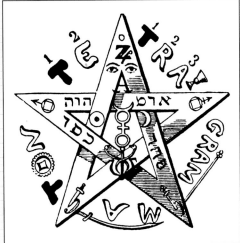

circle and its circumference - the Pi factor and the not so famous Phi factor -
the Golden Section of the ancient world. Could these be what they used ? The
qualities which these constants employ are several. They are both irrational
numbers - i.e. they never resolve to a finite number, even after millions of
places of decimals - and they are ratios and as such are 'universally' invariable
in the true sense of the word. Pi is the ratio of a circle, relating radius to
circumference and Phi is that of a line being able to be divided into two
unequal sections so that the length of the shorter part compared to the longer
part is the same as that of the longer part to the whole, (see appendix 2 for full
explanation).

Although these explanations may sound complex, they need not be so. The
Egyptians evaluated Pi by dividing two ropes of equal length into 22 equal
divisions. One rope was laid on the ground in the form of a circle. The second
rope was laid from the centre to the perimeter of the circle. The sections were
counted off in this radius and straight away a relationship could be seen. If the
circumference of the circle was 22 units, then the radius was just over 7. This
relationship is still evident today in hat sizes! Phi is not quite so simply derived,
but it is automatically generated when a regular pentagram is drawn
(see Fig. 2.). Here, whenever one line is intersected by another, the
intersection always occurs on the line according to the Golden Section ratio. Pi
and Phi have the numerical values:-

Pi π **= 3.14159265**   **Phi** $\emptyset$ **= 1.61803398**

In the case of Pi, four places of decimals are sufficient to accurately
describe the outermost limits of the universe at one end of the scale and the
circuit of electrons around an atom at the other end, so these figures are more
than adequate to define the Rennes-le-Château geometry. Nevertheless, to
accommodate the scaling we chose to work the ratios to eight places of
decimals in order to preserve accurate ground measure to the nearest inch.

The quality of these two irrational ratios is that they would be the same in
any part of the universe, whatever the unit of measure used. Furthermore, Phi
is seemingly one of the fundamental building blocks of life. It determines the
morphology or shape of nature. The leaves and branches of a tree, left to their
own devices, are all offset according to the Phi ratio, and this ratio efficiently
enables each leaf to have its fair share of sunlight, ensuring maximum benefit
to the plant. The Phi ratio also determines the exact point at which cell
division takes place. Even we human beings have navels which are situated at
the Golden Section ratio of the length of our bodies. Try measuring it sometime
- simply divide your height by 1.618 and then measure from the ground to the

navel.

Phi has other 'magical' qualities - its reciprocal is a harmonic of the number itself. In other words:-

Phi (Ø) = 1.618 and 1 ÷ Ø = 0.618 or 1 ÷ Ø = Ø - 1

Equally, the strange looking equation (X^2 = X + 1) can only be true when X = 1.618, because oddly enough X^2 also equals 2.618.

Six hundred years before the Christian era in Greece, there existed the Pythagorean School. Pythagoras was a prominent philosopher and in those days philosophy encompassed mathematics in its logical aspects. Geometry was certainly one of the subjects taught and the followers of Pythagoras were initiated into the 'mysteries' of the cult, which included showing them the qualities of secret geometrical shapes and arrangements. One of these was the pentagram, which, as we have already mentioned, contains the Golden Section or Phi Ratio. Indeed, this was reputedly such a closely guarded secret amongst the brotherhood, that to divulge it outside the group was a crime for which the punishment was death! However, it is unlikely that it was the simple regular pentagram which they held so sacred.

The Pythagoreans also used a secret sign of introduction as a means of revealing, one to another, that they were members of the Pythagorean school. Whenever a member wished to identify another member who he did not know, he would proffer an apple, which if the stranger cut laterally across the core, would display the seed pod in the shape of a pentagram. If the stranger executed this correctly, he would be known to be a member of the brotherhood.

We would now refer to the 'Wood Pentagram', which was discovered at Rennes-le-Château. In order to examine this pentagram thoroughly, we should return to *GENISIS*. This pentagram was of a strange construction, for although there were certain apparently regular pentagonal lines which could be placed, as from Rennes-le-Château to Bugarach, others, although not hitting markers on the circumference of the circle, still passed through quality markers which unavoidably generated the special pentagram. This pentagram was unique in that its northernmost tip projected outside the circumference of the circle, but it still preserved the requisite 36 degree angle on each of the star-points. Was this by accident or design? The thought occurred that there might well have been other peripheral markers on the rim of the circle, markers which had long since been reclaimed by nature. Was there a regularity in the spacing of the markers around the perimeter? Many experiments were carried out with different numbers of perimeter markers, but only one matched the geometry on the ground at Rennes-le-Château. It was that of a pentagram based on 15

THE EXTENDED PENTAGRAM

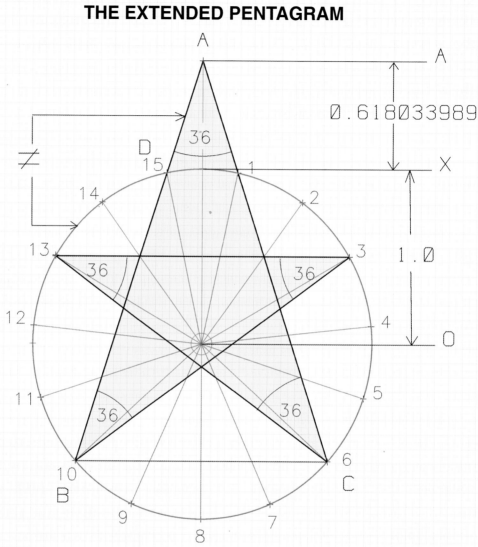

FIG 3. The circle circumference and the body perimeter **ABC** equate to within **1/6000** of **Pi**. The circle is divided into fifteen divisions of 24 degrees and by joining the positions indicated in the diagram a pentagonal figure is produced with one limb breaking the circle, but the star-points of 36 degrees are maintained. **BC** is in Golden Section to the chords comprising the Pentagonal body **AB** and **AC**. The axis of the extended head **AX**, is in Golden Section to the radius **OX**. (See Appendix 3 for a fuller analysis).

equal divisions of the circle. This arrangement was so accurate that only a very small amount of axial movement was necessary to hit all the markers which remain extant.

It was when this theoretical 15 division circle was analysed that David Wood knew he was on the right track. The problem with using a regular pentagram is that the dimensions generated are the same whichever way round it is oriented. The Rennes-le-Château theoretical pentagram however, throws out several different figures. The most impressive of these, is that the Phi ratio remains present in the new pentagram although the north point lays outside the circle. It is no longer apparent on the 'arms' of the figure but is generated where the perimeter of the circle cuts through the north point. This incredible figure also has other surprises in store. By studying Fig. 3, it can be seen that this enigmatic pentagram not only displays Phi ratio on its circle centre to north point dimension, but that the base of the body triangle, BC in the triangle ABC, is also in Phi ratio with both the west and east sides of the body. A comparison of the circumference of the circle also shows an almost identical length (within 1/6000 of Pi), to that of the perimeter of the body triangle which it generates. All this while still preserving the essential identity of 36 degrees on each star-point. A truly strange figure indeed! What is even stranger is that nowhere in the annals of Sacred or any other geometry have the remarkable qualities of this figure been commented on. On the contrary, a few supposedly learned mathematicians who we have approached have said that this irregular, but symmetrical, 15 division pentagram could not support an angle of 36 degrees on each of its points, and that we were quite mad to believe that it can. Check it for yourself!

Lastly, in this chapter, we should look at the Star Union - the fitting together of the perfect pentagram and hexagram into a seven pointed star. Legend has it that King Solomon carried a shield with the Star of David (a hexagram) emblazoned on its exterior and the pentagram on its interior. For what purpose? Certainly throughout history, these two geometrical figures have been generated into the most popular designs on the planet. If you doubt this, just count how many countries have embodied these designs into their national flags. Is there however, a method in this 'madness'? Curiously enough, we have only to turn to nature to find an indication of the answer, for plants bearing 5 petalled leaves are considered safe to eat whilst those embodying 6 folded symmetry are considered to be poisonous, invariably belonging to the alkaloid family.

Recent research also shows that plant growth can be speeded up or retarded by the application of either positive or negative electromagnetic currents in a pentagonal or hexagonal pattern. A whole new science will

THE STAR UNION

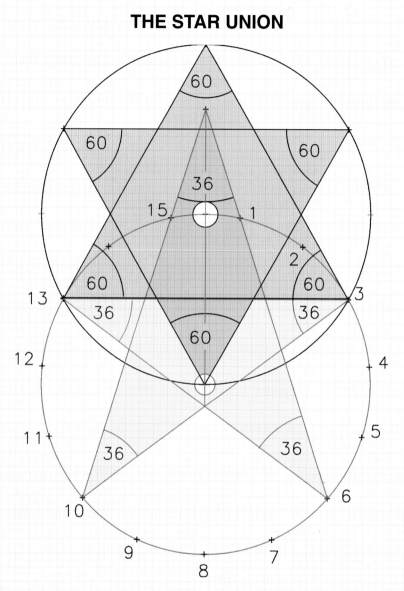

FIG 4. Only by the use of the fifteen division circle, can a pentagonal figure be generated which results in an arm chord which is the same as the chord of a hexagram **(3-13)**. In fact, all the chords of the female pentagram are the same dimension as the hexagonal chord. The hexagram can, therefore, be constructed from any of the pentagonal chords in the original circle.

probably grow up around the use of 'shaped' electromagnetic fields, which might, in future be used to control disease or promote growth. Curiously,in medieval times, witches when denounced, often cursed the land of their accusers by putting a 'hex' on the fields belonging to them. An Old Wives' Tale perhaps, but possibly with good reason.

At this point, we should remember that whereas geometry has always been regarded as the Cinderella of the mathematical sciences, it has, since the inception of the Nuclear Age become possibly the most important. From its original position as the fairly insignificant sibling branch of the other sciences, it is now regarded as the major tool for the understanding of the new physics of time and the molecular bonding processes.

In the Rennes geometry of the pentagram, it was noticed that the top arm of the figure runs from the church at Rennes-le-Château through the ruined chateau at Montferrand before hitting the perimeter of the circle. Although there is no marker at this point, its perimeter intersection is determined by Montferrand. This line creates a chord across the circle. A chord, the measure of which when divided by the radius of the Circle of Churches, generates the ratio of 1.732 : 1 . This is the root of 3, or ($\sqrt{3}$), the exact length of a chord which divides the two intersecting circles of the sacred Vesica Piscis, whose centres stand on the perimeter of each other's complementary circle. In other words, directly this $\sqrt{3}$ value (1.732), was noticed in the arm/chord of the pentagram, we knew it had another property, for this chord of $\sqrt{3}$ is the exact length of the base of an equilateral triangle (see Fig. 4), which would be generated by the same circle.

As an equilateral triangle is half of the figure required to make a Star of David or hexagram, we recognised that this 'arm' of the diagram was common to both figures and could unite both pentagram and hexagram. Once more, such a figure had never been revealed in any books on Sacred or Ordinary Geometry, until it was published in *GENISIS*. It would, however, have had devastating significance to the esoteric world, for the Star Union, the blending of both life forces, the Yin and the Yang of the Chinese school, was every alchemist's dream! Even the notorious Eliphas Levi (Alphonse Louis Constant), mysteriously stated that "whoever discovered the secret of uniting the Pentagram and the Hexagram, was halfway to solving the mysteries". How other than by way of an advanced intelligence could this figure manifest itself at such a scale in the valley of Rennes-le-Château?

We started this chapter explaining the necessity of the use of constants, reasoning that it would be a possible way for knowledge to be derived from the geometry. Now we have shown that both Phi and Pi, the Pentagram and the Hexagram, are indelibly represented in the ground figure of Rennes-le-

Château. If confirmation of the Star Union was needed, we had only to remember the lines of the poem by Charles Péguy :- "The arms of Satan and the Cross of Lorraine... The arms of Jesus and the Cross of Lorraine..." We concluded in *GENISIS* that the arms of Jesus are thereby being presented as the arms of Satan, precisely as the geometry of the star-union depicts. Jesus was of the line of King David and Solomon, whose emblem was the hexagram and the Christians certainly considered the pentagram to be the symbol of Satan. Symbolically, the hexagram has six points representing the head, arms, legs and phallus, whereas the pentagram represents the female figure.

At this time, it would serve us well to remember that to the Christian, Satan is a fallen angel, said to have been God's closest associate. As our inquiry proceeds, we will have no alternative but to identify the true nature of this Christian Satan. He was Seth in the Garden of Eden and Set in the Egyptian pantheon of gods. He was also the Typhon of the Greeks.

Although we were sure that Pi and Phi were two of the constants necessary for the solution of the geometry, we still needed confirmation that we were on the right track and furthermore, we needed to discover how a unit of linear measure could be defined from those ratios together with angles and the properties of the circle. Elsewhere in the solving of the mystery, such confirmations had always been forthcoming. Little did we expect that this one would occur with such clarity.

CHAPTER 6.
SINE LANGUAGE

The trigonometrical ratios. 'La Vraie Langue'.
We begin to see the signs. The sign which conquers.
Poussin and Teniers did hold the key. What was 681?

IN any right-angled triangle (a triangle which contains one angle of 90 degrees), it is comparatively simple to calculate all the values in that triangle as long as one knows either two sides or one side and one angle. This has been made possible by a series of tables which were constructed to determine the ratios which exist between the remaining angles in the triangle and their opposing sides. Dependent upon which function is chosen, one of the tables is selected. One may use the Tangent, Cosine, Sine or their reciprocals to facilitate the solution. Nowadays, we are fortunate to have scientific calculators which have dispensed with the need for tables and thus greatly accelerated trigonometrical calculation. The ratio we are particularly concerned with is the SINE, which is the side opposite the angle in question divided by the hypotenuse of the triangle.

To achieve a full understanding of the secret of Rennes-le-Château, it is necessary to at least recognise that more than one ratio has been used. In this chapter, we will introduce another form of mathematical language, SINE LANGUAGE.

Already, we have dealt with the literature written about the subject in English and French and referred to the coded documents which were in Latin and Greek. Abbé Boudet additionally brought Gaelic, Basque and other more exotic languages into the fray to explain his major opus *La Vraie Langue Celtique et le Cromlech de Rennes-les-Bains*.

Nevertheless, we will be staying with the language of number and in particular, the language of SINES. Before going too deeply into this new language, rest assured we are quite aware of the English/French dictionary translation of the mathematical word SINE. The French equivalent is SINUS and that is not the word which is mentioned in the church, so before anyone suspects that we have indeed caught a cold from this word/idea, please be patient. The French word we encounter in the church is SIGNE which although Collins/Robert translates as 'A MATHEMATICAL SIGN' it could easily be interpreted as a SINE. Remember, everyone we encounter in the mystery seems to be fond of playing word games and making puns.

John McLeish, in his book *Number* defines SINE thus :-

"The kuttaka is an extremely sophisticated procedure and points to a deep understanding of number theory. Aryabhata did work of equal insight in other areas."

He calculated the value of Pi as 62,832 ÷ 20,000, that is, about 3.1416. (He also recognised that this was an approximation). It is, nonetheless, an improvement on Archimedes' value of Pi as being 'between 22 ÷ 7 and 223 ÷ 71', i.e. between about 3.1408 and 3.1428. He laid a basis for trigonometry by developing a table of sines, which replaced Ptolemy's table of chords in astronomical calculations.

As Claudius Ptolemaius (Ptolemy) was active in about 150 A.D., we can see that the idea of such a trigonometrical function is at least as old as this and we have reason to believe that the Ancient Egyptians also had Tables of Chord lengths and calculations which were the same as those which today we call SINES. If you have been educated in 'maths' and 'trig' prior to the 1970's, then you will recall that the most common form of sine values used to be found in the form of Sine Tables, often listed in the back of a book of Logarithmic Tables. We also understand that many people who may have been educated after this period, may not be aware of them. This is one of the dangers of progress, as is the adoption of a metric system. Both make the puzzles of antiquity more difficult to see, let alone solve.

It is indeed curious that the small community surrounding Rennes-le-Château should need not one language, but three or even four to be able to make itself understood, but such is the enigma which surrounds the place. Most of us are aware that by far the greatest part of the literature on the subject is written in French, and it is only when you can read the authoritative accounts in that language that you can begin to see the complexities involved.

Before we move on to the language of Sines, let us return to the work of Abbé Boudet and his *La Vraie Langue Celtique et le Cromlech de Rennes-les-Bains*. It is, at the very least, an obscure and unapproachable piece of literature. It is one in which the author tries to draw similarities between the old language of the Languedoc and Breton, Celtic, Basque, Latin and English. Indeed, Boudet seems to implicitly suggest that English was the original language of the Gods and that it is that language which is represented in the place names found in the area of Rennes-le-Château. An astonishing claim, especially when you see Boudet really straining to make one obscure or abstruse connection after another. For example, Boudet gives us the flavour of his reasoning with his interpretation of the names of the months of the year, giving us first the French name, then the Basque, and then the way he thought the name originated from the English; two examples of which are:-

"Janvier, Urtharrilla-Le mauvais temps du mois de janvier arrête les travaux de ceux qui voudraient passer la herse dans leurs champs,-to hurt,nuire,-to harrow,herser, to will (ouill) désirer, vouloir."

"Mars, Martchoa-Les pluies continuel-les de Mars changent forcement les terrains en marécages - marsh, marais, un lieu marecageux - to owe (o), devoir."

This should give the reader an idea of the eccentric work of Boudet. For the month of Mars, for example, he makes no attempt to explain that the month was named after the Roman God of War. Instead he builds his explanation that Mars, Martchoa (in Basque) sounds like and takes its meaning from the English words 'marsh' and 'owe' and clearly he was mistaken. You do not have to search very far back into the English language to be aware that modern English is far removed from that of Shakespeare's day, which is only just comprehensible to a modern English speaker, but try to understand Chaucer's 13th century language and you will receive a rude awakening, for that requires scholarship and has little direct relevance to the modern tongue. Go back a century further than Chaucer and English was Norman French and before that, Saxon. Therefore, Boudet's idea that local names of the area surrounding Rennes-le-Château have their etymological stems in Modern English, is quite frankly, laughable. Even if Boudet had been correct in his etymological explanations of Languedocian terms in modern English, all it would indicate would be that it was a modern conundrum and not one from antiquity. But remember, Boudet was an erudite man, and presented his master-work to the literary society in Carcassonne and was universally snubbed for it. If the man was indeed nobody's fool, then what should we make of the feeble explanations such as are contained in his book. Could he even be suggesting that English would be needed to understand a cipher? Strangely this will be shown to be so when later we decode the famous 'ET IN ARCADIA EGO' inscription.

The first thing to be aware of is that Boudet undoubtedly knew that the work would not stand up to scrutiny by scholars in etymology, but remember we are dealing with the Languedoc, an area which takes its name from the old language of the area the 'langue' (tongue) of the 'oc' (old French for yes) and nothing is necessarily what it seems. Another language was referred to as the 'langue des oiseaux' - mentioned and used by Mozart in his occult/Masonic 'Magic Flute' and by Richard Wagner in 'Siegfried' and 'Götterdämmerung'. This language of the birds - la langue des oiseaux - refers to the fact that the word oiseaux is one of the very few words in French containing all the vowels A, E, I, O, U. In other words, la langue des oiseaux played with words and

phonetic meanings and was often said to be the language used by the birds. It was a secret language, and Boudet was in his element when using it, as was Jules Verne. Secret meaning was conveyed by the use of seemingly plain passages which had a hidden sound or meaning, although sometimes, it was necessary to transmute such phrases through several languages before being able to distil the wisdom of the message. Most people lacked the time to indulge Boudet and therefore his secrets remained very safe. However, in our condemnation of Boudet we must be careful not to discard the baby with the bath water, for some of the place names in the valley seem to be understandable as phonetic English.

Another of Saunière's clues in the church. In hindsight, the 'Signe' of the inscription is a blatant reference to the 'Sine' of trigonometry.

So what of SINE LANGUAGE. We believe it is a numerical precursor of what Boudet and Saunière and Jules Verne were doing when they deliberately left clues for others to discover in the centuries to come.

What we are also sure of, is that the numerical language is so complex and has been used so expertly to confirm the geometry, that it must be the product of a far older intelligence than our illustrious friends mentioned above. Its origins may even be older than 'thinking' man himself, for what we are able to do today with a simple pocket calculator would, a millennium ago, have taken a team of mathematicians years to work out.

We returned to the church of St. Mary Magdalen at Rennes-le-Château. A church unusually full of word games, puns, misspellings and misquotations. Usually, the Church just writes information which they wish to keep from the public in Latin or Greek, but not so at Rennes-le-Château. The quotation under the frieze which displays Jesus on a hillside on the west wall of the church reads in French:-

"VENEZ A MOI TOUS QUI SOUFFRE ET JE VOUS SOULAGERAI"
"COME UNTO ME ALL YE WHO LABOUR AND I WILL GIVE YOU REST".

Quite straightforward at first glance, except the words 'donner reste' have been replaced by 'soulagerai'. Coincidentally, Soulatgé, is the name of a hamlet near Rennes- les-Bains ! Another quote is:-

"PAR CE SIGNE TU LE VAINCRAS"

"BY THIS SIGN YOU WILL WIN/CONQUER"

except the word 'le' - meaning 'he' or 'it' has been inserted changing the sense of the phrase to:-

"BY THIS SIGN YOU WILL WIN/CONQUER IT"

So, obviously, word games and puns are the tools that Boudet and Saunière work with and hence there will be a need to examine the parchment code, "BERGERE, PAS DE TENTATION QUE POUSSIN, TENIERS GARDENT LE CLEF. PAX 681....".

We had seen the paintings and copies of the paintings and we had studied them carefully. We were aware of Professor Cornford's detailed examination of 'Les Bergers d'Arcadie' and his revelation of the pentagonal base for the painting, but we also knew what he had overlooked. We had seen the Lincoln/Chronicle tape, showing the juxtaposition and misalignment of the painting with the location of the 'Poussin' tomb near Les Pontils, but were we missing something? Something so simple that it lay under our noses. The interpretation of the coded phrase made little sense, or rather it made several senses, none clearer than the other. If the Poussin reference tied in to his 'Les Bergers d'Arcadie' painting, that would be important, but would it also imply that we were to consider that the Teniers reference involved a Teniers painting? This was a complex question, for a check with art historian Valerie Martin revealed that there had been three painters called Teniers, - a father and two sons, and that they had all painted similar biblical scenes in similar styles including a dozen or more, entitled 'The Temptations of St. Anthony'. Curiously enough, in only one of these was St. Anthony NOT being tempted.

Could this be what the code was referring to:- 'Shepherdess, No Temptation' - were we supposed to concentrate on this one painting in which he wasn't being tempted by the Devil? Or, was it the background of this painting that was important - the cave - in a similar way to the background of the Poussin painting?

It appeared to be insoluble until we realised that it might be the very names of Poussin and Teniers which held the key. What did they have in common? In the following chapter the reader will not only see how these names are related, but how it can be confirmed. Furthermore, later in the book we will see this information solve the famous 'ET IN ARCADIA EGO' inscription on the tomb featured in 'Les Bergers d'Arcadie'.

For the moment let us look at the rest of the coded phrase 'PAX 681'. PAX surely meant 'Peace', but what of 681? We played with the figure, tossed it around and made several observations. If it had been 'PAX 618', that might have implied Golden Section, but 681 continued to ring a tiny bell.

Allegedly, the year 681 was when Sigisbert IV , son of Dagobert II was brought to Rennes-le-Château, after being rescued from the assassination attempt which had killed his father in the forest of Woëvres. The timing fitted, and we already had a connection with Dagobert in the parchment:-

"A DAGOBERT II ET A SION EST CE TRESOR ET IL EST LA MORT"

The date 681 gave us nothing further than we already knew and the 'Intelligence' which had given us the conundrum of Rennes-le-Château was not given to wasting clues. As 681 was the only figure used in the entire decoded parchments, we felt it was bound to have a more specific meaning.

According to French author Franck Marie in his book, *La Résurrection du 'GRAND COCU'* (published by Anciennes Vérités, 1981), 681 might well refer to the PEACE Treaty signed between Thrace and Macedonia in the year A.D. 681. Marie's source for this information is given as *La Bulgarie* by G. Castellan. Although the link may seem tenuous, Franck Marie does link the Bulgars with the name Bugarach given to the highest mountain near Rennes-le-Château. This mountain reputedly contains one of the largest cave systems in Europe and there are tales of treasure associated with it. Although the nature of the treaty and the year seemingly match the encoded phrase 'PAX 681', we decided to stay with the mathematical connotations the number 681 brings and as the reader will see, we were right to do so.

First we broke the figure down into its component parts and analysed them. $681 \div 2 = 340.5$ Reminiscent of the 3,4,5 right-angled Pythagorean triangle, but was there a right-angled triangle featured in the geometry? Eventually we found it, but already we were seeing things that had escaped the notice of other investigators.

The SINE values of a 3,4,5 triangle are 0.**6**, 0.**8** and **1**.0. We knew there must be a connection. If a 3,4,5, right-angled triangle is enlarged or reduced proportionately, the sine values remain at 0.6, 0.8 and 1.0, and thereby the SINE LANGUAGE is general, whilst the recognisable numerical values of 3, 4 and 5 are restricted. Suddenly we realised that the sine value of any angle could be interpreted as a linear dimension and given the acceptance of a 360° circle, a universal measure could be established. So enigmatic was the 681 factor at Rennes-le-Château that we made a mental note to watch out for it as the figure developed. When it eventually manifested itself, it did so in a most convincing way.

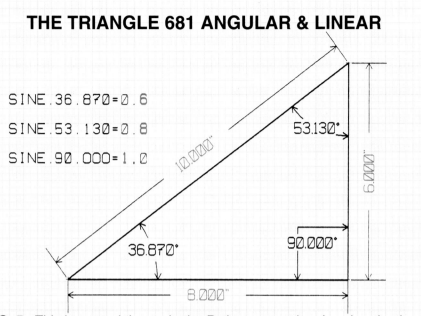

THE TRIANGLE 681 ANGULAR & LINEAR

SINE.36.870=0.6

SINE.53.130=0.8

SINE.90.000=1.0

53.130°

10.000"

6.000"

36.870°

90.000°

8.000"

FIG. 5. This is a special case in the Pythagorean triangle, whereby the lengths **6-8-10** correspond to the Sines of their angles **.6-.8-1.0**. As the reader will later realise, it was the sickening simplicity of this triangle - **681** which was the key to showing us that Sine values could be used to convey linear measure regardless of which unit the discoverer happened to be handicapped by at the time.

We were now in possession of the geometry of the Circle of Churches and the unique Extended Pentagram, but what did that extension mean? Remarkably it was to be the limiting factor of the length of the Temple of Rennes-le-Château. Under computer analysis, this Temple displayed many unbelievable properties. These will be dealt with in detail, but first let us return to some more signs (Sines) in the valley, sines which eventually will be seen to translate into the linear dimensions required to solve the geometry.

CHAPTER 7.
THE SECRET OF THE SIGNS

Slotted-templet exposes a pentagram. A sexual implication.
Is a sign a sine? Clues in Poussin's works. The half-staffs.
The pentagram is female. The search for the unit of measure.
Finding of the radius of the circle. Amazing correlations of area and
circumference reveal the ancient doctrine.
We find the ground multiple.

AT this stage of our exploration, it should be borne in mind that we have been working with the geometry of Rennes-le-Château for several years. Since *GENISIS*, we have lived and breathed number, Pi and Phi ratios and angles. So much so, that sometimes, when we chance upon a new number, subconscious connections force themselves into the frontal lobes of the mind. Where one person may see no significance whatsoever in a particular number, others, more familiar with the territory will make connections and deduce inferences. After months of calculating, multiples of the ratios are recognisable to us as familiar faces. For this, we make no apology. It is simply the way things are.

Returning to *GENISIS*, the pentagram in the Rennes valley was discovered by using the slotted-templet method (see Appendix), an aerial/trig surveyor's technique developed in World War II. What this meant was that when David Wood knew he was searching for a pentagram, he commenced the search by studying the maps of the area, looking for pentagonal angles in the landscape.

Templets could be considered to be simply lines drawn onto an acetate sheet at angles of 36 degrees to each other - a pentagonal angle. This acetate vector could be pinned on the map at a known point, rotated and any correlations noted through which the radials passed. In other words, if on the ground in the Rennes valley, you were to stand at any one point on a line of sight, you might have perceived important markers on a second line offset at 36 degrees to the first. It was noticed that several of these coincidences occurred in the valley and furthermore, corresponded with features related to the mystery.

It was also realised that some of the points which the lines identified stood on the perimeter of the Circle of Churches. An intensive survey and much computer work, has later confirmed this to be an irrefutable fact.

The pentagonal angles are principally those of 36 degrees (on each point), although other resultant angles, such as 72 degrees will appear within the figure. In fact, a series of angles such as 18, 27, 36, 72, etc. can be described as pentagonal. Curiously, their two figure numbers always add up to 9 !

The second important point to be aware of is that numbers are not chance events. They did not materialise by accident, but are part of an ancient order which we are only just beginning to grasp in depth. From early beginnings, 'thinking' Man has had a universal understanding of things.

Give a Chinese person a stick, and ask him or her to mark 3 in the earth and he or she will draw three lines. Pass the stick to a westerner and ask them to do the same thing and they will also draw three lines. The western 3 will be vertical and the Chinese 3 horizontal, but it is remarkable that such diverse representatives of modern man share a similar concept of number. This example was facile, but no less important for being so. Read philosophy and see the explanations for number. 1, Unity; 2, Duality ; 3 the Tripos - Three-in-One - the Trinity - the smallest number of straight lines which can be used to enclose a space, (the triangle); 4 the square - Man's building block - Construction; 5 The Pentagram - The Female Active principle - Life; 6 The Hexagram - The Male Principle, etc.,- all legacies from hoar antiquity.

Another illustration is even more explicit. The 1 represents the phallus, laying dormant on its side (as in the Chinese ideogram). The concept of zero represents the female, or the womb. The circle, after all, contains the female pentagram. Take either of these symbols on their own and you have just ONE or NOTHING, but combine them into a 10, by placing the nought alongside the one, and suddenly multiplication occurs. In order for the phallus, (the 1) to achieve its sexual conjugation, it has to become erect. i.e. it has to pass through 90 degrees and if you subtract this 90 degrees from the 360 degrees of the circle, the remainder, 270 degrees happens to be the equivalent of 9 x 30 day months, the period of human gestation. Don't forget that when we described the square as the male building block, the square is comprised of 4 x 90 degree angles. In other words, the concept of number is much more than a trite phrase and totally descriptive of its action.

Therefore, be aware, that playing with numbers can have surprising consequences. *GENISIS* listed a whole series of numbers with their meanings as attached to the pantheon of Egyptian gods and once aware of these values, it is impossible not to recognise them whenever they occur in the geometry. The idea of number can work on different levels simultaneously, just as many books can work on a simple and complex level at one and the same time, dependent upon the intelligence of the reader.

With all these left-brain-hemisphere activities reverberating around the mystery of the Rennes geometry, the right-brain brought one particular word to the surface. It was one that continually surfaced from the muddy waters of the mystery. It was everywhere and nowhere. In the church. Outside the church and alluded to in the decoded documents and featured in the Poussin painting of 'Les Bergers d'Arcadie'. The word in question was SIGN. Two items had caught our attention.

Incised above the portal of the church of St. Mary Magdalen at Rennes-le-Château is engraved:-

"IN HOC SIGNO VINCES"
"BY THIS SINE/SIGN YOU WILL CONQUER"

As we have mentioned, inside the church and under the tableau at the western end of the nave, we find:-

"PAR CE SIGNE TU LE VAINCRAS"
"BY THIS SINE/SIGN YOU WILL CONQUER IT"

Could the 'it' refer to something significant in the geometry of the mystery? In the decoded parchments:-

POUSSIN, TENIERS GARDENT LE CLEF

POUSSIN, TENIERS HOLD THE KEY. Could the key be a trigonometrical key or, as we refer to it, a ratio? Could the 'sign' in these two statements (SIGNO and SIGNE) be telling us to consider the trigonometrical 'SINE' ratio? SIGN(O) SIGN(E) In fact, as we said earlier, could it be simply the names of the artists we should examine (POUS)**SIN** and (TE)**NI**(ER)**S.**

Could   **SIGN = SIN = SINE?**

The name POUSSIN ends in SIN, the recognised mathematical abbreviation for a 'SINE' and the only common letters in POUSSIN and TENIERS are SIN, which in TENIERS are reversed and this process of a 'mirrored' image in occult matters is well-known. In fact, the tombstone of Poussin in Rome is a reversed version of 'Les Bergers d'Arcadie'. We examined the SINE values of the pentagonal angles and none of the values rang any bells, except one, -SIN 18°. It looked vaguely familiar, then the bell rang, as loud and clear as the cow-bells on the mountain slopes beneath the brooding fortress ruins of Montségur. When we had been investigating the qualities of the Golden Section (Phi, Ø, or 1.61803398), we had also looked at its reciprocal (1 ÷ Ø), or 0.61803398. Half the reciprocal is 0.3090169 (precisely the Sine value of 18°, the pentagonal angle par excellence).

Should the non-mathematical reader fail to appreciate the powerful significance of halving the reciprocal of Phi and obtaining the precise SINE value of 18°, we will expand the connection.

'La Peste d'Azoth' (The Plague of Azoth) by Nicolas Poussin. Azoth is
the alchemical name for Mercury. This work contains a great number of
confirmations of the secret doctrine concealed in its imagery.
This detail demonstrates the half-staff, the geometric adjustments to
the head and hand of the pentagram of Rennes-le-Château and finally
the God of the Deep, warning the Shepherds of impending disaster.

In Lincoln's Chronicle programme The Priest, The Painter and The Devil, you will recall Professor Cornford stated that 'Les Bergers d'Arcadie' by Poussin, was constructed by an unusual combination of Golden Section and pentagonal disciplines. Our identification of the relationship between the reciprocal of the Golden Section and the pentagonal angle of 18° is, therefore, both a confirmation and extension of this construction.

Lincoln also drew the viewers' attention to the fact that the staffs of the shepherds were 'halved' by various intersections of detail. Lincoln was sure this repetitive 'halving' was significant, but could see no reason for it. In examining other works by Poussin, we discovered the same technique and an outstanding example is where the carrying staffs of the Ark of the Covenant are precisely 'halved' in 'La Peste d'Azoth' (see illustration). The reader should also recall that the star angles of a pentagram are 36° and they must be 'bisected' or 'halved' to form the construction radii to the centre of the circle. Halving 36 produces 18. To summarise, therefore, both the control disciplines of the painting must be halved in order to recognise their correspondence and solve this part of the mystery.

Add to this the overpowering 'co-incidence' of the SIN in POUSSIN, and that the kneeling shepherd in 'Les Bergers d'Arcadie' points to the **'R'** in the inscription 'ET IN ARCADIA EGO'. The letter **'R'** is as we know the **18**th letter of the alphabet. Surely the most sceptical should be convinced.

POUSSIN - PHI - PENTAGRAM - HALF-STAFF - SINE 18° - 'R'

The link has been made, and how beautifully it has been done! In *GENISIS* the figure 18 was described as :- "The function of Isis and one of the keys to the mysteries. It is this number which appears to rationalise numerical descriptions in esoteric texts." The Ark of the Covenant, The Grail, The Round Table, Atlantis and many more artefacts, all respond to this number and become immediately meaningful.

With the name Isis meaning 'seat' in all respects, and assuming the standard height of a seat to be 18 inches, the number of man (4) is confirmed by the simple recognition that a 6-foot standard man has 4 divisions of 18 inches both in height and across his outstretched arms. In this position, the body of the man represents the 'crux ansata'. It is interesting to observe that the circular part in the emblem doubles as his head and the female genitals. Once again we find the equation - intellect, (the head of the man) = the womb, (source of intelligence)." (*GENISIS* p 216). "The complete symbol of the Isis principle is the caduceus - here we see the 'one-in-eight'. The two serpents are entwined to represent the vagina and the womb, through both of which passes the phallus."

Continuing with the pentagram, although 18 is not immediately apparent, the axes passing through the 36 degrees star-points bisect those angles to form 18 degrees. These five axes intersect at the centre of the circle containing the pentagram. If each of these axes is then extended, they divide the opposing legs of a regular pentagram at the positions which represent the female reproductive organ. Remembering that 360 divided by 18 is 20 - the number of the Holy of Holies - and that the pentagonal 5 multiplied by 18 equates with the 90 degrees of erection, it is hardly surprising that this number was so important in ancient doctrine.

Returning to our investigation, we now had confirmation that Phi would form an important part of the solution. In addition to this we had also established the Phi/Sine relationship to reinforce our assumption of the 'sign' references meaning 'sine'. When one considers that, whereas the SIN of Poussin indicates the use of SINE values so does the NIS of Teniers quite clearly suggest the necessity to use the 'inverse function'. As half the reciprocal of Phi (0.309016994) is the only factor of the universal constants capable of inversing to a perfect number of degrees (18°), we can be sure we have found the 'key'. Indeed the chances of the signs in the church, the artists names, the Phi and pentagonal construction of Poussin's painting, the 'R' of the inscription and the half-staff of the Phi reciprocal, all harmonising to only one common factor are nothing short of astronomical.

In the last chapter we mentioned how the design, which we knew it was, would have to be laid down using universal constants, such as Pi and Phi, interacting with an angular function. Now we had all three! Was this enough? Could the geometry of the Rennes valley be conceived purely by using these factors? If so, then we could free ourselves from the map and yet we would have a ready made test, for if we were right, then the purely theoretical layout of the geometry should, if correctly scaled to the map being used, fit all the locations. It should indeed be possible to draw the plan on the computer using the CAD system, print it to map scale, overlay it on the map and hit all the positions. There could be no finer confirmation! At this stage, we should point out that we were already convinced of the high intellect of the designers. Attempting to put ourselves in their position, we knew they would have no idea which units of measure would be in use at the time their construction was discovered. True, the geometry could confine itself to only interacting ratios and still be impressive, but to convey numerical values, an established unit of measure could do so much more. As we continued with the trigonometrical analysis, we began to recognise how they had interwoven the ratios of Phi and Pi with Sine values. Eventually we realised they had done this in such a manner as to establish the unit of measure they were using, and we knew they would clearly demonstrate its value.

We turned our attention to the computer and drew the basic Rennes-le-Château diagram, using a scale calibrated in what we refer to as Ancient Units without knowing its precise length (AUs in this book always refers to Ancient Units and not Astronomical Units or Ångstrom Units). We thought that this unit might approximate very closely to the British inch, but we did not know for sure, so we calibrated the diagram in AUs. In the days of *GENISIS*, Wood had noticed that one of the measurements which seemed to approximate the radius of the Circle of Churches was 186,282 inches of ground measure - the speed of light in inches of ground measure instead of miles per second, but he had discarded it because it involved miles. The difference between the early work and the modern work is largely one of resolution. Working by map and drawing equipment alone, you can be no more accurate than +/- 25 metres. With the Computer Aided Design system, we could work to within an inch of ground measure, which is to say, an inch on the computer screen representing an inch on the ground.

First we needed to find the correct radius for our Circle of Churches and one which was not open to different interpretation - a mathematical value would be fine. We knew it would probably approximate the figure 186,282 and also that it might be any number modified by Phi, Pi or sine ratio. A glance at the table below shows why sine values of various numbers between 1 and 90 on their own would not be large enough to fit within our ball-park figure of 186,282 :-

SINE 1° = 0.0174524   SINE 18° = 0.3090169
SINE 54° = 0.8090169   SINE 89° = 0.9998477

Clearly no sine value can ever be larger than 1. Therefore we knew that a scaling factor would be needed and one that would not change the characteristics of the number. This meant that we could only use numbers according to the base of ten - 100, 1000, 10000, 100000 or 1000000 etc.,

Multiplying the above numbers by 100,000 gave us values of:-

SINE 1° = 0.0174524 X 100,000 = 1,745.2406
SINE 18° = 0.3090169 X 100,000 = 30,901.699
SINE 54° = 0.8090169 X 100,000 = 80,901.699
SINE 89° = 0.9998477 X 100,000 = 99,984.77

but from this it was still clear that straightforward sine values would not even bring us within the ball-park, so we experimented with Pi values :-

3.1415927 X 100,000 = 314,159.27   3.1415927 ÷ 2 X 100,000 = 157,079.63

Again, the nearest we could approach the ball-park figure of 186,282 was

THE ALTERNATIVE RADII FOR
THE CIRCLE OF CHURCHES

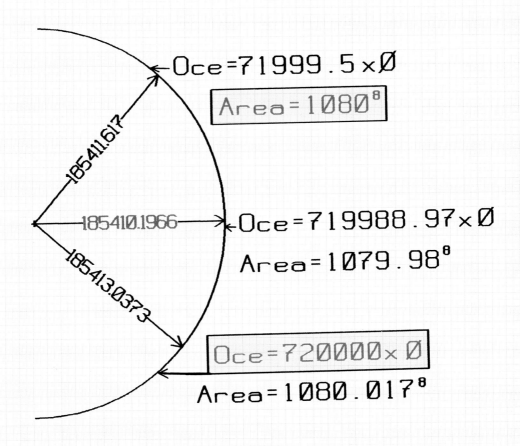

Fig.6. The three radii vary by only 2 inches over a distance of almost 3 miles. This could never be plotted on a map, but when one considers the correspondences these radii generate, it is nothing short of miraculous. Radius **185,411.6171** is the precise mean value of the other two radii and **185,410.1966** (3x0.618033989), is the doctrinal mean between the integer values of area **1080** and circumference **720,000**, the significance of which is explained in the text.

with 157,079.63, a difference in radius of 29,185 AUs, which was off-target by Lincolnian proportions ! Lastly, we tried the Phi ratio. Could there be a special figure which, if multiplied by, or divided by Phi would indicate the radius we sought :-

100,000 ÷ 1.618034 = 61,803.399 (our familiar friend, the Phi reciprocal). This figure was about a third of the one we sought, but we were aware of the possibility of three concentric circles in the construction, each decreasing in radius by one third of the larger.

300,000 ÷ 1.618034 = 185,410.2

This was certainly within the ball-park, but was it significant? Compared with the figure for the velocity of light in a vacuum, the discrepancy was less than 1,000 AUs - 872 to be precise and we realised that if we exchanged AUs for inches, we would be within 25 metres of the original radius for the Circle of Churches. We looked for confirmation. A circle, radius 185,410.2 AUs generates a circumference of 1,164,966.6 AUs and an area of 1,079,998,000,000 AUs. We wondered what values lay concealed in these figures. The area figure was certainly, strangely familiar. The 1,079,998,000,000 AUs was very close to 1080^8. Why was it ringing a bell? Luckily, not many books have been written on Sacred Geometry, so the search for the meaning and relevance did not take too long to find. It has been clearly stated by John Michell in his masterwork *The Dimension of Paradise.*

> "1080, the Lunar number. Of the forces or tendencies which, through their interactions, create the apparent universe, that which is called the "yin" or receptive - the lunar, earthly, inspirational as opposed to the solar, cosmic, rational side of nature - is subsumed under the number 1080...in the Cabalists' equation 666 + 1080 = 1746...identified by all its symbolism with the moon, the sublunary world, the waters below that are drawn to the moon, the lunar influence on the earth's vital currents, the periods of the female, the unconscious, intuitive   part of the mind and the spirit that moves oracles. The geometric image of that same principle, the pentagon, exhibits the angle of 108 degrees between its sides."

Even more significant to the nature of our construction, John Michell in *The View Over Atlantis* states:-

> "Throughout the world, in every traditional code of architectural proportion, computation of time and wherever else number is

involved, 1080 is always prominent."

As we progressed, we realised just how accurate his judgement was. Obviously, if the circle generated 1080 in harmonic form, it could be a clear indication that we were on the right track.

Accordingly, we worked the problem backwards. Assuming that the area was supposed to be 1080^8 AUs, what would be the radius? It is simply the square root of the area divided by Pi, or 185,411.62 AUs. This was less than 2 AUs from the original radius. If we could now find significance with the perimeter measure, then we might have another key to the geometry.

Unfortunately, the figure of 1,164,966.6 didn't seem very promising. It was a very large figure which suggested that it needed to be divided by some factor to render it meaningful and we were limited in our choice of such numbers by the use of the constant already enumerated - Phi.

1,164,966.6 is 719,998.95 x Ø (AUs). Again, this figure is so close to 720,000 x Ø (AUs) that it was possibly the figure intended. We worked backwards again. 720,000 multiplied by Phi (Ø) is 1,164,984.5 and this circumference is the result of a radius of 185,413.04 AUs, again only three inches of ground measure away from our preferred radius.

If the figure of 72 or 720,000 had significance then the proof would be clear. Once again we had recourse to John Michell's *The Dimensions of Paradise* :-

> "The Numbers of the Canon... In operations of simple arithmetic and throughout all the numerical manifestations of nature, such as the periods and intervals of the solar system, certain 'nodal' numbers occur, providing a link between the processes and phenomena which otherwise appear quite unconnected with each other. Most prominent among these are the multiples of 72, including the powers of 12 and numbers such as 5040..."

We had our answer. Our radius of **185,410.1966** AUs was itself the product of dividing **300,000** by **Phi** and it exhibited, by varying the radius by only two and a half ancient units, a perfect area of 1080^8 AUs, whilst the second minor variation resulted in a perimeter of **720,000 x Ø** AUs, echoing the New Jerusalem of Sacred Geometry and the number so prevalent in the SET/ISIS legend of the Egyptians.

Looking at this in tabulated summary and recognising that two or three inches of variation over a radius of nearly three miles can produce these most profound of doctrinal numbers, would be sufficient to shock any student of Sacred Geometry.

To summarise:-

1. **185,410.1967 is 300,000/Ø as the radius.**
2. **185,411.617 generates an area of 1080⁸ AUs.**
3. **185,413.0373 generates 720,000 x Ø AUs on the circumference.**

It is staggering to realise that the upper and lower figures produce a mean, which is precisely the one generating the doctrinal area.

Surely then, the radius of 185,410.1966 AUs, deduced by dividing 300,000 AUs by Phi was probably the intended radius of the Circle of Churches. Alternatively, if it was either of the others it would not materially effect the plot, as on the 1:25,000 scale map it would be only one eight hundred thousandth of an inch. By simply translating these radii to millimetres on the 1:25,000 map and noting the small difference in the Circle of Churches, we had the necessary conversion factor to change AUs to British Standard Inches and vice versa. The figures were 0.9953 and 1.0047 respectively.

GENISIS had identified the layout of the Temple and what we now needed was confirmation of its mathematical dimensions.

Could the dimensions of the circle and pentagram disclose a mathematical code in the Temple?

CHAPTER 8.
THE INVISIBLE TEMPLE OF RENNES-LE-CHATEAU

The mountain of Pech Cardou. The Temple of Solomon and Hiram Abiff.
A hidden goddess. The search for the temple walls.
The temple dimensions are found.
"And was Jerusalem builded here, amongst those dark Satanic hills!".(sic)

BEFORE we can explore the concept of the geometrical temple on the landscape of the Rennes-le-Château valley, we should have a clear idea of what we are exploring and why.

From ancient times, Man has built special places of 'worship' which he has deemed 'holy'. This term has, in modern times, degenerated into one which might be described as relating to 'a place where people gather to worship, whilst putting their hands together and uttering mundanities in the form of musical or non-musical chants'. Originally, though, the term holy had a precise, even geometrical meaning. To build a place which was holy, necessitated the creation of a building where the height of its roof equalled the radius, as calculated by treating the length of the perimeter of its walls as a circular one. The master masons would thus build a temple structure that was truly 'holy'. There were many other such idiosyncratic ideas involved in the construction of sacred places, all with their roots buried in deepest antiquity.

Godfrey Higgins, a historian of impeccable scholarship, incorporated explanations for many of them in his august work, *Anacalypsis*.

In order to appreciate the genius of this man, who to our knowledge knew nothing whatsoever about Rennes-le-Château, let us take one place name from the Rennes-le-Château valley and see what significance it has. 'CARDOU' as in 'Pech Cardou' is the name of the mountain which dominates the northern part of the Rennes-le-Château district and serves as one of the pentagonal markers. The Collins-Robert French dictionary does not list the word 'CARDOU' . The nearest word to it is 'CARDINAL' or 'CARDIOLOGUE'. Although these two words are different from 'CARDOU', they both seem to share the same Latin root.

'CARDINAL' means 'point' and 'CARDIOLOGUE' relates to the 'heart'. The Chambers English Dictionary explains 'CARDINAL' thus:-

> "Denoting that on which a thing hinges or depends, fundamental...one of the dignitaries next to the Pope in the R.C. Church hierarchy...the four points of the compass."

In *Anacalypsis*, however, Godfrey Higgins goes a little deeper,
"Cor was the Latin name for both heart and wisdom...
from this came the word CARDO. We have the meaning of it in the
'cor januæ quo movetur', as hinge, regulator of the door; and as
regulator, it gave name to the line drawn from North to South, - the
pole or axis of the earth, used by the Etruscan Agrimensores to
make their squares for the collection of the sacred tenths or tithes.
This line regulated all others. The word is 'cor-dis-di' - 'divus', and
from this it came, that where the Decumanus, crossed it from East
to West, the point of intersection at which a cross was set up, was
called 'cor', or 'cardo', 'car-di'. It was in each district the centre, the
heart, of all their operations: it was, from circumstance, the Arca-
polis, the Caput-lium. From this point of intersection two roads
always branched off, which is the reason why we have a cross or
merestone in the centre of every village, which arose by houses
collecting around the sacred X : for this was, for many evident
reasons, declared most sacred and holy, and in suitable places the
temples arose around or over these crosses. The whole circle was
divided into 360 parts; and, beginning at the Equator, the
Decumanus was drawn at every ten of these parts to North and
South, whence it had the name Deca. In a similar manner, I
believe, the mensuration by the Agrimensores took place in every
country. The Decumanus would always be the same, but the
'Cardo' would in one sense, vary. A 'Cardo' would run through
every capitol or principal town, which of course, would divide the
land into parallelograms of different length. The lengths would
vary according to the localities. Our system is the same : the
parallels of Latitude never vary, the Longitude each native reckons
from its own 'cardo'. It was from being the superintendents or
curators of the Seventy- two Bareichs, parishes or cardinal
divisions, into which the city of Rome was divided."

(Anacalypsis, p413)

"...each having its sacred Mount or Cardo or Acropolis or Olympus
or stone circle, around which the processions, the Deisuls, the
voyages of salvation, were made, and the collection of tithes
would be paid, as at Delphi and Jerusalem."

(Anacalypsis, p422)

The name 'Cardo' or 'Cardou' can therefore be seen to contain many layers
of meaning pertinent to the area being studied, the very name denoting its

original function and we will have reason to return to this definition later. It is we so-called educated, civilised people who read more or less into these names than is necessary. In a similar way, the thought behind describing a building as 'holy' has long since disappeared.As we have said originally, a building would only have been deemed 'holy' if the master masons (themselves a very secretive sect), had incorporated certain measures into its construction.In some ways, it is instructive to review the building of the Temple of Solomon by Hiram Abiff and to take as close a look as we are permitted, in order to gain some understanding of what these masons were doing, before we try to re-discover the Temple at Rennes-le-Château.

In the Bible's *First Book of Kings*, the construction of the Temple of Solomon is described thus :-

> "And the house which King Solomon built for the LORD, the length thereof was threescore cubits, and the breadth thereof twenty cubits, and the height thereof thirty cubits",
>
> (*I Kings, Chap.6, v.2*).

Now, if the temple was truly built according to the proportions quoted above, then it would not have been a 'holy' building as has already been described. But three chapters of the *First Book of Kings* are devoted to the description of the building of the Temple, another house and the Ark of the Covenant, which illustrates the importance that biblical writers have attributed to the scale and design of 'holy' places.

Why all the fuss? What was really going on? What should we make of it? Unfortunately, by the time the descriptions of the buildings were recorded in the King James Bible, they had been expurgated, abridged and edited by 'clerical' people with a strong bias as to which version of the 'truth' they wanted to be handed down. Therefore, we should not necessarily accept the stated dimensions at face value.

We really need to look more closely at the use of Sacred Geometry in Temple design, and for that, we need to look at the records of the master builders, the Masons. When King Solomon decided to build his Temple for the glorification of his God, he lacked the designer for it and had to look further afield for his architect. Luckily for Solomon, King Hiram of Tyre, a man with certain expertise in this department, upon hearing of Solomon's wish to build a temple, offered to contract a supply of craftsmen and materials for the project. Who was Hiram of Tyre? When we look into his background, we find that he had lived in and been educated by the priesthood, and had been inculcated into worshipping the goddess Astarte in his native Kingdom of Tyre. Astarte is another name for Ishtar also known as the Syrian goddess closely associated with Cybele or Isis.

Hiram Abiff's master stroke, in accepting the commission from Solomon to build his temple, was to construct the Temple of Solomon according to the secret doctrines of the worship of Ishtar. What Solomon may have never learnt was that his Temple was built to conform to the secret measure of the goddess, rather than anything to do with his own god Jehovah. It is indeed ironic that Solomon, commissioned to break away from the old gods,finished up with a temple conforming to their measure, whilst claiming his temple to be Jehovian. Perhaps Solomon in all his wisdom, was lacking in certain departments. Or was he wiser than we think? Were there so many differences between the old gods and the new ones? Yes, there certainly were and they were fundamental.

The old religion focused on female deities, whereas the new religion was entirely male in concept. The female dominated religions concentrated on the fecundity of the Earth Mother - and used rites which involved the sacrifice of the phallic corn god, necessary for the earth to bring forth her fruits.

Until the time of Solomon, religion had encompassed both sexes in its gods and goddesses, but suddenly the Jehovian concept wanted god to be thought of as purely male. (N.B. This schism is still echoing around the world as we write this book, with the division caused by the Church of England accepting women into the priesthood.) Indeed, one British Member of Parliament has just embraced the Roman religion because of it. Women priests are nothing new! The female influence was paramount in the world, and most of the religious rites were focused around the idea of the female Earth Mother being fertilised by male seed.

During the construction of the temple we are told it was visited by Balkis, the Queen of Sheba, a beauty renowned for her sexual appetites, and one who we might best regard as a 'liberated' lady in today's parlance. Things went well between Solomon and Balkis until she met and fell for Hiram. Normally, Solomon might well have arranged for an accident to befall his rival, Hiram, but he needed him to finish his work on the Temple. So until then, Hiram was comparatively safe, but after the completion of the majority of the work, Solomon failed to warn Hiram of a plot by three dissatisfied apprentices to kill him. The first plot failed and the affair between Hiram and Balkis continued until a second attempt on Hiram's life was successful. Before he died, Hiram said that he had left many sons who would finish the great work. It is these sons who gave rise to the masonic orders and later on, the Knights Templar, who considered themselves to be the custodians of the secrets and the appointed architects of secret measure.

Why should the construction of the Temple of Solomon have been placed in the hands of Hiram Abiff in the first place? In C.W.Heckthorne's *Secret Societies of All Ages and Countries*, it has been suggested that Cain was the son of the gods - the Elohim, and that this was the bloodline from which Hiram Abiff descended. These Elohim were the 'fire people' to whom were attributed all the sciences and the secrets contained in its use. The issue from this superior race presumably died in the Flood, stories of which are common to nearly all races. The survivors of this catastrophe are said to have been Tubal-Cain and his son, from whom is descended Nimrod, the Mighty Hunter and in turn Hiram Abiff. It is possible therefore, if not likely, that Hiram Abiff was thought by Solomon to have inherited the secret wisdom of the sciences of the Elohim, and that he incorporated them in his temple constructions, especially encoded in the careful use of proportion.

We are told of the proportion of the Temple of Solomon in the *First Book of Kings*, that it was 60 x 20 cubits. Now accepting the length for a cubit as being 18 inches, this building would have measured some 1080 x 360 inches thereby covertly incorporating the fundamental female proportions. It also may amuse the reader to realise that the product of these two numbers (60 x 20) divided by 2 Phi* is the precise integer value of the diameter of the circle of Rennes-le-Château. We are then told that this minor construction took seven years to accomplish, even though there was a work force of 153,300 men engaged on the project. Not even the cost over-runs of the Anglo-French Channel Tunnel project were arrayed like this! Quite obviously the figures and construction methods to which 3 chapters of the *First Book of Kings* is devoted, do not make sense if taken at face value. This is why, in *GENISIS* we looked at the number code which had been used.

We learn in the Bible that the Temple of Solomon took 7 years to construct, and that the palace for his Egyptian wife took 13 years. If we multiply each of these two figures by the secret key number of the active principle of Isis or the cubit (18), then we see:- 7 x 18 = **126** and 13 x 18 = **234.**

The sum of these two figures is **126 + 234 = 360** , which once again is representative of the circle and is the symbol of Nuit as absolute femininity.

Now, although the Temple of Solomon is reputed to have been one of the 'holiest' places on earth and should have been indestructible, it is wise to remember that the physical temple was destroyed on three different occasions. But if the temple plan, conforming to a secret/sacred measure, had been overlaid on the surface of the planet, then it would have been truly indestructible! Perhaps this then is what we have in the valley of Rennes-le-Château; a vast temple, etched into the landscape by markers of antiquity which conforms to sacred geometrical measure.

Several authorities have studied sacred buildings and sacred geometry, and

* or multiplied by Sine 18°

FIRST TRIAL POSITION

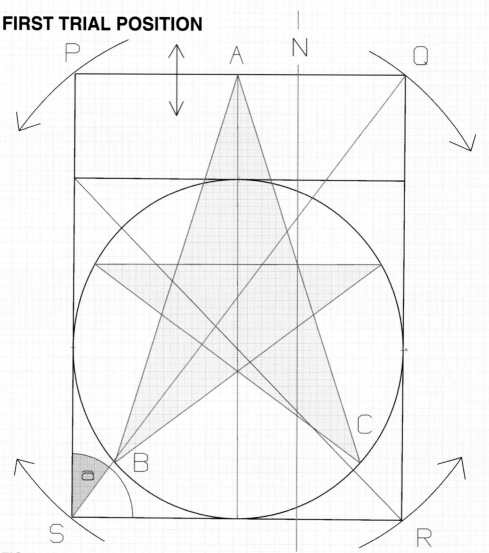

FIG.7. Using the apex of the pentagram (**A**) as the controlling factor of the position of the North Wall (**PQ**), any tangential rotation from the position shown will cause the length of the Temple diagonal (**SQ**) to reduce as **PS** and **QR** diminish. Equally the diagonal angle (**a**) will also vary. With **A** as shown, **SQ** is at maximum. Sine (**a**) = **0.607061998** = 37.37736813 degrees. Whereas the sine of the Golden Section is **0.618033989** = 38.17270765 degrees. i.e. the sine of the angle is short of perfection.
The diagonal (**SQ**) is **3.294556414** as opposed to the perfect **2Ø** (**3.236067977**) i.e. in excess of perfection.

we have only to turn to the works of John Michell once again to see that many such buildings started with a circular plan, contained in a square. In his *Dimensions of Paradise*, Michell gives two examples, St. Mary's Chapel, Glastonbury and Stonehenge, both of which seem to have been designed using this idea. John Michell also gives his own plan of the 'New Jerusalem', which is composed of the same geometry and uses 'Sacred Measure'.

At Rennes-le-Château, we have already established that we have the Circle of Churches (marked by churches and a château of antiquity), and we have seen it divided into 15 sections (theoretically), which produces a unique pentagram. Unique, because its north point breaks out of the circle. We have seen also that this figure incredibly displays special Phi relationships in its dimensions. Although a containing square could be oriented in any direction around the circle, we felt that the rectangular extension to it (the Temple Courtyard), would contain this northern point of the pentagram. Even so, this gives a lot of latitude to the positioning/orientation of the rectangle. Therefore, we started with a neutral position for the rectangle, one in which the north point of the pentagram met the north wall of the temple at its central point (See Fig. 7). In this diagram, we noted that the diagonal of such a rectangle makes an angle of 37.377368140° with the side of the rectangle and that the sine of this angle is 0.607061998. This, we realised was close to the reciprocal of Phi (0.618033989) which might be important because we already knew that we were dealing with a Phi diagram! The length of the diagonal SQ in this diagram measures 3.294556414 units and we knew that this was close to the value of **2Ø** (3.236067977). In other words, by orienting the rectangle so that the north point of the pentagram bisects the north wall, the sine of the diagonal angle of PSQ fails to match the value of **1÷Ø** by only 0.01097199 and the diagonal fails to equal 2Ø by as little as 0.058488436 units. There would ordinarily be no reason as to why we should expect the Temple Rectangle to equate these measures, but we were aware of the regard for the Golden Section (Ø) by the ancient civilisations, and realised that if we were missing Phi values by only such small amounts, we had to investigate the possibility that such an orientation had been intended to conform to Phi.

In our second attempt, we rotated the rectangle as far clockwise as it would reasonably go i.e. to a point where the line AB is parallel to the west wall PS, (See Fig.8). Any further rotation in this dimension would be pointless. In this diagram, we can see that the angle PSQ has now become 38.229654° and that the sine of this angle is now very close to **1÷Ø** or 0.618815035 as opposed to the true value for **1÷Ø** which is 0.618033989. The diagonal SQ is now 3.231983528 as opposed to 2Ø which is 3.236067977. The conclusion from this variation was that we had slightly over rotated the rectangle in a clockwise

SECOND TRIAL POSITION

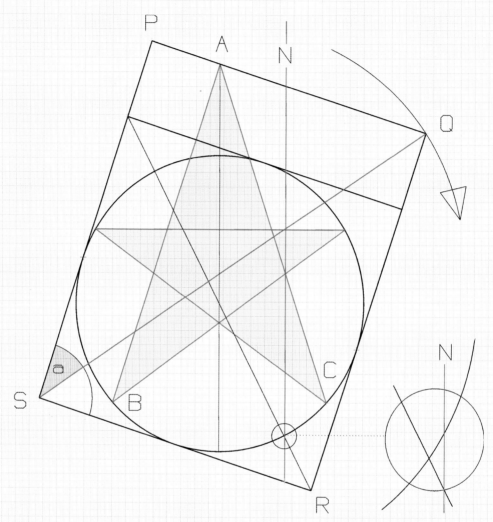

FIG.8. By clockwise rotation until **PS** is parallel to **AB** the rectangle has diminished. In this position the values are:- **sine (a)** = **0.618814999** - 38.229651 degrees. Whereas the sine of the Golden Section is **0.618033989** = 38.17270765 degrees i.e. the sine of the angle is in excess of perfection. The diagonal (**SQ**) is 3.231983528 as opposed to the perfect **2Ø** **(3.236067977)** i.e. short of perfection.

Also note the position of the Meridian relative to the intersection of the circle with the diagonal of the Temple Square.

direction. However, we were very close to both dimensions.

The next step was to construct therefore, a diagram in which the PSQ angle was made to be exactly **1÷Ø** in order to see whether the diagonal would hold its almost perfect **2Ø** length (See Fig. 9). As you will observe in this diagram, this subtle change of angle generates a perfect diagonal length of **3.236067976** units, which is of course, **2Ø**! Now came the acid test. Could we transpose the theoretical geometry of the diagram to the ground. In other words, would we find any significance in the diagonal ground measure of the temple which would confirm that we were on the right lines? In the theoretical diagrams we have related everything to a circle radius of unity. This is simply to aid transposition and to clearly recognise any special relationships. As we have already mentioned in the previous chapter, we had arrived at an actual circle radius of 185,410.1966 AUs, which we realised would be fairly close to the British inch. We should not have been surprised therefore in the following transposition :-

Diagonal SQ = 2 Ø Radii (185,410.1966 AUs)

i.e. **185,410.1966 X 2 X 1.618033989 = 600,000 AUs**

But we were surprised. When we applied this solution to the ground figure overlay on the map, further confirmation was forthcoming. When the Temple Rectangle was oriented as discussed above, we discovered that the north wall of the Temple passed through the summit of Mont Rédond and the north wall of the containing square of the circle passed exactly through the château at Serres. Remember, the Circle of Churches also passes through both the church and the château at Serres.

To recap, we now have a Circle of Churches based on a radius of 185,410.1966 AUs which is derived from **300,000÷Ø**. We have a pentagram based on a 15 division circle, which generates a north point that breaks the circle exactly at the Phi ratio point on a radial line extended from the centre of the circle to the north point of the pentagram. The body base of the triangle is in Phi ratio to the side of the body triangle and now, we have the Temple rectangle - a rectangle whose width is controlled by the radius of the circle and is then tangentially rotated to the only point whereby its north wall just meets the apex of the extended pentagram. This point of contact locks the position of the north wall and in so doing, transcribes the apparently random numbers of the radius and Phi into the diagonal's precise measure of 600,000 AUs. By subjecting this 'holy' number to the conversion factor, the rectangle synchronises with the ground features associated with the mystery. In particular, the diagonal passes through the outstanding rock feature of La

FINAL POSITION

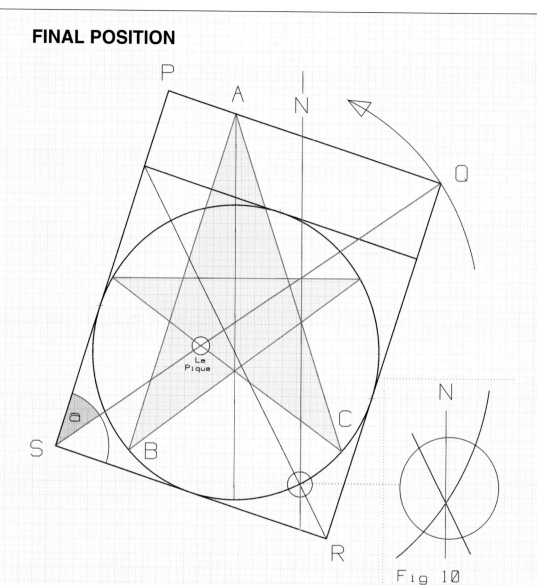

FIG. 9. By a slight anti-clockwise correction perfection is achieved with:- **sine (a) = 0.618033989** an angle of 38.17270765 degrees, and the diagonal **(SQ)** - **2Ø (3.236067977)**. This is further evidence of Geometric regularity being sacrificed for Trigonometrical perfection.

Also note that apart from other ground confirmations the diagonal of the Temple Square now coincides with the circle / Meridian intersection. (Fig.10 Inset).

Pique, which is also a pentagonal marker on the line from Rennes-le-Château to the Church of Bugarach. We are surely privileged to witness the work of an advanced intelligence from remote times!

Echoes of this type of construction were mentioned by John Michell, when referring to the squared circle idea, as stated in *The Dimensions of Paradise* :-

> "As the matrix and synthesis of every order of geometry it can be drawn so as to accommodate many other figures, but its framework is firmly tied to its foundation figure, the squared circle.
>
> Religious symbols and cosmological patterns the world over, from the mandalas of eastern mysticism to the rose windows of Gothic cathedrals, are versions of this same diagram. The earliest example known of it, the plan of Stonehenge, was laid out some four thousand years ago, but the universality of New Jerusalem imagery and of the units of measure associated with it suggest an even greater antiquity.
>
> In constructing the New Jerusalem the geometer begins by imitating the first act described in the Old Testament, 'In the beginning God created the heaven and the earth.' The corresponding geometric operation is to draw the circle of the heavens together with the earthly square and to harmonise them by giving them both equal perimeter."

We would do well to remember that in the previous chapter's explanation of the significance of number, Man was represented by the 90 degree right-angle, four of which compose the square - Man's building block. Before we move on to discuss the missing piece of information, SINE LANGUAGE, we offer one last thought on the meaning and use of number and measure. We looked at the meaning of number in the previous chapter, but there are some who think measure is arbitrary, something merely inherited from the past. Inherited, yes, but merely no? Those who think in metric terms wonder why Sacred Geometry always seems to relate to Imperial Measure and the cubit, apparently not realising that the metric system was devised at the behest of Louis Napoléon in order to sever France from a world dominated by Imperial Measure, which at that time was mainly wielded by the British who ruled the commercial world.

However, whilst the metre is acknowledged as being derived from earth measure (1/20,000,000 part of the longitudinal distance between the poles), the Imperial Foot has hitherto been regarded as an arbitrary measure, even though its history reaches back into the dark shadows of antiquity. We know that the Romans had a 'foot' as did the Ancient Egyptians and the Greeks. We also know that they differed in length from country to country, and even varied according to the degree of latitude at which the measurement was used. Hence the Roman and Greek 'shorter' and 'longer' foot, or more appositely, the equatorial and northern 'foot'. John Michell reveals more about the humble 'foot' in his book *Ancient Metrology.*

If we consider the Earth's equatorial circumference, a good reference book such as Whitaker's Almanac reveals it to be:-

24,901.8 miles or 131,481,504.00 feet.

If we divide this circumference into 360 equal parts (degrees):-

69.171667 miles or 365,226.4 feet

and if we divide these degrees into 1000 parts then each part =

0.0691716 miles or 365.2264 feet

Is it not curious that the 1/360,000 part of the planet's equatorial circumference should reflect the length of the Equinoctal year so precisely - 365.2264 versus 365.2240 days?

If this is not coincidence, then the implication is clear that someone had the ability to measure Earth's equatorial circumference in antiquity, to a magnitude of error which we are only just accomplishing today with the benefits of satellite surveillance. It is also one of the reasons why we have chosen to make our investigations into the temple in an arbitrary measure of AUs, for these units avoid the pitfalls of argument over which type of measure was used and reveal the true significance of the numbers involved.

And what of Pech Cardou? How does that fit into the picture? Well, remember that when the rectangle is properly oriented, its northern wall passes through the summit of Mont Rédond and the parallel line of the north wall of the containing square passes through Château Serres. Amazingly, Pech Cardou not only is situated precisely on the line which runs from Mont Rédond to La Pique (previously mentioned), but also it sits astride the line from the Château d'Arques to the church at St. Ferriol; the northern lateral arm of the pentagram from the church at Rennes-le-Château to the Les Toustounnes marker and the line from the north point of the pentagonal axis to the church at Bugarach. In other words, Pech Cardou supports lines which locate four of the circle markers and five of the pentagram markers, some of which confirm the orientation of the rectangle. That rather puts it at the heart of things, just as Godfrey Higgins had predicted it would, but later we will see it has an even greater significance. Higgins mentioned two more things which are relevant here - Arca-polis and a stone circle. Could Arca-polis be reflected in the village of Arques? It is certainly possible. As to the stone circle, we have only to remember the Boudet book *La Vraie Langue Celtique et le Cromlech de Rennes-les-Bains*, in which cromlech is a stone circle. Later we will consider an even more famous stone circle and its connection to the geometry at Rennes - Stonehenge.

Is it still coincidence that all three words referred to by Higgins, Cardo, Arca-polis and stone circle are all represented in such a small area, and function as Higgins predicted they should? What strange language of signs are we being shown? Although not a shadow of doubt remained in our minds that we had correctly oriented the Temple Rectangle, the computer plot revealed a further startling confirmation. In geometric analysis, one always adds the construction axes of the resultant figures, and one of the diagonals of the tangential square of the Temple left us in awe, for it passed through the circumference of the Circle of Churches at precisely the same point where it was intersected by the Paris Meridian (See Fig. 10).

The mathematically minded reader will immediately appreciate that we were now in possession of sufficient data to enumerate and delineate the Temple structure, both by formulæ and unit of measure.

With a radius of:-

300,000/Ø or 600,000 x Sine 18 degrees = 185,410.1966 AUs

the diameter of the circle, which is also the width of the temple becomes:-

600,000/Ø or 1,200,000 x Sine 18 degrees = 370,820.3933

which could also be denoted as:-

Radius ÷ (Ø x Sine18°) or Radius ÷ (Ø x Cos72°)

As previously explained, the diagonal is 600,000 AUs or alternatively,

Radius/Cos 72 degrees or Radius/Sine 18 degrees.
The diagonal angle of 38.173° is Sine 1/Ø and its complimentary 51.827° is Cos 1/Ø.

We are now able to use either the Pythagorean or sine formulæ to calculate the Temple length of:-

471,690.8266 AUs

THE TEMPLE DIMENSIONS & FORMULÆ

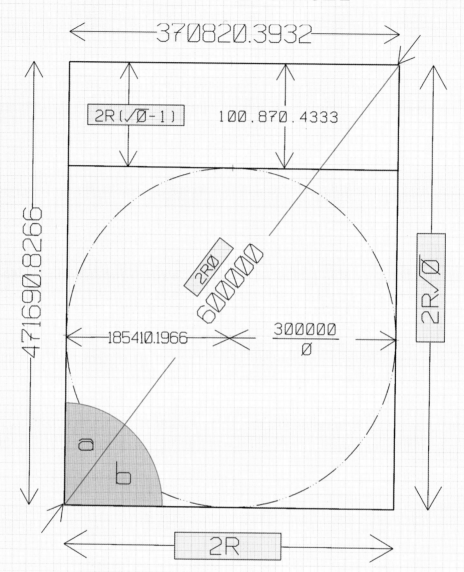

FIG.11. With **R = 600,000 Sine 18 degrees = 185410.1966** the dimensions shown can all be translated in terms of Sine 18 or formulated by simply remembering that **sine 18 degrees = 1/2Ø**

Angle (a)=Sine 1/Ø(38.173 degrees)

Angle (b)=Cosine 1/Ø(51.827 degrees)

i.e. with 'R' denoting the radius, the line formula for the length of the Temple is:-

2R √Ø or 600,000/√Ø

The length of the Temple extension beyond the Temple square, is simply found by subtracting the circle diameter from the Temple length:-

471,690.8266 - 370,820.3933 = 100,870.4333

which may be formulated as:- **2R(√Ø-1)**

Remembering that sine 18 degrees is half the reciprocal of Ø one may substitute all the formulæ to read in terms of sine 18 degrees (see Fig.11).

At this point in the investigation we should all know we are witnessing a geometric miracle. In plain language we began with an unlikely, but possibly coincidental circle of features. We were led to a pentagonal figure with remarkable geometric and doctrinal properties, a figure previously unknown or certainly never disclosed until we identified it and it is indelibly inscribed on the landscape by outstanding markers. This in turn led to the identification of the Temple Rectangle, equally confirmed by ground markers and asymmetrically locked to the previous figures, but nevertheless trigonometrically controlled by Phi, which was the original factor of the circle which generated it.

Furthermore, this Temple construction complied in all its measures to the formulæ of Phi and Pi. It also introduced the sine relationship with Phi, enabling linear formulæ to be translated into trigonometrical values. Consider next the wealth of artistic cipher and historical confirmation which was subsequently constructed to confirm the path of this investigation, and the mind reels.

On and on we were led by the mathematical genius of the designers, knowing by now we were under their control and being taken inexorably to the message they intended to convey. We also knew that the comparatively recent embellishments of Poussin and the like were nothing but glimmering candles at the early junctions of the labyrinth; placed there by those who had never been able to continue to the end of the tunnel, but felt duty bound to assist those who followed. Slowly we progressed, and we knew we would be confronted with further and more profound revelations, but we also knew we had the trigonometrical torch to light the way, something our predecessors were unlikely to have possessed, even though the designers did.

The next task loomed before us, and inevitably it was the Meridian. Slicing the Temple as we have shown and geometrically related to it, we knew that behind its simple mask we must find its linear and angular significance. We would eventually be back on the computer, but for the moment we must scrutinise other factors which may help us on our way.

CHAPTER 9.
THE MERIDIAN IS SET

The Paris Meridian. Clues at Saint Sulpice.
An inexplicable letter. The enclosed Meridian.
'Le Serpent Rouge' and the God Set. The Osirian legend.
The time is Set. The Seed of Set. Hybrid Man.

THE lines we find marked on a globe which run parallel to the equator are referred to as lines of latitude. The values given to them are in degrees, being the angle measured from the centre of the Earth to the position of the circle on the surface. Hence we progress from 0 degrees at the equator to 90 degrees at the poles, either north or south.

Meridians are the great circle lines which encompass the Earth and pass through the north and south poles at which points they converge. These lines are also given a value in degrees measured from the Earth's centre laterally. Contrary to the latitude, it is Man's decision as to which of these shall be the zero or starting point from which we number east or west. Currently it is the line of longitude passing through the observatory at Greenwich which is the international zero meridian and this was, of course, the result of the British being the predominant seafaring nation at the time when accurate celestial measures were established. In view of the manner in which the Earth rotates, these are in effect, time lines.

We must, however, concede that this was not always the case.

Old maps are extant showing a central Atlantic Ocean Meridian and one must wonder what would have been the reason to have chosen such a position and from which cultural centre the observations were taken. Suffice to say that one of the ancient Meridians was of French origin, and the adoption of Greenwich was hotly contested by them. The French zero Meridian is referred to as the Paris Meridian and seeing it pass through the Paris Observatory misleads one into an acceptance of it having originated from that location. Strangely this is not the case.

In 1660, Louis XIV began to take steps to lessen the power of the 'Compagnie du Saint Sacrement'. The church of Saint Sulpice was constructed on the site of the abbey Saint Germain-des-Prés a previous burial ground of the Merovingian kings. The position of the church preserved a marker of the ancient Meridian which divides France. It existed as a line of copper on a stone obelisk and was referred to as 'The Red Line'. It may be difficult for us to associate a line of longitude with a religious conviction, but there obviously was one at that time.

Whether to make an arbitrary change or whether to perfect its position, Louis XIV commissioned the building of the Observatory of Paris in 1671.The new Meridian was painstakingly positioned some 100 metres or so off the original 'Red Line' narrowly missing the position of the recently destroyed tomb featured in Poussin's famous 'Les Bergers d'Arcadie', far to the south. The original tomb was destroyed in 1789 and was at that time thought to be positioned on the ancient Meridian.

The recently destroyed one was a reconstruction, built at the beginning of this century and was probably the work of the Abbés, Boudet and Saunière.

Whether the two tombs were precisely in the same place is not known, but there was certainly no attempt to conceal them as they occupied a roadside position between Peyrolles (a 'phonetagram' of Perrault who designed the Paris Observatory) and Serres, this road is the only one of significance which crosses the Meridian in the commune of Rennes-les-Bains.

In the centuries which followed the establishment of the church at Saint Sulpice, many paintings came to be in the church which form an indelible link with the area of Rennes-les-Bains and Rennes-le-Château. Once one has realised that a Meridian is an origin of the measure of time, these paintings take upon themselves a new meaning. It soon becomes obvious that the 'time-meridian' had a religious and political import, the meaning of which, while being preserved, must also be kept secret. It is an established fact that the paintings of Delacroix and Emile Signol (featured in Saint Sulpice), direct one's attention to the valley of Rennes-les-Bains. Even more significant for this particular facet of our enquiry, is the importance attributed to the Meridian, or in other words, Time.

In 1622, Cardinal Rospigliosi commissioned Guerchin (Guercino), to execute a work entitled 'Time Discovers Truth' which is an obtuse way of saying the Meridian will disclose the secret. It was at this time that the 'ET IN ARCADIA EGO' motto of the House of Plantard, was used.

The same theme was emphasised in the painting by Poussin, 'Les Bergers d'Arcadie'. As we have previously discussed, Poussin's name was linked with Teniers in 'the parchments discovered in the church at Rennes-le-Château'. There seems to be no historical connection between the two painters, but that they both hold the 'key' was made clear previously and the key was the Sine.

Before leaving this page of history, it is worth noting Cardinal Rospigliosi had made it very clear that he knew the 'secret' of the Meridian and its significance in the mystery of Rennes-le-Château. It is, therefore, not surprising to find that the Court of France arranged that he should become Pope Clément IX, probably in return for the promise that 'Time' would not reveal the secret of the Meridian.

In his *Meaning of the Visual Arts*, art historian Erwin Panofsky devotes a chapter to the enigma of the 'ET IN ARCADIA EGO' theme and in particular refers to Rospigliosi having a 'special interest' in the subject. Furthermore, he suggests that Poussin admitted to the fact that Rospigliosi not only commissioned the Louvre version of 'Les Bergers d'Arcadie', but also claimed to be the 'inventor' of the subject.

The 'secret' seems to be woven intrinsically into religious antiquity and in such a manner as to deny that it could be a simple case of treasure.

We should remember the inexplicable letter received by the King's Superintendent of Finances, Nicolas Fouquet.

Fouquet's brother had met Poussin in Rome and in part wrote as follows:-

"He and I discussed certain things, which I shall with ease be able
to explain to you in detail - things which will give you, through
Monsieur Poussin, advantages which even kings would have great
pains to draw from him and which, according to him, it is possible
that nobody else will ever rediscover in the centuries to come. And
what is more, these are things so difficult to discover that nothing
now on this Earth can prove of better fortune nor be their equal."

At the earliest stages of our enquiry into the mystery, these words struck us as ominous and seemed to be exaggerated, but as the jigsaw slowly forms, an image begins to appear which shows them to merely hint at the enormity of what lies behind the geometric analysis of the hidden temple. The language is, to say the least, excessive. Simple buried treasure could never qualify for such a description as "nothing now on this Earth can be of better fortune nor be their equal". The plurality of "things" and "their" equal imply a number of either items or pieces of information or possibly artefacts possessing remarkable powers. We are told that these are "things so difficult to discover", but anything which is buried or concealed can be discovered, whether intentionally or by accident. Is there then a category which will match the exaggerated language of this description? If a primitive witnessed the transformation of the formula $E = MC^2$ into a nuclear explosion, he may well use similar language. Had he stolen the secret files of the scientist he would treat them with great reverence, but having seen the equipment required to execute the explosion, the information would have been of no use to him at the time. He may well have decided to record his experience in the words similar to that of the Fouquet letter. Looking at his 'spear-throwing' tribe, he could be excused for doubting whether they would ever attain the wherewithal to use the information in the file and to execute the explosion. This would not, however, detract from his knowledge of the awesome event or from the fact that the secret was in his hands. He may well have considered it to be his duty to preserve the information for posterity by the best means available to him. Subsequent generations may look in awe at the $E = MC^2$ carved in stone outside the witch doctor's hut and he, like some priests of today, may pretend to having a great insight not available to the masses. Poussin may have been in possession of a great secret and may have chosen, or been instructed, to record it artistically. If this were so we should look carefully at the features of the mystery associated with him:-

SINE - ARK - MERIDIAN - 681

As we have said, when we had taken the geometry to a level of accuracy which was beyond one's ability to measure on the available mapping of the area, the diagram had been converted to a CAD program. Now with the ability to measure to within one inch on the ground, some problems were resolved but others were created.

The distance from where the Meridian enters the northern extremity of the Temple Rectangle to where it leaves in the south is almost 500,000 AUs (see Fig. 12), but not close enough to attribute the difference to map error. Hour after hour we pondered as to why this measure could not have been exactly 500,000 AUs. With a Temple Diagonal of 600,000 the relationship would have been doctrinally perfect. What more could one ask of the diagram than to find the hexagonal **6** factor on the diagonal and the pentagonal **5** factor on the Meridian. Nevertheless, the actual distance involved was some figure slightly in excess of 497,400 AUs. What could it mean? Bearing in mind the intensity of the religious interest in the Meridian and particularly in respect of its presence in the valley, there had to be a decipherable meaning to the value if the geometric plot which we had produced was valid. Despite the various criticisms which have been directed at our interpretation of the figures, our minds reverted to Egypt and its influence on Gnostic teaching. From a kaleidoscope of related information, an image began to crystallise.

Consider that the RED line of the Meridian at Saint Sulpice is SET, god of the desert and god of TIME. The colour attributed to him was RED and Meridian means time.

Equally significant were the title and contents of another work which can be found in the Bibliothèque Nationale and is known to be related to the mystery - *Le Serpent Rouge*. The colour was correct and there is no denying the connection between the Serpent - Satan and thereby SET. Equally pointed is the enigmatic zodiac quoted in the document composed of thirteen signs, the additional one being the Ophiuchus - the Serpent Holder, a well-known zootype of Satan from the Garden of Eden, who in turn is associated with SET.

Le Serpent Rouge also contains a genealogical table of the Merovingians and two simple sketch maps of the 1st century divisions of France. A ground plan of Saint Sulpice and two oblique sketches portray the Meridian.

The Egyptian connection is clearly indicated in the paragraphs of the signs of the zodiac, by obvious references to Isis. The author of the document also intended to demonstrate that 'Nôtre Dame Des Cross', Isis and the Magdalene were one and the same. Again the correspondences can be identified. SERPENT - RED - TIME - EGYPT. The connection is undeniable; we are identifying the God SET. From the translation of the Rosetta Stone in 1821 by Champollion, the world realised that hieroglyphics were more than a childish collection of pictographs. Almost begrudgingly at first, scholars were forced to admit to the existence of a highly developed culture, which had appeared from nowhere. Search as we may, we find no evidence in Egypt of the normal development of a primitive society and what is more, in lands which demonstrate sophisticated architecture on a gigantic scale.

Avoid it as we may, the day must come when we address ourselves to the question - From whence did they come?

The Christian Church was equally shocked to find their most cherished legends appeared to be no more than a re-write of something which had been recorded thousands of years before the New Testament story of Christ had been conceived and we will return to evidence of this later.

What then if the Egyptians or their ancestors were more widely travelled than we had previously thought? Even well within the recorded dynasties of the Egyptians, links with countries far afield are considered proven by some authorities.

One such authority, Winthrop Palmer Boswell M.A., claims old Irish sources state that Cain was Set and Abel was Osiris.

She goes on to reveal, that the Egyptian treatment of the SET-OSIRIS legend depicts Osiris as the dark-skinned brother of the red-haired white-skinned SET. This would seem to be in direct contrast to the accepted association of white as pure and black as evil. Boswell continues by saying:-

"Set is not only the god of the Hyksos, but also the god of some Irish monasteries. The Hyksos were Phoenician Shepherd Kings and they gradually took over Lower Egypt, the lands to which SET had been relegated since the gradual passage of his symbolic star Sirius had sunk into the underworld - or below the southern horizon."

At first this seems contradictory when one considers SET was worshipped as one of the most ancient of the Egyptian Gods, but the plot thickens further. If indeed at the very outset of the Egyptian culture, a seafaring white-skinned 'visiting' race had interbred with a dark-skinned African tribe, we could have the perfect admixture to explain many of the confusing and embarrassing coincidences of culture, religion and philology. Undoubtedly the Phoenicians had all the necessary attributes.

Even their Greek name discloses more than one would at first realise.These intrepid sailors called themselves the Sidonians, but it is their Greek name that we find in the history books. As they plied the seas, these white-skinned Canaanite sailors suffered from sunburn and were referred to by the Greeks as the 'Phoinos' - the blood red, hence their name Phoenicians.

Returning to Boswell's treatise and entering even more troubled waters, we find the Exodus involved the dismissal of the priests of SET, who left Egypt taking their god with them. The cult of SET was now firmly placed in the camp of the foreign white race and the ensuing hatred of it survives to this day. The subsequent invasion of Lower Egypt in later times can, therefore, be considered in the category of a crusade to re-establish their discredited god.

To find where these expelled peoples went, we look to the Encyclopedia Britannica and we are told that some 240,000 of them went to Judaea and built Jerusalem. Little wonder that it was on the back of the despised and unclean ass that Jesus chose to enter the sacred city of SET. Still searching for connections with Rennes-le-Château, we see that Boswell considers the Druids were also Phoenicians or Sidonians and there is no doubt that the area we have identified at Rennes-le-Château was a Druid centre of worship. As strange and peculiar as at first it appears, the area of Rennes-le-Château and Rennes-les-Bains is saturated with connections to the God of the Hyksos - The SET of the Egyptians and The Cain of the Old Testament.

Furthermore, we begin to understand why, if the religions of the white-skinned peoples are associated with a fornicating destructive warlord and a dismembering murderer of his brother, they would wish to conceal these connections. One must question as to whether definitive proof of this origin of Christianity was in the hands of Cardinal Rospigliosi when he accepted the bribe of the Throne of St. Paul to become Pope Clément IX.

It would be simple to condemn SET out of hand for his well recorded act of savagery, but what if these gods of the Egyptians were only human after all ? Legend states that Osiris was said to have shared the bed of Nephthys, wife of SET and it is reasonable to understand SET's anger. When the Priests of Heliopolis got together to write the 'authorised version' of the legends they wished to have 'good guys' who did no wrong and 'bad guys' who could do nothing right. Their solution was to say that Nephthys made Osiris drunk and then seduced him. If this were true, it would seem that SET would have exacted the dismembering process on his wife rather than his brother.

Another interpretation of this unacceptable facet of Osiris's sexual behaviour was to say that Osiris, representing the inundation, might occasionally flood the barren land represented by Nephthys and bring the dormant seeds to life. Indeed it did, for the result of this union was another Canine zootype, Anubis. Even knowing this, SET did not disown him and he dwelt with his father in the underworld. Regardless of this shadow of doubt in the parentage of Anubis, he and SET are generally linked as father and son. In the underworld, the jackal-headed Anubis is found checking the scales, when judging the heart of the deceased. It is interesting to note that it is to Thoth, the Lord of Measures he reports his findings.

Further evidence of the correspondence we seek can be found in the function of the SET-Anubis relationship as the 'stellar guide and announcer of the new cosmic cycle'. This implies a 'celestial re-arrangement', the significance of which will emerge later. Also Anubis was considered to have a close relationship with the Greek Mercury, both having the attribute of being swift. Subsequently, due to the more frequent periodicities of the planet Mercury, it was preferred by the Egyptians as being a more reliable measurer of time. It is not surprising, therefore, to find SET as the god of Mercury even as recently as the Graeco-Roman period. What is surprising, however, is that the metal of SET is iron, not mercury, so we appear to have a contradiction. However, we now know Mercury has a higher density than any other planet and this is attributed to its having a greater percentage volume of iron than even the Earth has, and so the contradiction is resolved. Surely the ancient Egyptian could not have known of this, but what he could have known was that from time to time a fearsome fiery bolt fell from the sky, sometimes composed of solid iron - a meteorite.

On the subject of Mercury, we should consider one of Poussin's famous works 'La Peste d'Azoth'. Several factors relating this painting to our mystery were mentioned in *GENISIS* including the Ark of the Covenant exhibiting the half staff system of 'Les Bergers d'Arcadie' and the representation of the tomb of Arques. Further consideration should now be given to the possible connection with SET. The word AZOTH is the alchemical name for Mercury and once more we must marvel at these incessant 'coincidences'.

Continuing with the identification of the imagery of SET, we will return to his association with the ass, and in particular with any one of these creatures which had the slightest red colouring. After the Exodus, the revulsion for this animal in Egypt, resulted in it being cruelly sacrificed.

SET has often been illustrated as having the head of an ass, thereby confirming various references to the god of the Jews having the head of an ass. In *The Secret Books of the Egyptian Gnostics*, Jean Doresse points out that after the period of the Persian invasions, the Egyptians represented SET with the head of an ass and afterwards this god SET was definitely regarded, in accordance with a myth mentioned by Plutarch in *De Iside,* as the father of the legendary heroes Hierosolymus and Judaeus, which is to say he was the ancestor of the Jews. In 335 A.D., St. Epiphanius went to Egypt to further his education and was deeply shocked by certain Gnostic practices of which he was totally unaware and which he equally could not understand.

Another shock was in store for him when he found in one of the Gnostic books, *On the Generation of Mary,* an account of Zacharias witnessing a human form with the head of an ass in the Temple of Jerusalem. Having reproached the congregation for worshipping such a monstrous god, the Jews put him to death.

Without wishing to excuse the Gnostics for their strange sexual ceremonies, we must at least take account of their 'desire to know' which has now been replaced in modern religious cults by a demand for unquestioning 'blind belief'. Little wonder that some of these suppressed pages in Man's development are now beginning to show from under the carpet where they were swept.

One of these is that to which we referred earlier, *The Secret Books of the Egyptian Gnostics* by Jean Doresse, which is the story and translations of a number of scrolls discovered in 1945 near Hamra-Dum in Upper Egypt. These papyri date from the sixth century and give a remarkable insight into Gnostic thought of the day.

For our purposes, it is the references to SET which must be mentioned. On the subject of the salvation of the human race of the 'Perfect', of the seed of Seth, Sacla who is the author of this particular section states that a seed is:-
"planted in the aeons that have been engendered" - aeons of which "the number is the figure of Sodom", and about which this word has been uttered:

"The great Seth has taken his seed from Gomorrha and has transplanted it into the second place which was called Sodom. Three divine visitations, including flood and fire, will come to persecute the great, incorruptible generation. But we are also told that the great Seth appealed to the great Invisible Spirit and to the other powers on high to obtain guardians for them - entities, no doubt supernatural, who are to protect his seed even to the end of this lower world. Moreover, the great Seth has had a holy baptism prepared, the five seals of which will enable his race to escape from the evil god 'of the thirteen aeons'".

Later there is clarification on the subject of Sodom and Gomorrha.

".....and, finally, Sodom and Gomorrha whose names, far from being associated with the maledictions of the Old Testament, here denote the earthly dwelling - places of the perfect seed of the Great Seth......"

Another passage reads :-

"The great Seth came and brought his seed, and sowed it in the aeons that have been engendered and of which the number is the number of Sodom. Some say: 'Sodom is the dwelling place of the great Seth, which is Gomorrha'. And others say: 'The great Seth took the seed of Gomorrha, and he has transplanted it to the second place which has been called Sodom!'"

At first sight, seeing the rather mysterious context in which these sentences occur, one might think they were concerned - as are the preceding pages of the same writing - with the continuation of a cosmogony of the higher worlds, where there can be no question of anything but spiritual, immaterial entities outside our mundane history. But here two facts are to be reckoned with: first, that "the seed of Seth" is an expression which denotes precisely the race of the elect - that is, the sectaries themselves. As our enquiry progresses, the stature and importance of SET grows. It can now be seen to have started at the very dawn of Egyptian culture and to be 'hidden' in beliefs which exist to this very day.

At this stage it is necessary for the sake of new readers, to quickly summarise some of the findings of *GENISIS* in relation to the God SET. As we now know, the SET - ASS - RED relationship is well established. Remarkably, the French for a Jerusalem pony is a 'roussin d'Arcadie' with 'roussin' meaning rust-coloured and Arcadie pointing us most obviously in the direction of 'ET IN ARCADIA EGO', the theme of the tomb featured in Poussin's 'Les Bergers d'Arcadie'. Shepherds suggest the Shepherd Kings of the Hyksos and the tomb is situated on the Meridian of SET, identified as the ass of Judaea. Furthermore the tomb of Arques displayed **56** face stones, the inexplicable number attributed to Set in Plutarch's *De Iside* where he states:-

"..... even the Pythagoreans looked upon Typhon (SET) to have been of the rank or order of Demons produced according to them ....the even number 56."

One always needs flashes of insight when confronted with insurmountable problems. Thankfully at this stage, we were so granted. With the additional knowledge that the geometry was composed of SINE language, we looked at the sine of **56 degrees**. It is **0.829037572**, which when subjected to the 100,000 factor previously explained, would mean we should be searching the diagram for a linear measure of 82,903.7572 AUs and we found it exactly where it should be - on the Meridian of SET! The precise and unbelievable function of this figure will be described later, but for the moment consider the sixth multiple of this number which is **497,422. 5436** AUs - the precise number required by the CAD program on the computer to satisfy the length of the

THE MERIDIAN SECTIONS

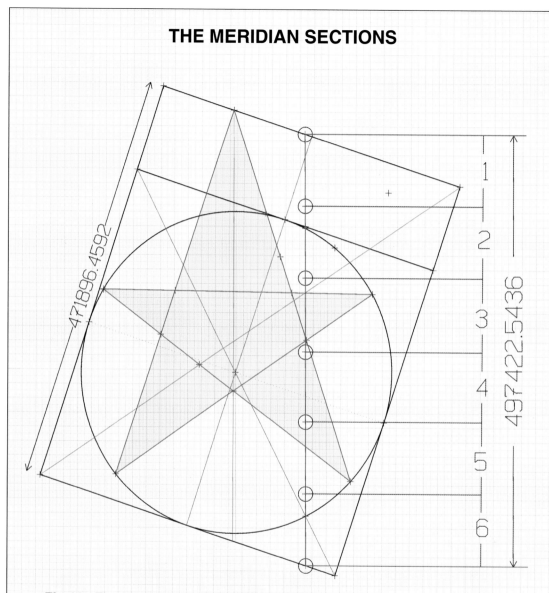

Fig.12. The Meridian length of **497422.5436** is composed of six sections of **100,000 x Sine 56 degrees. (82,903.7572)**. Proof that these divisions are correct follows later. This linear identification of the Meridian, forces the Temple length to increase to the measures shown, but on a 1:25,000 map it is only 0.2mm and therefore unrecognisable.

Meridian enclosed within the Temple Rectangle! Six equal divisions rang another bell. We had seen it before in *Le Serpent Rouge.*

"AQUARIUS - HOW STRANGE ARE THE MANUSCRIPTS OF THIS FRIEND, GREAT TRAVELLER OF THE UNKNOWN. THEY COME TOGETHER AS WHITE LIGHT BUT FOR ONE WHO KNOWS SEPARATELY, THEY ARE THE COLOURS OF THE RAINBOW; FOR THE ARTIST THESE SIX COLOURS UNITE LIKE MAGIC IN HIS PALETTE AND FORM BLACK."

Now we knew why the length of the Meridian in the Temple was not a perfect 500,000 AUs for it had revealed the secret of another key, the SINE of the TYPHON which was controlling the zero degree Paris Meridian! To understand the next function of the Meridian, we must again return to Egypt, to the myth of creation itself.

Nuit, the Sun-god Ra's wife, was the goddess of the celestial sphere and as

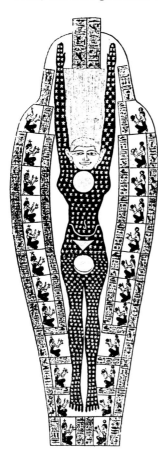

such she was represented by the inevitable symbol of femininity - the circle. Furthermore, when shown as a star - spangled body, it is her womb which adopts the circular shape (see illustration). Remaining for the moment with the simplistic notion of the gods having human foibles, she is said to have committed adultery with Geb - the Earth god.

Once again we must sympathise with Ra and understand how angry he must have been to find his wife had been unfaithful to him. Suspecting, quite rightly, that she was pregnant, he placed a curse on her, forbidding her to deliver her offspring on any of his 360 days. (This apparently being the length of the Egyptian year of those times). Not wishing to be pregnant forever, she sought the advice of another of her admirers - the mighty Thoth - Lord of Measures.

The only other source of light which was

Left: NUIT (The starry one). No satisfactory explanation has ever been given for the positioning of the two orbs on the body of Nuit, but a strange echo of this occurs in the confirmation of the 'Seed' locations which follows later.

available was that of the moon, so Thoth played draughts with the moon and won a **seventy - second** part of her yearly light. The mathematics are comparatively simple; 360 divided by 72 is 5, so, unbeknown to Ra the year had suddenly become 365 days. These additional days are variously referred to as the intercalory or epagomenal days and Nuit took full advantage of them to produce a child on each day. In this manner were born the famous group of gods we all know so well:- Osiris, Horus, Set, Isis and Nephthys. There are alternative versions of the actual sequence of these births, but the outcome is generally agreed : Osiris married Isis, Set married Nephthys and Horus was the resultant offspring of Osiris and Isis who had consorted while still in the womb of Nuit. Now all this seems a little unlikely, but we should give consideration to the possibility of these stories being a graphic method of teaching primitives how to understand the interaction of cosmic forces. We will deal with a possible explanation for these legends in more detail later. For the moment, a passing reference to the salient points should be sufficient to alert the reader to what will follow.

Consider what would be necessary to change the terrestrial year ; surely only a cataclysmic celestial event would achieve the necessary variation in our orbit. In the Egyptian legends, we are told the Moon lost some of her light. This implies either a shielding of the Moon's light by dust or an increase in the Moon's distance from the Earth - both cataclysmic events! Later we will examine these factors which, together with others, leave little doubt that our Earth has been involved in catastrophes of such proportion as to question how Man could have survived them.

For our purposes, two variations of the legend seem to be immediately represented in the geometry of the Temple of Rennes-le-Château in a truly remarkable fashion and as we progress, the correspondences increase.

We have previously discussed the dimension between the entry and exit of the Meridian in the Temple Rectangle. Now we will examine the dimension of the chord of the Circle of Churches formed by the intersection of it by the Meridian (See Fig. 13).

Let us assume the circle to be the womb of Nuit and that the section of the Meridian enclosed within it should portray a doctrinal confirmation of our assumption. This it most certainly does, for the length of the chord is **331,615** AUs, which is the fourth multiple of the sine of **56** degrees - the sine of SET. There is a reference by Holwerda who believed that the Typhon (SET) was only in his mother's (Nuit's) womb for 224 days (**4 x 56**).

Shocked by the accuracy of these representations, we examined the figure further and found yet another remarkable 'co-incidence'. Speaking of SET, Plutarch states "that he was born unseasonably on the third of the epagomenal days". There are also references to the fact that SET tore through the side of his mother's womb and at first sight it would appear to be impossible to portray such an act geometrically in the diagram, but it is there! By a subtle combination of the geometrical and trigonometrical, the strange nature of this birth is clearly represented. The shortest distance from the centre of the womb (i.e. the circle's centre) to the Meridian (SET) is a line from the centre drawn perpendicular to the Meridian; this distance is **82,903** AUs the 100,000 multiple of the sine of **56** degrees (See fig. 13). In summary, we have four of the five gods represented by the chord in the circle with SET projected from the centre of the circle and identified by his number.

To see these legendary gods manifest themselves trigonometrically in confirmation of the religious implications of the mystery was awesome. Even taken piecemeal, coincidence was out of the question, but viewed as a whole these latest discoveries locked into the Circle of Churches which had projected a previously undiscovered pentagonal figure marked over a vast mountainous region, were truly unbelievable. Now we are confronted with all these figures, including the Temple Walls interwoven to conform to a strict trigonometrical discipline, allowing no deviation whatsoever.

The complexity of the mystery under investigation demands that we should take account of every relative clue and some correspondences which may at first seem weak, but by repetition of their associations, they become stronger. On the other hand some relationships are so vast, one could fall into the trap of not seeing 'the wood for the trees'. The connection, to which we refer, is the Gnostic belief which dominated the Languedoc prior to Pope Innocent III dispatching an army under Simon de Montfort to destroy it. This vicious action designed to annihilate the Cathars is referred to as the Albigensian Crusade.

The Cathars or Cathari, as they were known, were 'dualists', with the conviction that this material world was not the creation of God, but rather the creation of the Demiurge - or evil spirit. They argued, quite reasonably, that the reproductive processes of some animal and insect life were too heinous to have been conceived by a God of love. They favoured the concept that God implanted a consciousness in 'animal - man' which permitted him to rise above his animal instincts, and by so doing become part of the cosmic awareness. This idea supports the ever increasing evidence to suggest that Man is the hybrid result of a genetic manipulation by a superior race.

Furthermore, it was generally accepted by most Gnostic groups that they were not of the Earth, but had originated from the Sirius system. Once more it is the Dog-Star of SET and ISIS to which we are directed. Even closer to our studies, we find that the very symbols most discredited by Christianity - SET, the Serpent and Cain, are those most revered by the Gnostics. They considered

THE WOMB OF NUIT

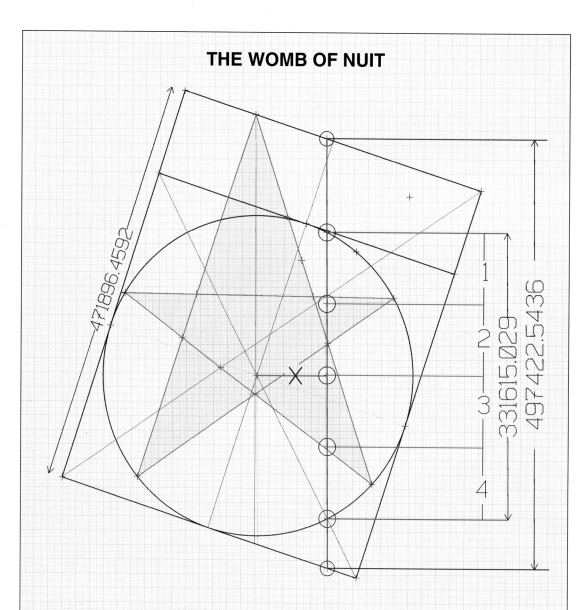

Fig.13. From the point where the Meridian enters the Circle of churches to its point of departure is precisely **4 x Sine 56 degrees = 331,615.029** AUs. Remarkably the perpendicular distance **(X)** to the centre of the circle is Sine 56 degrees i.e. **82,903.7572**. Both these figures have naturally been subjected to the 100,000 multiple, to translate them into ground measure. Refer to the text for the doctrinal correspondences to these figures.

SET to be the 'First of the Race of Perfects' and this is something which rests easily in our investigation, for it was the 'Parfaits' - the perfected - who were the preachers who instructed the Cathari of the Languedoc.

We should pause to consider how convincingly all these pieces of the jigsaw are coming together, and how geometry along with its numerical interpretation, trigonometry, can also be accommodated under the Pythagorean banner. Pythagoras was, as we are well aware, a mathematician and he laid down a major part of the Euclidean geometry taught in our schools. As has been previously stated, he was a philosopher and his beliefs were closely allied to the Orphic school which was undoubtedly Gnostic.

Unlike religious beliefs, geometry and mathematics are impossible to suppress and it is our intention to prove the geometry of the Rennes-le-Château mystery is also indestructible, despite the suppression to which it has been subjected. It is encouraging to find that of all geometric figures, it was the pentagram which was used as a symbol of recognition between the members of the Pythagorean school and it is equally surprising to see that this figure does not appear in our geometry books; but is it so surprising after all, when one realises the influence religion used to exercise over our teaching? Of one thing we can be sure - the pentagram and furthermore an extremely refined version of it, is indelibly marked in the vicinity of Rennes-le-Château and it was put there by a highly intellectual creature.

To summarise all these findings is as involved as it is to enumerate them in the first place. Instead, see them in tabulated form and appreciate the impossibility of coincidence forming such a pattern of correspondences.

MERIDIAN - SAINT SULPICE - TIME - RED - SERPENT - EVE - SET - EXODUS - HYKSOS - PHOENICIANS - SIDONIANS - CAIN - CANINE - DOG STAR - SIRIUS - SET - ANUBIS - DOG - TIME - MERCURY - POUSSIN - SINE - TOMB - 56 - NUIT - HOLWERDA - PLUTARCH - SET - PERFECT - PARFAITS - CATHARI - GNOSTICS - PYTHAGORAS - PENTAGRAM.

Inexorably the image forms, exhibiting both the skeleton of the secret and at the same time the reason for its suppression. Successful as the suppression has been and achieved with such loss of human life, the indestructible geometry remains - as precisely and demonstrably powerful as the day it was conceived and it is our intention to reveal it! Always self-critical, one reservation remaining was our failure to find why there was no obvious reference to SET in more recent times. 'Seek and you will find' has always been the key to the mystery of Rennes-le-Château. We sought it and we found it in a most convincing manner!

CHAPTER 10.
A STRANGE CONFIRMATION (David Wood)

The Jules Verne connection. The Theosophical Society.
A clear sign appears. Clue in a meteor. A strange
marriage. Satan's fort. Valhalla and the Valkyries.
A proven link.

TO identify the clues which are relevant to the solution of our mystery, we must follow strict disciplines. Even so, hunches and intuition are initially as acceptable as are the co-incidences tracked down by various investigators, including ourselves. The test of any data, regardless of its source, is to subject it to a series of discriminatory sieves and if it survives, to search for its associations. In this context, the power of the so-called subconscious human mind should not be underestimated and thankfully it is now coming to be recognised as a super-consciousness. It can often be found struggling to convey correct solutions to the stubborn and arrogant academic conscious mind through the medium of dreams.

Several great scientific discoveries have presented themselves in this fashion and those receiving it are often hard put as to how to attribute it. On some occasions it could be considered as the ability of the subconscious to store and associate vast amounts of data, in the style of a computer hard disk.

Sometimes, however, it appears to be so spontaneous as to suggest it is tapping into a race memory - something installed on the hard disk long before we were born and then being seen for the first time by one having inadvertently triggered the access code. It was an incident of this nature which led us to discover a profound confirmation of the identity of the Paris Meridian.

I had been working all night on the geometry of Rennes-le-Château and was in a state of physical and mental exhaustion. My daughter entered my drawing office with a cup of tea and in her other hand was a book by Jules Verne. The author's name seemed to leap from the cover and in a fraction of a second some of his famous stories raced through my mind. Almost instantly I knew Jules Verne must be connected with the mystery.

Jules Verne lived between 1828 and 1905. His first success was the well-known *Five Weeks in a Balloon* published by Hetzel, who continued with Verne's work until his death. Verne was a prolific writer and made it his business to stay abreast of the scientific achievements of the period. These he extended in an imaginative manner in his *Voyages Extraordinaires* series to produce a mixture of adventure and science fiction which greatly appealed to the youth of his day. *Journey to the Centre of the Earth, 20,000 Leagues Under the Sea* and *Around the World in Eighty Days* (which coincidentally first appeared in Le Temps in 1872), are three of his outstanding successes.

Having received this psychic prompt, I did little more, at that time, than to ascertain as to whether Jules Verne was in the right place and right time to have been associated with the occult fringe of Parisian society to which Bérenger Saunière was introduced. A society which included the notorious Eliphas Levi (Alphonse Louis Constant), Maeterlinck, Emma Calvé and other celebrities.

It was to the Theosophical Society that many of these 'searchers' gravitated, hoping to find the truth of the Gnostic teaching which had been stifled under the banner of profanity. Madame Blavatsky, one of the founder members, produced *The Secret Doctrine* and *Isis Unveiled* which did a considerable service to those who wished to open their minds preparatory to elevating them to unfettered knowledge.

Far-sighted as he was, I was convinced of Jules Verne's association with other enlightened minds of his time and confirmation of this came when my co-author appeared with a book by Michel Lamy, *Jules Verne Initié et Initiateur*, subtitled *Le secret du trésor royal de Rennes-le-Château.*

The author refers to the inevitable connections of Verne with the Theosophical Society, The Order of the Golden Dawn and the O.T.O. (Ordo Templi Orientis). The latter of these secret societies may be considered the academy of the occult sciences and it was there that Aleister Crowley achieved great recognition before passing the baton to the present-day British custodian Kenneth Grant. The work of Kenneth Grant delves into the origins not only of Man's existence, but to the birth of thought itself, involving additional dimensions and relationships between thought and matter which most find difficult to comprehend. This is not to suggest a lack of intelligence, but rather one's inability to shed the effects upon the mind of the pressures of living in a society of creeds, which suffocate the conscious mind from receiving the truth. So effectively have these creeds distorted and mislabelled progressive thinking, that one needs to spend years clearing one's mental processes sufficiently to be able to understand simple expressions such as:- 'Seek and you will find' – 'Knock and the door will open' – 'Where there's a will there's a way'.

Indeed, cause and effect and the rigours of scientific dogma are but putty in the hands of a liberated mind. 'Knowing that random chaos prefers to event', is all that is required to achieve creation. But - and the 'but' is immense - the tool must be spotless, or the fuel will poison!

Returning to Jules Verne, we are told by Lamy that Verne's works are a

LES VOYAGES EXTRAORDINAIRES

JULES VERNE

CLOVIS DARDENTOR

COLLECTION HETZEL

118

massive cryptogram into which are coded endless clues concerning his Gnostic beliefs and in particular, his knowledge of the secret of Rennes-le-Château. Lamy points out how the complexity of Verne's ciphers do not permit the application of simple rules. Anagrams created by Verne may well have a letter added or missing. Sometimes the true meaning is found phonetically and sometimes by nothing other than innuendo. The most critical clues, however, are to be found in the names of places and characters for, as Verne knew, these would survive translation to other languages.

On the other hand, rather than requiring close scrutiny, some messages could only be understood by reflecting on a story in its entirety. *Journey to the Centre of the Earth* for example, may be seen as a parallel to the descent of Ishtar, the goddess of Babylon, into the underworld. Journeying underground can be a reference to the labyrinth and Verne uses this imagery in some twenty of his stories. Closer to our studies, he also seems to be obsessed with the Meridian, which incessantly occurs in his works. Lamy also considers the name of 'Axel' in *Journey to the Centre of the Earth*, is merely a disguised form of AXIS, which we can recognise as a sigil of SET. In his epilogue, Lamy hints at a rebirth of Satan in connection with the return of the Grand Monarch of our mystery and he warns us of the dangers of opening the gates of the underworld. Interestingly, it was the activation of a volcano which brought Verne's heroes from the Earth's centre - another reference to SET, to whom the volcano is attributed. But none of this would be enough to convince the sceptic that our reading of the Paris Meridian was correct. The search had to go on until our findings were undeniably confirmed.

Continuing with Michel Lamy and flying in the face of the critics who denied the Egyptian connection when *GENISIS* was published, he mentioned several factors in Verne's works to reassure us.

The story in question is *Clovis d'Ardentor*, and Clovis I was the most famous of the Merovingian kings. He was the father of Dagobert II, who was mentioned in the coded parchments allegedly found in the church at Rennes-le-Château by Saunière, so we are safely entrenched in our mystery with this story.

It opens with a boat journey from a port in the South of France to Palma, Majorca and then on to Algiers. It is a light-hearted holiday trip and is largely concerned with the interplay of the passengers. Lamy considers that by referring to a travelling 'valise', Verne is suggesting Val d'Isis, which just about works in the French language. More to the point, however, is the name of the captain of the ship - **Bugarach**.

Until the publication of *GENISIS*, which disclosed the Circle of Churches, the name of Bugarach had not been associated with the mystery. The

LE PORT DE CETTE ET LE MONT SAINT-CLAIR.

identification of the extended pentagram disclosed a position on the circle close to the church of Bugarach, as one of the feet of the pentagram - something which Lamy could never have known.

Despite his admirable work, there were other things, which Lamy, not knowing the geometric structure, could never have identified, but which should surely have attracted his attention. We refer to the port of departure of the boat - it is, according to Verne, a port called **CETTE**. The phonetics are sufficient to immediately alert one to our hidden god SET, but the correspondence does not end there. The description of this port leaves one in absolutely no doubt that Verne is referring to **SETE** as it is presently named. Here we have an example of one of Jules Verne's ciphers being inadvertently exposed by a change of name. The phonetic cloak has, by chance or design been removed, to nakedly display the hidden god, SET.

An illustration occurs in the first edition publication of *Clovis d'Ardentor* by Hetzel which tells us even more (see illustration). To understand it, we must return to the Merovingian blood line wherein we find the family of Saint - Clair. Under their English name of **SINCLAIR,** they are the accepted founders of the Scottish Masons. In a recent book *The Sword and the Grail* the author, Andrew Sinclair traces the history of the family through a maze of detail revealing its close association to a number of things in the mystery which we have found in the course of our enquiries.

Jules Verne, involved as we now know he was, would certainly have been aware of the connections of the family of SAINT - CLAIR and would have seen the English name SINCLAIR as the ideal way to say a '**CLEAR-SINE**'. Ideal, but possibly too obvious for Verne's devious mind. Left in its original form SAINT-CLAIR, it could be used with impunity, concealed to all but those who knew that it was the SINE value of SET which was involved in the solution of the Meridian of the temple of Rennes-le-Château.

It is for this reason we find the illustration in the first edition of *Clovis d'Ardentor* carrying the title 'LE PORT DE CETTE ET LE MONT SAINT-CLAIR'. In this title Verne has excelled himself both SET and the CLEAR SINE are interwoven as a demonstration of his knowledge of the geometry. At last we appeared to have a comparatively modern proof of both SET and the trigonometrical ratio of the SINE being used in Verne's codes. With only a few more of his works to read, however, we continued to search.

The reward for our devotion came in the form of a lesser-known work by Verne which was significantly not published until after his death. It was *La Chasse au Météore* (The Hunt for the Meteor). Following the rules, or lack of them, we initially took a broad view of the story. It begins with two astronomers each claiming to have been the first to identify a meteor circling the Earth, with a slowly deteriorating orbit.

Prior to its fall, it is discovered that the meteor is composed of gold. An unlikely group of people set off for the estimated point of impact being unaware that a scientist, one ZEPHYRIN XIRDAL, has controlled the descent of the meteor and purchased a plot of land in Greenland, where he has arranged for it to fall. Due to a technical hitch it falls on the edge of a cliff and slips slowly into the sea, where it disintegrates and is lost. The gold-seekers, therefore achieve nothing, but the godfather of the scientist makes a fortune on the stock exchange by buying futures in gold. He knew the value of gold would fall if the meteor landed safely and he knew it would recover its value if the meteor were lost and that was all he needed to know, in order to manipulate the stock market. In this story, therefore, Verne is giving us a good indication that the gold-hunters of the mystery will be disappointed, but at the same time he shows us how knowledge of a secret can be invaluable. Cardinal Rospigliosi's bribe would certainly appear to confirm this and the large sum of money which came into the hands of Abbé Boudet of Rennes-les-Bains may well have occurred for the same reason.

The next consideration was to look at what appeared to be a gross error on the author's part. As we know, Verne made a point of keeping abreast of scientific knowledge and he would have known that an orbiting meteor of the type he describes is impossible. On the other hand comets do, of course, follow orbits, but these orbits are solar and elliptical. We should remember that the comet is the cosmic dragon, the winged serpent and every ancient culture is seen to carry in their legends reports of its celestial combats. The destruction caused when one of these warring factions falls to earth was good reason to strike terror into the hearts of the witnesses.

Now the identity of this 'Dragon of Chaos', is of course the Typhon - the SET of the Egyptians, which may be a worthwhile connection to follow.

Why then should Verne make such a blunder? First let us consider the possible origin of meteors. The two favoured alternatives, are that they either come from the asteroid belt or from a comet. Rocks of various size can at times, be gravitationally dislodged from the asteroid belt, whereupon they fall towards the sun. Some of them are of sufficient size to cause wholesale destruction should they strike the Earth. If they miss, however, they hurtle past the Earth unseen. Comets are, unfortunately, altogether different propositions. As they approach the sun from outer space, dust and debris is drawn from them, forming the well known tail of the serpent. As they continue their orbit, the head remains facing the sun and the tail lashes everything outside these orbits for millions of miles. To be 'missed' by one of these messengers of doom is of little consolation if it passes between you and the Sun, for the tail may

LES MONDES CONNUS ET INCONNUS

still lash you to oblivion. The composition of a comet is that of a solid rocky core with smaller rocks and dust, all bound together by frozen ammonia, methane, carbon dioxide and water in other words a ball of ice and rock.

Now we can see why Verne chose Greenland as the ground-zero for his celestial missile. Greenland is probably the greatest misnomer of any country, for more than Iceland, it is a land of ice. By virtue of its size, it would have been implausible, even for Verne, to have selected Iceland as the crash site. We have, therefore, been presented with this comet - SET, in the form of an 'iceland' - the celestial serpent or father of the meteor.

Returning to the strange name of the scientist who arranges the descent of the meteor - **ZEPHYRIN XIRDAL** we need no more licence than Michel Lamy uses for this to read as the **PHY RADIAL**. In the English language a 'Z' with an 'E' is interchangeable with 'S', such as in 'emphasize' and 'emphasise'. This conveniently introduces SINE into **ZEPHYRIN = SEPHYRIN = SINE PHY R**. It would appear we are being told to look for the SINE of PHY in a radius or radial. The reader will recall that this is, of course, the factor which we had previously identified as controlling the radius of the Circle of Churches.

Equally obvious, to those acquainted with the mystery, is the nickname of one of the astronomer's assistants. It is OMICRON, being a reference to either CHRONUS - TIME or ominously, the *NECRONOMICON*, which will be explained later.

Continuing with our examination of the story, we found the name of the street in which the scientist lived exhibited a further obvious reference to SET. The street was called Rue **CASSETTE**.

One has simply to remove the ASS, an obvious reference to SET, and we are left with CETTE, another reference to SET which we have previously demonstrated as coming from *Clovis d'Ardentor*.

Also the '**ASS**' immediately alerted us to its presence in the title of the book, 'La ch-**ASS**-e au Météore'. Assuming Verne to be fully acquainted with the French language, we wondered why he would have chosen the word 'CHASSE' which specifically means 'hunt'. There was certainly no hunt required as the landfall of the meteor had been exactly determined. Furthermore, the French use the term 'la chasse' more in respect of hunting animals than objects. An object such as a meteor was more likely to have been 'searched for' and the sensible title of the book would have been 'Recherche du Météore'. Obviously Verne was determined to exhibit the '**ASS**' in the title. Equally obvious is the composition of the 'METEORE' in that it displays '**OR**' - gold, but it could also suggest **METER**, which means measure. We are obviously speaking of the metal and also that famous measure, the Golden Section - Phi.

We looked again at the name of one of the astronomers, Mr Dean FORSYTH and in it found yet another connection with gold.

FORSYTHIE is French for the English flower FORSYTHIA, the common name for which is '**GOLDEN BELL**'.

Continuing in the same vein, the scientist's godfather and financial adviser was called Monsieur Lecoeur, a simple reference to a 'heart of gold' or gold **LACQUER**.

On one occasion Verne, describing the vacant stare of one of the astronomers says, "as if he comes from Sirius", which you will recall is the 'Dog - Star' of SET.

Step by step, Verne takes us deeper and deeper into the labyrinth of his mind and his obsessive desire to reveal the truth of the Meridian of SET, but the message is always concealed in cipher, allowing only those who know, to see.

Sometimes the message was vague and we wondered if it were real, but suddenly, almost violently, the door opened and the message became all too clear.

At the very beginning of the story, two characters, a woman and a man have arranged to meet outside a judge's house where they are to be married. The couple are both riding horses, one black and one white. The ceremony takes place in the street without either one of them dismounting. Halfway through the story and only two months later, the couple amicably agree to a divorce which is carried out on foot, once again outside the judge's house. A few weeks later, on the last page of the book, they remarry, this time inside the judge's house.

Now these marital anomalies have no bearing on the story whatsoever, but the names of the couple provide the potent confirmation that we have correctly analysed the god of the Meridian as SET.

The reader will recall the tomb featured in 'Les Bergers d'Arcadie' by Poussin carried the inscription 'ET IN ARCADIA EGO'. This tomb was supposedly positioned to mark the line of the Meridian. We have also established any number of historical references relating SET to the Meridian, but we felt that Verne of all people must have been aware of this connection. He most certainly was ! The names of the couple who were united, parted and re-united were:-

MR SETH STANFORT and MISS ARCADIA WALKER.

The **SETH = SET** and **ARCADIA = MERIDIAN** equations need no further explanation, but as is always the case with Verne, there is more.

« AU NOM DE LA LOI, JE VOUS DÉCLARE UNIS. » (Page 14.)

The strange marriage

Using the Jules Verne rules, it is quite simple to read STANFORT as SATAN's FORT and we could have left it at that.

There is, nevertheless, another 'coincidence' here for there is a fort at Stenay, (Ardennes) which was at one time the capital of the Merovingians and that FORT was called **SATANICUM**.

To understand the reason for the surname of MISS ARCADIA WALKER we must remind our readers of the Norse legend of VALHALLA. This is the palace of ODIN, where he dwells with the bravest of warriors, awaiting the coming of RAGNAROK, at which time the fallen will rise from the dead. RAGNAROK is the age of 'fire and gravel' when the celestial serpent will engulf the Earth. This is the Norse legend of the Earth's destruction by a comet - SET. The warriors who wait in VALHALLA were taken there by the VALKYRIES, demons or witches of the air, who ride out to bring the souls of the bravest warriors back to VALHALLA.

South of the valley of Rennes-les-Bains and following the line of the Meridian we come to Villefranche-de-Conflent, and further south towards Vernet-les-Bains are the Grottoes of the Canalettes. There, owned by the family of Fuilla, we find the castle of VALHALLA. We must now consider how a French person would view, or rather pronounce, the name of these ghostly riders. The French have very little use for words beginning with 'W' and we are, therefore, surprised to see them refer to the VALKYRIE as WALKYRIE! In fact, if a French person were to decide to find the word WALKER in a dictionary, they would be confronted with WALKYRIE.

Verne, of course, realised this would complete the equation.

SETH = SET = SATAN = SATAN'S FORT = STENAY = SATANICUM.

ARCADIA = MERIDIAN = WALKER = WALKYRIE = VALHALLA = RAGNAROK = COMET = MERIDIAN = SET.

Once having opened the Pandora's Box of clues, we can see that Verne has saturated his story with the necessary references for us to identify the 'hidden god' SET. He refers to Eric the **RED**, a 10th century sailor from Scandinavia as the godfather of Greenland. To emphasise the connection, he states that it was 'IRONical' for him to have so misnamed the country as Greenland.

Here we have **RED = SET = IRON**, with another reference to the Norse land of Scandinavia. He continues by saying meteors had previously landed in Greenland - three to be precise. He describes them as blocks of IRON, weighing **24** tons each. Now, 3 x 24 = **72**, the pentagonal number closely associated with SET in the Egyptian legends and the pentagram of Rennes-le-Château, but an even closer association lies in the fact that the 15 divisions of the Circle of Churches are **24** degrees.

It seemed as if Jules Verne had provided the means for us to prove beyond reasonable doubt that the identity of the Meridian was SET, and furthermore it was now obvious that this had been, and still is, a closely guarded secret. But why? If we are dealing only in legend, albeit marked with astounding accuracy on the ground, why in Verne's time should it still need to be a secret? Was it the combination of accuracy and dating that had to be suppressed? Was it because these two factors would prove the geometry to be the work of the 'gods'? Or was it to whom the Temple of Rennes-le-Château was dedicated, which had to be hidden? If this were so, there was good reason for self-righteous religion to fear it, for its disclosure would destroy the myths of their origins. This may well account for a good deal of the suppression, but was there an even larger shadow which loomed over all that we had found? A shadow so large as to be difficult to identify - a phantom which seemed to fade whenever we approached it directly, and yet with every new revelation we were more and more convinced it was there. If this were indeed the Temple of the mighty Typhon, what message is concealed within its walls?

CHAPTER 11.
CONFIRMATION OF THE SEED POSITIONS

The powerful alignment. The separation of the seeds.
The Triangle of Arques. Pech Cardou becomes the pivot.
The divisions of the Meridian. Poussin's Ark.
The 681 triangle. The R.l.C. triangle.

W HEN the primary geometry of Rennes-le-Château was first published in *GENISIS*, a number of people found the sexual implications of it offensive. Even more readers were disturbed by the evidence of cataclysmic events in the history of our planet and the high probability of their recurrence. Our further research and that of some other authors who have investigated the mystery has, however, leant strongly towards the possibility that the origins of the subject are extremely ancient. They have also moved from the biblical and comparatively recent historical connections outlined in *The Holy Blood and the Holy Grail,* more to the Gnostic, Pagan and thereby sexual reading of the mystery. Together with this, there is now indisputable proof that the celestial collisions referred to in myth and legend are a reality.

We can do no more than state the truth as we find it, and apologise if it should disturb or offend. In our opinion there can be no justification, in factual research, to avoid disclosures which may shock belief in religious dogma or show our planet to be less than the safe haven we have assumed our God provided for us. We would have been only too pleased, had the mystery moved towards strengthening belief in the Christian story, but our findings take us far from those orthodox concepts and we have no alternative other than to pursue the mathematical solution together with all the interwoven material, regardless of where it may lead us, or what it may reveal. Although we would never close the door on any facet of the subject, we were reasonably satisfied our reading of the Meridian was correct, both doctrinally and mathematically. The reader will have realised by now, how differently we approach the subject compared to others. Many authors seem to believe they are justified in publishing a conglomerate of the evidence of those who have pioneered the research and then proceeding to snipe at it, when it contradicts their calling. We, on the other hand, identify the components of the geometric structure and then look for evidence which coincidentally confirms the geometric, mathematical and doctrinal relationship of the part to the whole. That is the essential difference between researching and rehashing.

Using our new key of Meridian data, so powerfully confirmed by Plutarch and Jules Verne, we applied it to the existing geometric locks of the Circle of

Churches and the Temple Rectangle. If it were correct it would fit, and as we have previously shown, it must fit like any other key, with a small degree of tolerance. This tolerance is indeed so small as to be immeasurable on the 1:25,000 scale mapping; only the computer will disclose it. One of our most important objectives has always been to confirm the two critical but unmarked positions identified in *GENISIS* as the 'SEEDS'.

The South Seed was considered to lie at the intersection of the axis of the ground pentagonal figure and a powerful alignment of features as yet unrelated to the established geometric figure. This line extends from the Château d'Arques to Les Toustounes, then through the fortress of Montferrand. Next it passes through the church of Rennes-les-Bains and finally to the church at St. Just-et-le-Bézu. An almost equally convincing alignment established the intersection on the pentagonal axis which we have referred to as the North Seed.

The obvious action was to determine the distance between the Seeds and identify its significance, for if the positions were valid, the distance between them must conform to the mathematical controls we had discovered. Within our previously determined tolerance, the map measure indicated this distance to be in the region of 154,000 AUs. Two possible confirmations immediately presented themselves. The first was simply to assume it to be 5/6ths of the radius of the Circle of Churches (185,410.1966), this figure being **154,508.4972** AUs which could also be identified as **250,000/Ø**, and therefore confirming the Phi control discipline already established. Effectively we had divided the inter-seed distance into the radius of the circle, and the use of the factors 6 and 5 were doctrinally acceptable to the existing geometry.

Another test gave a figure which was also within map measure. This was found by dividing the Meridian, being 600,000 x sine 56 degrees (497,422.5436 AUs) by 2 Phi, with the result being 153,712.0194 AUs. However, had the Meridian not deteriorated from the ideal 500,000 to 497,422.5936, the result would have been the same as that resulting from 5/6ths of the radius of the Circle of Churches i.e. 500,000/2Ø = 154,508.4902. It was also interesting to note that 500,000/Ø is 3090.169944, the numerical sine value of 18 degrees (0.3090169944). Were we once more being shown the remarkable 'near-miss' strategy which only the computer could recognise? Now just outside the village of Arques, is the Château d'Arques, a huge structure which was said to be built on ancient foundations and since the publication of *GENISIS*, generally agreed to be an integral part of the mystery (See *GENISIS* p283). A number of clues had led us to believe that it had even more significance than just being the origin of the two alignments to the Seeds.

We decided to analyse the triangle formed by the Château d'Arques and the

The Pech Cardou - pentagonal marker and the 'gunsight' which locks the North and South Seed positions. The 'pivot' and point of landing.

The Château d'Arques critically positioned to terminate the most powerful alignment in the Temple and to form the pantograph controlling the Seed locations and the divisions of the Meridian.

**The ruined 'keep' at the South Seed; previously undiscovered until
revealed by the geometry.**

two Seed positions (see Fig. 14) and other oddities began to surface. The
distance from Château d'Arques to the North Seed was equal to the radius of
the Circle of Churches. This line is, of course, intersected by the Meridian and
the intersection occurred at 100,000 AUs from the château! That in itself is
remarkable, but this intersection was significant in another way. Remembering
that we had identified the Meridian as six divisions of sine 56 degrees, the
ground value of each is naturally 82,903.76 AUs.

Imagine how dumbfounded we were when we discovered that this was the
precise distance from the north wall of the Temple to the Meridian intersection
we had just described. It was the first point of the division of the Meridian into
six parts. Moving south along the Meridian to the next division, we then found
it was precisely on the amazing alignment from the Château d'Arques to the
church of St. Just-et-le-Bézu and passing through the South Seed - yet another
incredible correspondence! The Meridian divisions of SET (Sine 56 degrees)
were being confirmed and in a totally unexpected way and another function of
the largest château in the area had been identified.

When we measured the perimeter of the triangle formed by the Château
d'Arques and the two Seed positions, the result was remarkable. It was 600,000
AUs, literally a feast of mathematical perfection! Also within this triangle there
were several points which had aroused the interest of other investigators. Most
notable of these were the Roque Nègre and the ruins of Château Blanchefort,

THE SEED/ARQUES TRIANGLE

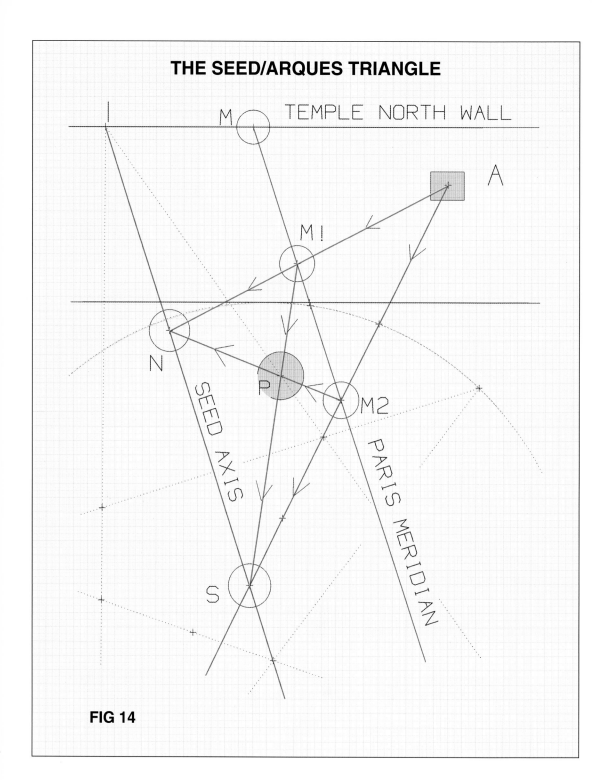

FIG 14

FIG.14. To fully appreciate the ingenuity of this illustration we should review its component parts, some of which the reader is already aware and some which will be demonstrated later. It is, however, essential that we remember the largest château in the geometry (Château d'Arques-**A**) and the largest mountain in the geometry (Pech Cardou-**P**) are inter-acting with the Meridian to disclose the Seed Positions.

1) The Meridian is composed of six divisions of **82,903.76** AUs (6 x Sine 56 degrees x 100,000)

2) From the point of entry of the Meridian into the Temple (**M**) to the intersection (**M1**) of the line from the Château d'Arques (**A**) to the North Seed (**N**) is one division of Sine 56 degrees.

3) From this point to the intersection of the Meridian with the line from the Château d'Arques to the South Seed is another section of Sine 56 degrees.

4) From each of these positions (**M1** and **M2**) and using the Pech Cardou (**P**) as the foresight, the **M1** to **P** line extended, and the **A** to **M2** line extended, intersect on the seed axis of the pentagram at the South Seed (**S**).

5) By the same method, the line **M2** to **P** and extended to meet the **A** to **M1** line extended, forms an intersection on the seed pentagonal axis at the North Seed (**N**).

6) The position of **N** on the seed pentagonal axis is also confirmed numerically in that its distance from the apex of the pentagram (**T**) at the North wall of the Temple is **123,606.8** AUs or **200,000/Ø**

7) The interseed distance (**154,508.5** AUs) **NS** is also confirmed as it is **250,000/Ø**. It is also five sixths of the radius of the Circle of Churches (**185,410.2**AUs).

8) The distance **AN** is the same as the radius of the Circle of Churches and the intersection **M1** occurs where **A** to **M1** is **100,000** AUs.

the home of the Blanchefort family whose name seems to be interwoven into the history and mysterious codes in the church of Rennes-le-Château. As interesting and striking as these positions are, none of them coincided with the geometry which we had presently identified. However, also within the triangle is the extremely obvious Pech Cardou, the largest mountain within the area which we had defined as the Temple Rectangle. As obvious as it was, this mountain had not attracted the attention of other investigators until it was identified in *GENISIS* to be one of the markers for the pentagonal body. Even so this seemed a trifle demeaning for so prominent a feature. When the South Seed location was first investigated (see *GENISIS* p197) we had been surprised to find in one room of the building, the ruined remains of a circular window. By standing precisely in the centre of that room it became obvious that the window had been so positioned as to target the Pech Cardou. We decided to look more closely at this mountain feature. Naturally, the first consideration was the name; we returned to Higgins, the master in the origin of words, and we were not disappointed. We have previously referred to the name Cardou and as you will recall, in the *Anacalypsis - The Saitic Isis* - Higgins begins by stating that every country had a Templum or Cardo, a microcosm of the temple of the globe, a Pole Star or position which acted as a regulator. He considered it 'the centre of measurements'.

There is also the obvious parallel to the prefix CARD..., which describes all things related to the heart. CARDO, he continues, was the the name given to the line drawn from North to South - 'the pole or axis of the earth'. Even more remarkably, Higgins tells us that from this CARDO, were laid out the 72 divisions of the circle and we are well-versed with this number and its pentagonal relationships to the geometry. The religious rank of Cardinal is, of course, already well known to us, but we should give consideration to another reference - 'cardinal RED', a deep scarlet dye, a colour undoubtedly associated with the god SET of the Meridian and we will show it to be inexorably linked to the nearby Pech Cardou.

One would consider the connections must be exhausted, but they run still deeper and closer to the mystery. Almost as if Higgins were looking over our shoulder at the geometry, he calls our attention to the fact that CARDOS and ARARAT are interchangeable and he reminds us that the Ark of Noah came to rest on Mount ARARAT or the Mountain CORDI. There at the apex of the triangle is the Château d'ARQUES, an obvious parallel to the ARK and you will also recall CARDO had another meaning. From Latin we saw it defined as A PIVOT, A HINGE, A SOCKET, A POINT ABOUT WHICH SOMETHING TURNS, A PLACE OF CROSSING.

We examined the triangle more closely and more particularly the

'L' Hiver' (Winter) from 'Les Quatre Saisons'
by Poussin, often referred to as 'The Deluge'.
Here we see that Poussin is creating a parallel between the annual
seasons and the progression of Mankind from his inception in the
Garden of Eden (Spring), to his eventual demise by a winter of total
destruction. The agent of the disaster is prominently displayed; it is
the serpent - the comet!

intersections on the Meridian. Suddenly all became clear and we realised how ingenious had been the choice of the name of Pech Cardou.

The reader will recall that the lines from the Château d'Arques to the North and South Seed locations are intersected by the Meridian. These intersections you will remember are the first two divisions of 82903.7572 AUs (Sine 56 degrees) measuring down the Meridian from its origin at the north wall of the Temple. Now imagine yourself standing on either of those intersections and using the Pech Cardou as a gunsight, just as the view through the circular window had suggested.

The first division which is on the line of the North Seed goes through Pech Cardou to the South Seed. Now imagine standing at the second intersection on the line from Arques to the South Seed and fire through Pech Cardou again; it goes directly to the North Seed! Exactly as its meaning is defined, the Pech Cardou becomes THE PIVOT POINT - THE HINGE - THE POINT OF THE CROSSING OF LINES. Furthermore, it can now been seen that both seed positions may be pin-pointed by nothing other than two axes, the pentagonal and the Meridian together with only two points, the Pech Cardou and the Château d'Arques - both having the same meaning. We are witnessing perfection in geometry and philology, both confirming the Seed positions found in *GENISIS*, but requiring none of the complex geometry of the Temple or the Circle of Churches. Obviously, the designers were determined to preserve the secret locations by more than one method. When one considers that this pantograph could only exist by the precise positioning of the Château d'Arques in its relationship to the Pech Cardou and the Meridian intersections, one must realise how sophisticated the designers must have been in ground surveying techniques.

Gone now were thoughts of the Ark of the Covenant - we had a symbolic Ark of Noah, (Château d'Arques) and the symbolic point of grounding - Ararat (Pech Cardou). As the reader probably knows, the Ark was afloat for 150 days and as if by confirmation of this, the distance from the Château d'Arques to the mountain top of Pech Cardou is 150,000 AUs.

We had found the words, the mathematics and the geometry of the Arques/Seed triangle with the time Meridian of SET controlling their inter-relationship. Could this also be coded into the works of Jules Verne? Probably it is, but we baulked at the thought of re-reading such a mass of literature again to find it. Nevertheless, as the reader will see later,we are far from having heard the last word on the subject from Jules Verne. The time had come to leave the dictionaries and computer. Somewhere there had to be an obvious confirmation and all we needed to do was allow the subconscious mind to recognise the correspondences.

ARK - NOAH - RAIN - FLOOD - MOUNTAIN -
CARDOU - CARDINAL - RED - SET - SERPENT

Once again with blinding simplicity the answer came in another of Poussin's works, 'The Deluge'.

As the reader will recall, it has been firmly established that several of the works of Poussin are coded to contain keys to the mystery, but before the publication of *GENISIS* , 'The Deluge' was not considered to be relevant. 'The Deluge' is also referred to as 'L'Hiver' (The Winter) being the last of a set of four paintings collectively known as 'Les Quatre Saisons'; Spring, Summer, Autumn and Winter. The 'Spring' depicts the Garden of Eden with the inevitable 'forbidden fruit' and we realise Poussin is showing us the four seasons of Man from his Biblical creation to his Biblical destruction.

In his 'Spring', Eve is shown tempting Adam to take the forbidden fruit and the influence of the serpent - SET is well-documented in this legend. It is regrettable that the story of Adam and Eve has been misinterpreted to represent the creation of the physical form of homo sapiens when it is far more likely to be a graphical illustration of his acquisition of knowledge - the time when by some means or another he was genetically elevated from a primitive to a large brained creature.

The agent responsible for this rapid elevation was, of course, the serpent SET and with few exceptions the serpent was revered in ancient doctrine as the origin of intelligence. We should also remember that many scholars consider the Ark of Noah to signify a process of preserving intelligence. Although it would be unlikely for the celestial cataclysms, to which we have referred, to destroy every life form on the planet, it could easily cause the demise of intelligent Mankind.

Returning to Poussin's 'The Deluge', we see the Ark of Noah in a flooded landscape, not of drowning animals, but drowning humanity. In all four paintings there is a distant mountain - almost obscured in 'The Deluge' and it may well be meant to represent the mountain of Pech Cardou. In the foreground, however, with stark clarity we see a **SERPENT** on a rock watching the destruction of Mankind and providing indisputable proof of our reading of the triangle of Arques.

Poussin knew; and once again the shadow looms over the valley. This artist has certainly provided a number of leads and we decided to consider whether he may provide a link between the church of Rennes-le-Château and the Meridian. When the documents, which were allegedly found in the church were decoded, a strange message was revealed and it has never been fully understood. The first sentence states:-

SHEPHERDESS, NO TEMPTATION, THAT POUSSIN
TENIERS, HOLD THE KEY, PEACE 681.

As we have previously shown, Poussin and Teniers did hold the key - it was the trigonometrical Sine (SIN). We had wondered whether 681 could also respond to Sine treatment and it did. A triangle with Sine values of **.6 .8** and **1**, is the famous Pythagorean right-angled triangle of 3-4-5, where, with whole numbers, one demonstrates the square on the hypotenuse equals the sum of the squares on the other two sides (9 + 16 = 25). Was it the Pythagorean triangle which was being referred to in the coded parchment? The 3, 4, 5 ratio is, of course, true of any multiples of those numbers, but only by doubling them do we arrive at a coincidence of length and angular sines.

137

THE 681 TEMPLE TRIANGLE

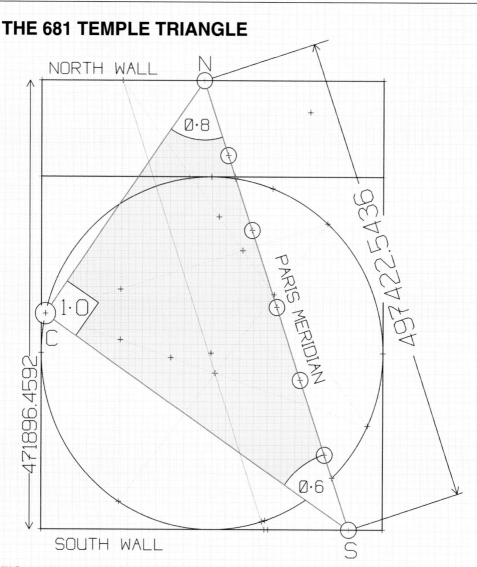

FIG.15. The orientation of the Temple rectangle is uniquely confirmed by the fact that the intersection of the Paris Meridian with the North and South walls of the Temple form the hypotenuse **NS** of a Pythagorean triangle whose third point is Rennes-le-Château (**C**). The dimensions of the triangle are only slightly, proportionately, modified from that of the perfect **3,4** and **5,** hundred thousand AUs, but the angles of the triangle still conform to the **.6, .8, 1** Sine values.

These lengths would, of course, be **6**, **8** and **10**, where 6 + 8 = 10 or 36 + 64 = 100, but the same numerical values are uniquely exhibited in the Sines of the angles generated by the lengths of the sides in this triangle. Reverting to the 3, 4, 5 values, causes us to consider bringing them to scale by the 100,000 multiple which has already become a feature of the geometric layout and the Meridian was theoretically 500,000 AUs. It was a simple case of striking two arcs, one of 300,000 AUs and one of 400,000 AUs from the point of entry and exit of the Meridian into the Temple Rectangle. They intersected at Rennes-le-Château! (See Fig. 15). Could this curious yet enigmatic number contain anything else? Incredibly, it does, and in such a way as to leave us in no doubt that we had solved this part of the code.

To discover this last meaning, it was necessary to treat the figure 681 as a decimal fraction and turn it into angular measure. This is accomplished by looking up the Inverse-Sine value of the figure on a calculator :-

Inverse-Sine 0.681 = 42.9218360 = 42° 55' 18.6"

And this incredibly precise angular measure when interpreted as a line of latitude, passes east/west across the landscape, just south of the village of Rennes-le-Château. It even echoes its numerical progenitor in its final detail of 18.6 seconds of arc which is the reverse of the enigmatic code. Furthermore, it reminds one of the Saros cycle of Stonehenge (18.61), which we will examine later.

To recap, some consider 681 could mean the year in which Sigisbert IV came to Rennes-le-Château, but we think this is probably coincidental. Numerically, however, it emphatically indicates a 3,4,5, Pythagorean triangle based on the zero degree Meridian and Rennes-le-Château, (confirmed by the Sine values of its components) and the latitude north of the equator which passes through the very landscape with which we are concerned. It is worth mentioning that if the code had been 682, then its line of latitude would have passed approximately 28 miles north in the region of Carcassonne, whereas if it had been 680, then it would have been 28 miles to the south. Also, at these slightly different values, there would have been no Pythagorean triangle indicated and therefore no indication of the importance of the zero degree Meridian. All in all, a magnificent piece of work! The enigma of 681 is solved! Furthermore, it disclosed that the Meridian casts the angle of 90 degrees at the church of Rennes-le-Château. In masonic terms it is saying, the church is 'on the square' and the floor of the church has alternate black and white squares as do the masonic temples. Seeing the mystery unfolding before as in this fashion left us dumbfounded, always wondering what new revelations might lay hidden in the geometric skeleton. Once again we had the overpowering conception of being led through the labyrinth of the geometry and slowly being

THE SEED PROJECTIONS

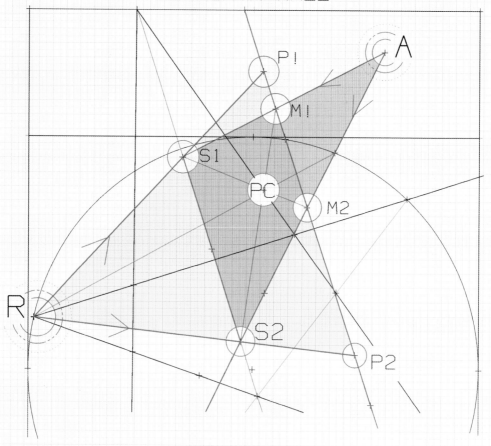

TEMPLE NORTH WALL

FIG.16. Using Rennes-le-Château **(R)** as a light source, the projection of the Seed separation **S1/S2** (**154,580.5** AUs) on to the Paris Meridian is a magnification factor of **1.545085**; the same integers as the Seed separation distance. **P1** to **P2** is therefore **238,728.8** AUs.
The triangle **R-S1-S2** perimeter is **500,000**AUs!
Using the Château d'Arques **(A)** as the light source the Meridian section **M1/M2** (sine 56 degrees) is projected on to the pentagonal Seed axis to disclose the Seed positions **S1** and **S2**.
The triangle **A-S1-S2** is **600,000** AUs!

taught where to look for the next confirmation.

We reconsidered the use of Sine 18 degrees, which as an alternative to Phi, had served to solve the Temple dimensions.

Applied to 600,000 it displayed the radius of the Circle of Churches. 600,000 x Sine 18 degrees = 185,410.1966 and with 500,000 it revealed the distance between the seeds. 500,000 x Sine 18 degrees = 154,508.4972

Both these measures occur on the perimeter of the Arques/Seed Triangle which graphically gives one the impression of the Meridian section of Sine 56 (82,903.7572) being projected on to the pentagonal axis as if Château d'Arques were a light source (see Fig. 16).

Seeing the right-angle from Rennes-le-Château projecting back on to the Meridian caused us to consider projecting the Seed dimension on to the Meridian as if Rennes-le-Château was also a light source. (see Fig. 16).

The lines were drawn from Rennes-le-Château to both the North and South Seed and then extended until they intersected the Meridian. The distance between the projected images of the Seeds on to the Meridian was 238,728.757 AUs, and by squaring the inter-seed distance of 154,508.4972 the harmonic figure of 2.38728757 occurs. Alternatively, it could be considered that, to the inter-seed distance of 154,508.9972 a magnification factor of 1.54508.4972 had been applied. Yet again we are confronted with a mathematical miracle made even more so by knowing that this, as with all the other figures, was trigonometrically locked into the whole construction.

It would seem unreasonable to expect any further confirmation, but there was; when we examined the perimeter of the triangle formed by Rennes-le-Château and the two Seed positions, it was inconceivable! It was 500,000 AUs. What possible meaning could cause the designers to inter-relate the MERIDIAN - TIME with the SEEDS, if indeed they were SEEDS.

Were we being shown the time when they would germinate? Or were they protected, to germinate after a danger had passed? Here our imagination could run wild and surmise the concealed sperm bank of a creature whose intellect surpassed ours by aeons. A seed, which if artificially inseminated, would create a species which would accelerate our anthropological ascent thousands of years. This would be a true 'Ark of Knowing'.

The thought prompted us to consider recent evidence which could account for the uncertainty of the origin of intelligence in the form of homo sapiens.

CHAPTER 12.
IN THE BEGINNING

Learning to SEE mathematics. The 'Will' of God.
The mind at work. Man 'evolves'. The Mitochondria factor.
Genetic engineering. Man as a slave. The super-sub-conscious.

A T times we will have to leave the nuts and bolts of the mystery and review things which seem far removed from Rennes-le-Château. The reason for this will be obvious to some readers, but to those who find it frustrating we owe an explanation.

If you have absorbed all we have presented, you should be, by now, at the point whereby it is obvious that the mathematical expertise displayed in the diagrams could never have been executed in recent historical times. We, the authors, are in the privileged position of knowing how the construction develops and furthermore why we must consider by whom it was constructed, seemingly at a time when Man was not in possession of the wherewithal to achieve it. We know all that will be presented in this book and a good deal more which is too complex to describe. We are, therefore, forced to consider first an indigenous intelligence on this planet which has become extinct or secondly, the likelihood of an extra-terrestrial visitation. With the evidence presently at hand, we may be forced to admit to a combination of both these possibilities.

Mathematics are essentially mind games and by not being visual they are less impressive than the obvious miracles of ancient pyramid construction. This is not to say that some of those monumental buildings do not conceal mathematics which are unrecognisable to the casual observer. At Rennes-le-Château, however, the monument itself is invisible until the mathematical solution unveils it. There is no place for the casual observer at Rennes-le-Château other than in viewing the comparatively recent debris left by those who sought to understand or preserve it piecemeal. It requires an intensive study of the mathematical and visual detail. Satisfy yourself with the validity of the detail and the mind will eventually reward the searcher with a mental image of the whole.

As in the construction of an aircraft, every tiny component must be tested, but the day will come when they are all obscured by the aerodynamically designed skin which determines whether or not the 'edifice' will fly. No amount of examination of the tiny component will allow its examiner to visualise the whole. To do this one must step back a long way, but always with the understanding that only if those components are within tolerance will the whole achieve its purpose.

The task before us is, therefore, to present the components to the readers in order that they may examine them individually and satisfy themselves as to their veracity. Next we must ask them to step back and with the global understanding with which Mankind has been blessed, see the message of the whole.

To do this we must give some attention to the viewing mechanism which in this case is not the eyes, but the mind. It is unfortunate that in many ways our academic methods of teaching handicaps the mind from functioning laterally.

We are all well-acquainted with the learning process experienced by a child as it slowly acquires sufficient knowledge to allow it to function in our society. Given equal opportunity and incentive, it is surprising how little difference is displayed in them by the time this happens. There are naturally exceptions, but in percentage terms it is smaller than one might imagine and furthermore, we must be cautious as to the particular measuring device we use in making our judgements. It is all too easy to refer to the 'average', both in terms of education and intellect, when in fact these attributes are only loosely linked. A considerable difference can be noticed, however, when one compares a highly educated 'linear' mind with a far less educated 'lateral intelligence'.

As reference material has become cheaper in the form of technical publications and computerised data, it has become the lateral thinkers who have made the 'break-throughs'. Academic qualifications are admirable, but they are largely awarded on a basis of the recipient having learnt, 'parrot-fashion' the results of 'established' disciplines. Unfortunately, these are inevitably those which the 'establishment' find acceptable.

Teaching children to conform to acceptable behaviour patterns is essential for the existence of an orderly society, but the creative abilities of the mind can be easily suffocated by superimposing unproven doctrines of belief which contradict the experience and logic of the individual. A primitive mind can be easily convinced that a natural disaster is the outcome of the annoyance of a neglected god. However, intelligent beings, fully conversant with the forces of causation do have a problem when they are confronted with hundreds of innocent men, women and children subjected to untold suffering. Reasonably they pose the question. 'Is this the will of God and if so, why?' How can they reconcile praying to God to relieve the suffering of the victims, if the event was of his doing? One would seriously doubt the outcome if he were to stand for re-election. The clash between intelligence and faith is unavoidable and eventually the liberated mind must come to terms with it. Superimposing human emotions on the forces of nature and on their causes will only confuse. One of the most important and neglected subjects is that of learning HOW to exercise the mind.

Countless millions are spent and countless profit is made convincing us to follow 'keep-fit' programmes, but we know of no organisation concerned with teaching us HOW to think clearly. Here we are not speaking of education, which is collecting, collating and remembering information. This we could think of as hard-disk memory capacity. Although it is an inadequate analogy, we are here referring more to the CONFIGURATION of the mind.

How one distinguishes brain from mind is largely a matter of choice, but to avoid confusion we will speak of the physical object as the brain and its electrochemical processes as the mind. The brain has been partially mapped and the locations of some of the areas responsible for various functions are known. On the left side, we find two small areas concerned with the production and comprehension of language. On the right are the musical and visual sections. An arch across the head is known as the Motor Cortex which controls the elementary functions of the body. These areas are, however, responsible for only a tiny fraction of the brain's activity.

The composition of the brain tissue can best be imagined as a long established bramble bush that has intertwined to such a degree that it is virtually impossible to distinguish between the shoots. It also has a self- propagating root system which is equally complex underground. Here the analogy ends, for in the case of the brain each shoot and root are grafted on to hundreds of other shoots. Each of these connections is fitted with 'switches' or ' valves' known as synapses, of which the brain may contain some 100 trillion. Through this labyrinth passes a 'thought', but not in a linear motion. The electrochemical function of thinking flashes through the brain in every direction until it is satisfied that all the departments requiring the information have been contacted. Unfortunately, it is possible to consciously shut off the 'valves' if the individual feels threatened by the incoming data. A blind belief can misroute the information and thereby hamper the logical function of the mind to arrive at the result of its best endeavours.

Continuing with the analogy, certain of these valves are, during our normal daily experience, one way 'gates', in that they allow information to flow into the subconscious and remain trapped there. This wealth of information is probably passed from generation to generation through the genes and is only accessed by the conscious mind when the 'gate' is partially ajar. We are here referring to dreams or moments of emotional stress when we glimpse the vast storehouse of knowledge accumulated by our ancestors over thousands of years. We may even, at times, intuitively see the solution to a problem beyond the capability of our conscious mind.

We are told that this all-powerful computer is the result of aeons of evolution, but this is not so. The average adult brain has rapidly expanded from 500 to some 1400 or 1500cc's in a very short space of time, so let us use a little of it and see what happens. It is now generally agreed that we only employ a small proportion of our brain and our rapid progress is attributable to being able to utilise more of its present capacity. This is certainly not the scenario of an evolving mind gradually increasing in capacity to satisfy the mental processes required of it, otherwise each scientific development would be delayed by thousands of years, waiting for the brain to enlarge itself sufficiently to accommodate the additional input.

It has now been proven beyond reasonable doubt that the dinosaurs were destroyed by cometary or asteroid impact at the end of the Cretaceous era, having survived for millions of years in near perfect conditions, not only for the development of their bodies, but also their brains. However, their fossilised remains show us that at best they only achieved 500cc's of brain capacity; so much for the speed of evolution! Next, let us consider Neanderthal man, the creature who was once erroneously considered to bridge the gap between ape and our direct ancestor Cro-Magnon. The idea could never hold water when we consider the 500cc brain capacity of the ape with the massive 1500 cc brain of Neanderthal. It was even possibly larger than homo sapiens. Given time - countless millions of years - such an evolution might possibly occur, but the Earth would have been littered with countless intermediate creatures developing painfully slowly from 500 to 1500 cc's - a process requiring hundreds of thousands of years. Neanderthal's origin would then be pushed back to a time when we know he could not have existed. In fact, our latest findings show Neanderthal to have become extinct some 40,000 years back, having only existed for some 35,000 years from his appearance on Earth. Despite his massive brain, his achievements were very limited. We know he used stone implements and certainly used fire, but although we are in doubt as to why he became extinct, it could be something to do with the 'sudden' arrival of Cro-Magnon who appears out of nowhere with a complete toolbox of skills previously unknown.

In recent years, dozens of authors have considered that Man may have been a genetically engineered creature, created by visitors from outer space. Their quite reasonable logic has, of course, been ridiculed by the academics who, nevertheless, offer nothing better in return. They dismiss these theories as a sensational offshoot of the UFO phenomenon - just another facet of scientific fiction spreading its wings into the past instead of the future.

We decided to look back to some early books on the subject to see if the explosive development of Man had captured the attention of previous men of science. Consider, for example, this comment by Professor Henry Drummond in *The Ascent of Man* published as far back as 1894. In the chapter significantly titled 'The Dawn of Mind' he states:-

> "The enormous distance travelled by the Mind of Man beyond the utmost limit of intelligence reached by any animal is a puzzling circumstance, a circumstance only equalled in strangeness by another - the suddenness with which that rise took place. Both facts are without a parallel in nature. Why, of the countless thousands of species of animals, each with some shadowy rudiment of a Mind, all should have remained comparatively at the same dead level, while Man alone shot past and developed powers of a quality and with a speed unknown in the world's history, is a question which it is impossible not to raise. That by far the greatest step in the world's history should not only have been taken at the eleventh hour, but that it took only an hour to do it - for compared with the time when animals began their first activities, the birth of Man is a thing of yesterday - seems almost the denial of Evolution. What was it in Man's case that gave his mental powers their unprecedented start or facilitated a growth so rapid and so vast?"

Now this learned man was not influenced by UFOs or sci-fi stories, but his disbelief is apparent.

In the epilogue of *GENISIS*, a possible scenario to explain this enigma was presented which suggested that the origin of the accelerated intelligence probably dated from only 200,000 years ago. A year later it was gratifying to read that:-

> "Scientists at the University of California at Berkely lead by Dr. Alan C. Wilson, support the view that modern man, homo sapiens, originated in Africa about 200,000 years ago and later spread throughout the rest of the world".
>
> (Harold M Schmeck. *New York Times 26/3/86*)

These finds are based upon a study of the DNA from the cell structures of Mitochondria which are only inherited through the mother. The Mitochondrial DNA has a known rate of change which has allowed scientists to date its origin. It is even more revealing to hear that from the study of the DNA of human blood, no connection whatsoever has been found to relate homo sapiens to the previous apes and bipeds.

The time has come for the reader to use his 'open' mind. An 'ape-like' creature suddenly appears on planet Earth equipped with an enormous brain which could never have evolved in the available time. This simple fact cannot be easily dismissed for we, his ancestors, are living proof of it.

Naturally, not all scientists agree with the findings of Dr. Wilson. Dr. Wallace, a professor of biochemistry at Emory University in Atlanta considers the origin to be not in Africa, but in Asia. He also doubts the single person origin, but admits the research suggests only a small number of ancestors. He also questions the date of that origin which he estimates at the remarkably recent time of 100,000 years ago. This, of course, only strengthens the argument against evolution and leans in favour of the possibility of genetic interference.

If this were indeed so, the medical engineers responsible would have to have used their own genetics to elevate us, but at the same time to have ensured that something less than a hundred per cent transfer occurred, otherwise they would have created a creature with powers equal to their own. These powers may have been their telepathic, telekinetic and telesthetic powers which are those that our psychics occasionally activate.

Consider the possibility of even greater powers which may lie hidden in our subconscious, such as the knowledge of how to manipulate time and space in a manner inconceivable to us at this time. Acceptance of this theory certainly explains all the mysteries, paranormal or otherwise, with which we are now confronted.

Finally, consider why and by whom these genetic changes were made and furthermore, whether the theory can be supported in any other way. Certainly there is a mass of substantiating evidence in the myths and legends of every ancient civilisation. Even psychologically, there is the human conviction of someone superior to ourselves giving rise to the Father or God concept. This incorporates the idea of someone who fashioned us in his own image, and our theory finds no argument there. However, the human mind appears to be offended by the thought of a race of 'gods' who created us, not out of love, but to do the work they found too menial and uncomfortable. Our arrogance strongly objects to the possibility of having been created as workhorses for a superior being.

Economically, there is no question that a self-generating clone is a cheaper and more efficient proposition than mechanical robots. Even Hollywood now accepts the robot as a poor choice compared to a flexible self-healing human, but on moral grounds they seem to have compromised by using androids.

This leads us to the physiological considerations. It would be supportive of our theory if our bodies had anything which appeared to be 'not of this world'. The first and most obvious in this category is our heads which are disproportionately far too large and heavy for our bodies. This was the unavoidable consequence of the massive brain which we inherited and the equally massive skull needed to accommodate and protect it. Most of it is, as

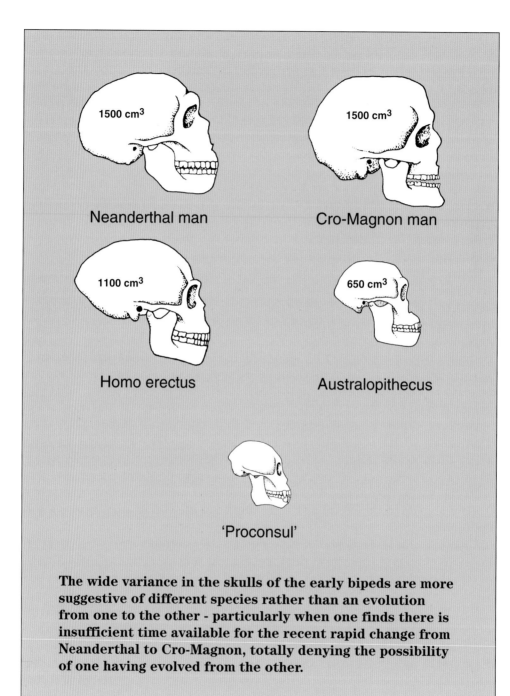

1500 cm³

Neanderthal man

1500 cm³

Cro-Magnon man

1100 cm³

Homo erectus

650 cm³

Australopithecus

'Proconsul'

The wide variance in the skulls of the early bipeds are more suggestive of different species rather than an evolution from one to the other - particularly when one finds there is insufficient time available for the recent rapid change from Neanderthal to Cro-Magnon, totally denying the possibility of one having evolved from the other.

previously explained, completely unnecessary for us to have reached our present stage of advancement, and as a brain would only need to expand by having used up its capacity, we have further evidence that we inherited it. Neanderthal was handicapped with an even larger brain and an even thicker skull. Obviously, he also found it quite difficult to use and our theory would classify him as the Mark I version of the genetically manufactured creatures. This probably accounts for his brief stay on the planet.

Modern man, the improved version, still suffers from backache, tired legs and heart problems associated with pumping blood round an overburdened body. Slowly this had the effect of reducing the lifespan enjoyed by our ancestors, which is well-documented in the legends. Eventually, having reached rock bottom, the body began to recover and adapt itself to counteract these deficiencies, first by natural physical development and then by technology. Confronted with his inability to move anything other than the lightest items, Mankind has been forced to develop machines which can lift and carry. Beginning with the wheel and the lever, he continued until hydraulics satisfied his desire to move bulk by the magnification of his body movements. Our creators however, may well have had the ability to levitate objects, thereby obviating the necessity for machines of the type we require.

Being early offspring from the 'gods' possibly some of our ancestors also had this ability. This could be a part of the answer to the mysteries of the massive constructions of the past where powers of mind were used and which we have since lost.

The evidence of the improving records set in the Olympic games could also be seen as indicative of a species adapting itself to overcome the burden of carrying excessive weight, for which its body was not designed. If this were not so, a graphical representation of the achievements would by now be in the form of a slightly fluctuating level line.

We must come to terms with the fact that if we were genetically modified there must have been a very good reason. It may well have been that our planet was a superstore of 'goodies'. First, it is not unreasonable to assume that an advanced intelligence could use water as an environmentally acceptable fuel. This would put planet Earth in the category of a super fuel-tanker; probably the best in this part of the galaxy. This abundance of water also created the necessary climate to make planet Earth the perfect market garden. It probably enjoyed a far more stable orbit than it does at present, and that would mean a continuous harvest at established and invariable latitudes. The mineral wealth could also have been an attraction; but was there something about our planet which even their technical or mental expertise could not overcome? If the 'gods' had developed on a smaller planet than ours, they may have found our gravitational field totally overpowering. Nearby, the planet Mars may have been less environmentally accommodating but at least tolerable. In suggesting this, we should be mindful of the fact that in those times Mars was a life-supporting planet, and not the airless hostile neighbour as we now see it. It is, therefore, not unreasonable to suggest that the 'gods' settled on Mars and used the nearby Earth - the Garden of Eden - as their hypermarket. In fact, Earth satisfied all their requirements, but above all, there were these ape-like creatures wandering around who were almost ideally suited to do all the arduous work, if only their imbecilic brains could be adjusted to carry out instructions.

Courtesy *Sunday Express*

Consider, however, that we now decided on a similar programme to elevate the intelligence of apes and then put them to work in the mines. This is not a fictional idea, for we are already at a point where we could probably genetically create an intermediate subhuman between us and them. There are certain dangers inherent in such an operation. In the process of producing such a creature we would be forced to use the only available genes - our own! Inevitably the subconscious powers which we now know to be latent in homo sapiens would pass to the sub-species and, in the absence of strict control, the sub-species could breed and progress in much the same way that we have. If some selectively virulent disease totally or almost destroyed us, our subhuman creation might rule supreme. Imagine after a thousand years, how confused that creature would be. Imagine its subconscious race memory recalling our achievements, or even worse, consider that after thousands of years it found evidence of us having created it. Their spiritual leaders would probably go to some lengths to suppress that evidence. Suffice to say, many recent articles have appeared which leave us in no doubt that our scientists are currently involved in experimental genetic engineering, as the cartoon by Cummings so clearly illustrates.

We feel sure that the reader will accept mental telepathy as a reality, and it is probably a latent power which would have been at the disposal of our creators. They would obviously have done their utmost to ensure that this particular ability was not transferred to us; but genetic engineering may not be that precise. It may even be that telepathic communication is an inevitable result of the function of the intelligent mind. It could also be, that if it were tampered with, the species would have a natural self-rectifying ability to reinstate it. This could explain the remarkable powers possessed by some people which has been recorded throughout our past history.

Sufficiently developed by enough people, telepathy becomes a 'group-mind', whereby a number of people can concentrate on a given problem and solve it spontaneously. Many consider that ant colonies use this system to overcome obstacles when they migrate. The process of gathering together to pray may well be a weak echo of the subconscious knowledge that once we had the ability to achieve so-called miracles by this method. Even in our everyday lives, we are often confronted with coincidences which seem to stretch mathematical probability formulæ to breaking point and we are forced to ask ourselves whether there is an overall consciousness at work. It may even be that the 'group-mind' could also be capable of assessing the likelihood of catastrophes and directing individuals to create works which would alert the masses to that possibility.

CHAPTER 13.
THE COLLECTIVE SUBCONSCIOUS
(Ian Campbell)

Psychic help. Answers in dreams. Race memory.
Coincidence or co-incidence. Dowsing.
Intuitive knowledge. Drugs.

THE idea of a collective subconscious is an old and hackneyed one, regurgitated at regular intervals by various psychologists since it was proposed by Jung. However, we will be discussing the idea in its metaphysical rather than its purely psychological sense.

To date, throughout our adventures along the Rennes-le-Château trail, we, the authors, and no doubt countless other investigators of this or other mysteries, have felt that we have been led by the nose in certain directions. When we have become stuck, relevant clues have materialised in front of us. When we have strayed away from the mystery and left it well alone, something has always happened to nudge us back into it. It is almost as though we have become necessary parts of the machine which constitutes Rennes-le-Château. However much we may have wished to distance ourselves from it, both mentally and physically, there has always been something, sometimes an insignificantly small thing, which re-kindles the fire. In this chapter, we shall try to analyse this feeling of being manipulated. During his compilation of *GENISIS*, I know my co-author was subjected to any number of these experiences, and in our time together he has received many more.

In my own experience, even my first trip to Rennes-le-Château included several psychic nudges - the temptation whilst climbing the hill to the village to quench my thirst by eating large bunches of succulent black grapes, was stymied by the thought that the grapes may be poisoned. The temptation was still there, but after I stepped off the road into the vineyard and actually had my hand on a bunch of grapes, incredibly, I saw a weathered sign which read "EMPOISONNE" under the motif of a skull and crossbones.

On that same first trip, I found the church locked and was unable to find anyone who had the key. I had tried the key-holder's house three times with no success, but as I was leaving the village, the elderly caretaker of the church appeared in the street. He was the only person I had seen in the whole village.

Later, in England, I tried to obtain several books which David Wood had referred to in *GENISIS*, hoping to facilitate my understanding of the phenomenon which is Rennes. I was unable to find any of them through the usual channels and many readers of this book will also experience the same difficulties with some of the literature to which we refer. However, one by one, I was led to each of these books and often in most curious circumstances. I had spent a good deal of time trying to trace a copy of Peter Tompkin's *Magic of the Obelisk* and I found it in an unknown bookshop in Chester - I had walked in to browse, and not knowing the layout of the shop, had leant against a pile of books. Yes, as you have guessed there was a copy of the Tompkin's work at a reduced price. Another of my quests was *The Lost Light* by Alvin Boyd Kuhn which I found in the Liverpool City Library the day after a friend had told me it would be there. So, considering I had searched for both of these books for nearly two years, it was quite impressive.

On the same trip whilst staying with friends on the Wirral, because of the Poussin connection, I had decided to take them to visit Shugborough Hall in Staffordshire. We left early enough in the morning for the 100 mile drive, but it was not to be. Thwarted at every turn by traffic diversions and road works, after three hours on the road, we had only driven as far as Crewe. Something was preventing us attaining our objective.

We turned around and headed for my favourite city in the north-west, Chester. Once there, we did the rounds of the antiquarian bookshops. The first one bore my name. The second had an Egyptian work by Wallis Budge in the window for £1.50. Now this book was not on my list, but remembering the Egyptian connection to Rennes-le-Château, I went inside. We browsed in vain and found nothing worthy of attention, until we decided to leave. My friend pointed to a box full of books, stooped and removed the top booklet in the box and handed it to me - it was the *Guide to Shugborough Hall!* The point I am making through these otherwise mundane anecdotes is that it would seem that another agency was at work. Something which was leading me to things which were important for my research. It is my contention that this is what Jung loosely referred to as the 'collective subconscious' and possibly what Robert Anton Wilson would say is related to my 'reality tunnel'.

Since those early days, I have been led to information, or books, or ideas, by fortuitous chance, or by this collective subconscious and many others who are engaged in similar work have had these experiences. This includes my co-author and no one could be a greater advocate than him of:-

"Knock, and the door shall be opened"
"Ask and ye shall receive"
"Seek and ye shall find"

These three phrases would seem to be alive and well and working overtime for some of us. Although it seems a crazy idea, we also know it pays dividends. It has served me in foreign countries where I did not know the local language.

In order to be able to approach what we think is happening, we need to have a basic understanding of how the 'mind' works. As previously explained, the brain is divided into two hemispheres; these are then further subdivided into different parts, but we will only consider the left and right hemispheres. The considered advice from many experts is that the brain hemispheres are cross-wired - that is to say that the right hemisphere controls the functions of the left side of the body, whilst the left hemisphere controls those of the right.

The left hemisphere is responsible for logic - things scientific and mechanical; the right deals with things artistic - emotional and intuitive. Most people develop one hemisphere more than the other, and therefore tend to live their lives accordingly. The logical, technical people are left hemisphere dominated whereas artists, writers and musicians are often right hemisphere dominated.

These developments are noticeable in the study of phrenology - the study of the morphology of the human head, where if you look closely at a mature adult, you will see that hardly any face is symmetrical. Nearly all are asymmetric, which means that one side of the face is physically larger than the other.

Look around at members of your family to test this. Imagine three lines drawn across their faces; one through the corners of the eyes; one across the base of the nose and the third through the corners of the mouth. Are the lines parallel? If they are not, then the side of the face which is the smallest will be the side where its muscles have done the most work and tightened the facial structure. This will indicate that this person is dominated by the opposing hemisphere of their brain. It is an interesting exercise to do and it illustrates different types of people.

The problem is that for someone to be a good mathematician, they need to be left hemisphere dominated, but to be a brilliant mathematician, like Hilbert or Dirac, they probably need to be both! Earlier this century, a mathematician concerned himself with trying to work out a formula for testing prime numbers. A prime number is one which can only be divided by one and itself. No even numbers are or can be prime numbers, and the simple test to check whether any given number is a prime is to simply try dividing it by all the numbers less than itself. If you try doing it with all the numbers up to 100 you will soon see that it is a lengthy process. In fact, our mathematician quickly recognised that it would take so long to do the checking that even if he had started at the time of the alleged Big Bang, he would never have had enough time to make all the check calculations! This much was given to him through his left hemisphere logical brain. However, he didn't give up. He was a man who kept a note pad and pencil by his bedside, just in case he thought of something in the night. One morning, he awoke to find that he had written an equation on the note pad. Although he could not recollect having done so, he recognised that it was concerned with prime numbers. Having applied and tested it thoroughly, he found that it worked. He had discovered the formula for testing prime numbers! Then came the problem. He knew, logically, that there had not been long enough since the beginning of time, to arrive at the formula. It could only have manifested itself from his creative, intuitive, right hemisphere. Luckily, he recognised the phenomenon for what it was and did not waste too much time in trying to work out the psychological intricacies involved. As you may have guessed, he always sleeps with a note pad and pencil beside his bed! The same technique is advised for people who want to remember their dreams. Everybody dreams, but some cannot remember them. Neurologically speaking, if we didn't dream, we would probably die because the brain 'signals' and 'interrogates' the whole organism to make various repairs, each time we enter the alpha-rhythm dream state. If you have trouble remembering your dreams, try this note pad approach and when you awake, record the first thought which is passing through your mind at the time. This will in turn stimulate the thought which immediately preceded it, and by that means one can often access a forgotten dream. This is not just an interesting pastime; it can be beneficial and even profitable.

There are many cases on record of problems being solved through dreams and many instances when we, the authors, have been rewarded by the use of this technique. It is also recognised quite widely by the scientific community as a means to an end if nothing else. Before you can solve any problem or invent anything , the imagination must have conceived it first. Before the imagination can present it to the conscious mind, the subconscious mind, in its many layers, must have already dealt with the problem. So whether you dream of having met the Comte de St. Germain and gained instruction from him or whether like Dr. Timothy Leary and his 'Star Seed' accomplices you believe you have intercepted telepathic messages from Sirius, or whether you just have a premonition to do, or not to do something, you are probably encountering your subconscious mind breaking through to the conscious level.

Of course, the implications are far deeper than they at first appear. For our mathematician to have intuited his solution, the presumption is and has to be, that the solution already existed in another place, even if that other place was not in the physical world and the problem may never before have been solved by Mankind.

The inference here, is that all the answers to all the questions, including those which have yet to be thought of, already exist in a sort of universal subconscious, and that the subconscious mind has the ability to visit the great library of the universal subconscious and access the necessary material. It could also be that we are accessing the hidden subconscious of our creators who used their 'down-loaded' intelligence to accelerate ours.

On a more physical plane, a similar system could well explain some of the coincidences that each of us have enjoyed or suffered in our everyday experiences. How many times have we as individuals been travelling in distant places or countries where no-one knew where we were, only to run into someone we know. We put it down to coincidence of course and forget about it, but if you record all these little coincidences and review them every year, you will be amazed how many you experience. Indeed, it is not long before a rational mind starts to wonder whether the word coincidence disguises a more profound function. In fact we seem to be observing a 'contemporaneously contrived incident' and furthermore, it seems to be 'contrived' by the subconscious minds of the participants who have been led into contact with each other through a maze of subconscious alternatives.

Consider how your brain works in everyday situations. How often do you think of something from the past? A memory is triggered by one of the senses, and a full implication or association of that event takes place in your mind. In fact we should marvel that so small an input can bring all the memories flooding back. In computer terms, it is like having a hard disk of almost infinite capacity, completely cross-referenced to any event, memory or piece of knowledge you have ever experienced and it happens instantly! If we continue with the computer analogy, this book is being written on a word processor with a mere 30,000,000 byte capacity of information. The central processing unit works at 8 million bytes per second and the whole of the book can be stored on two 720k floppy disks.

Nevertheless, if we want to load a chapter from floppy disk into the machine it takes several seconds and if you wish to search for a particular word or phrase, then you can hear the clockwork whirr for quite long periods of time. Our minds easily outrun that performance and furthermore, the computer's powers of access are dependent on our loading the correct disk and choosing the correct directory.

So now that we have given ourselves a pat on the back and seen how wonderful our minds really are, let us return to the subconscious mind. Many experiments have been done to illustrate that not only do we share a collective subconscious, but that we also inherit a race memory and one which may, or may not be genetically based. For example, experiments have been done with rats, where in order to receive food, the rat has to negotiate a maze. Gradually, over a period of time, the rats learn by trial and error, the shortest route to the food reward. It then becomes ingrained on their conscious mind. Amazingly, a hundred miles away the offspring of the rats are able to immediately cope with an identical maze and earn their reward without the learning period! Even rats born after all the first group rats had been killed and not genetically connected with the second group rats, have also been demonstrated to be able to cope with the maze. In other words, they have not learnt either genetically or telepathically. They appear to have accessed a collective subconscious.

This use of the subconscious mind prevails through many areas and may well be the reason that techniques such as dowsing, can work. Most of the world's population could dowse without putting their minds to it and those who cannot could be taught. In some ways, it is similar to the game of golf. It is a very simple game to play, if you can keep your conscious mind out of it. It is essentially a game of relaxed concentration. Unfortunately, those two terms are diametrically opposed. Have you ever tried to relax and concentrate at the same time? The real problem is that the rational, thinking mind interferes, when it should be leaving everything to the right hemisphere and allowing the intuitive mind to work.

With the game of golf, the brain knows exactly how far it is from the hands to the club face and the ball and if it is allowed to take control of the swing, most people would naturally hit the ball a fair distance straight down the middle of the fairway. However, once the conscious mind intrudes, the grip on the club, posture, stance, aim and swing all require attention and this results in so much information being fed into the logic centres that the circuits are overloaded and the shot is invariably muffed.

Returning to the dowsing analogy, the dowsing rod, which can be made of almost any suitable material, probably acts as an antenna or aerial whilst the right hemisphere performs the part of the tuning coil. The radio receiver, (the dowser) then tunes in to the object or thing he wants to pick up by thinking the thought and then relaxing. Now, with a dowser able to locate physical things, the whole process can be thought of in terms of the dowser picking up magnetic radiation or the shadows upon magnetic fields. But this does not explain how some dowsers are able to dowse remotely.

For example, the British Society of Dowsers receives from time to time, requests from farmers in arid countries - South Africa and Australia, for help in locating water. Quite often this request is passed on to members who are skilled at map dowsing, and they, armed only with a map, sometimes only a sketch map, are able to locate water. Not only can they give accurate directions as to where the well should be sunk, but they can also predict the flow-rate and purity of the water.

For map dowsing to be a possibility therefore, implies that there exists knowledge of the event, (the flow of water) and that the dowser is somehow able to tap into it. Once again, although this is remote dowsing,it does involve water flowing, which in itself involves the mass movement of electric particles. This enables the physicist to at least speculate on what is happening. So much so, that most physicists and engineers will admit, at least in private, that dowsing in some areas, works. This is probably part of the reason why dowsers are employed by the Water , Electricity and Gas companies as well as by farmers and mineral prospectors. It does not come anywhere near to explaining how dowsers are able to dowse people's auras, missing pieces of paper, or missing persons, but they can and quite often do this successfully.

In other words, the information or piece of knowledge must exist before the dowser can tune in to it. Perhaps this is something that the dowser shares with the clairvoyant and psychic. We live in a society which specialises in telling its citizens what they cannot do, and these remarkable gifts remain in the province of eccentrics. They remain apart and aloof because they think differently or would rather trust their intuition. Unfortunately, these gifted people are often those who infuriate the logical component of the population by knowing that something is so without being able to explain why.

With regard to Robert Anton Wilson, his idea of reality tunnels, which he has developed at length in his book *The New Inquisition* (New Falcon Publications, Scottsdale, Arizona, 1986) seems to be most pertinent. Briefly, each of us has his or her own reality tunnel - a way of looking at the world in an individual way. Whereas we may all think that we see or experience the same things, possibly nothing could be further from the truth. We are each sensitised differently, and each of us only experiences that which we have programmed into our individual minds to experience. The rider to this, is that if we do not share the same reality tunnel, how can we ever be sure that what exists for one, exists for the other. Possibly everybody's reality tunnel is different and we are all tuned to different parts of the spectrum.

One example is to consider the way that we see. Our optical equipment is superb, but consists of a fairly simple flexible lens. The image which passes through the lens of the eye behaves as it would through any other lens - it records an inverted image on to the retina of the eye. This image is then sent through the neuron system via the optic nerve to the brain, where our on board computer sees it the right-way up. Once again, nothing is quite as it seems.

In the late 1960's, Tony Buzzan made a series of educational television programmes on the way in which the brain works, or more explicitly, how to order information for presentation to the brain in the most efficient way. He suggested that the brain does not assimilate linear information such as long passages learned by rote, as well as it does highly coloured 'bubble' diagrams. This was a boon to people entering educational systems. Even so, there were other areas where the breakthrough has taken longer. One of these was to analyse the way in which we could compare two totally different ideas.

Edward de Bono, a great lateral thinker, wondered whether it would be easier to compare disparate ideas if he first coined a term for it. He thought that while it was easy to think of things which were the same, similar, or even opposite, it was impossible to think of unlike things in comparison to one another because we lacked the term for doing it. So he called the 'other' state 'Po' - and applied it to the usual systems of 'reality' which we think we have. By changing from an either/or or positive statement/negative statement to a 'Po' statement, de Bono manages to open up areas which we would not usually think exist - due to there being no obvious link. Here are a few to think about which may, or may not be connected with Rennes-le-Château:-

St. Germain Po Pierre Plantard de St. Clair
Rennes-le-Château Po St. Veronica
Simony Po Otto Rahn
Saunière Po Ordo Templi Orientis
Marie Denarnaud Po Tout Paris
Abbé Boudet Po P2
Red Tassles Po Umberto Eco
Marquis de Chambord Po The British Labour Party

As you will have observed, just encountering these strange bedfellows, linked only by the 'Po' concept, sparks some interesting thoughts. Would you have had them if you had not encountered the 'Po' concept? To illustrate this point concisely look at the following 'Po' statement:-

President Kennedy Po The Ophiuchus

Initially this would seem to be a nonsensical statement, but consider the following line. Ophiuchus is the constellation of the serpent holder at the cusp of Scorpius. Scorpius (Scorpio) is the name of the private island of Onassis and after Kennedy's assassination, Onassis married Kennedy's widow, Jackie Kennedy. Now curiously, the date of the cusp of Scorpius is given as the 22nd of November, the day of the Kennedy assassination. Now you know how useful the Po concept can be. Was this a modern Greek tragedy? More recently, Britain's Margaret Thatcher resigned her prime-ministership on 22nd November 1990!

To close this chapter, since we have been dealing with the mystery of Rennes-le-Château, we have experienced the effects that we have mentioned and we have met people who seem to 'know'. Also, quite often, we have known that we were being led to certain information and conclusions. If you analyse some of the more astounding geometrical and doctrinal relationships in this book you may wonder how on earth we discovered them.

In some cases, they came to us in a dream or in a moment of enlightenment from the collective subconscious. Time and time again, an apparently unrelated clue presented itself in a persistent manner and although our conscious analysis found it unacceptable, eventually in defiance of our logic, it proved itself. With this in mind, the reader will realise how deeply we have wished that the message of Rennes-le-Château could have been in a lighter vein. There are many ways to tap into this intuitive knowledge - the eastern traditions prefer meditation over many years. Adolf Hitler preferred mescaline as did Huxley, whilst Dr. Timothy Leary favoured the careful use of L.S.D. Aleister Crowley favoured sexual techniques as did Wilhelm Reich. Whatever the method, the result was the opening of the subconscious to the conscious mind and the release into that conscious mind of a vast array of knowledge.

The drug route, although shorter, is of course fraught with danger and curiously enough, as both Aleister Crowley and Dr. Leary found out to their cost, experimentation even upon yourself with drugs, is forbidden in all countries of the developed world. Apparently, the only people allowed to carry out such experiments are the governments using their armed forces as guinea pigs. As for ourselves, we will settle for the lily of the valley, wherein it was said a great, but veiled understanding could be found. It may even be the conglomerate intelligence of our own subconscious minds which we have personified as an omnipotent father figure.

As a closing thought, consider how often scientific events and discoveries have been foreshadowed by artistic fiction. This is demonstrably true with respect to Jules Verne, for as the reader will later be shown, he anticipated the magnitude and danger of comets long before scientific progress considered them as a threat to our continuing existence.

CHAPTER 14.
IN THE END

Imaginary UFOs and the Aurora. The Condon Report.
Danger in the sky. 'Ground-Zero' is found.
The Cretaceous destruction and the aftermath.
Did the Church know? Does God care?

UNTIL very recently, space and astronomy were of little interest to the average person. In its early days even Star Trek was considered risky by Hollywood, but the exploration of space was imminent and Man, or at least youth, looked to the stars. The Moon was suddenly within reach and the achievements were sufficient to suppress the voices complaining about the cost. Eventually, there may have been a ground swell of objection, but the advantages to communication, defence and satellite television placated the masses.

On the technical side, unmanned probes roamed the solar system transmitting planetary spectaculars into the comfort of our lounges. Responsibly minded television producers presented explanatory programmes to acquaint us with the conditions prevailing on our celestial neighbours.

During the same period other designers were busy producing aircraft to fly faster and higher than had previously been thought possible. ICBM's, MERV's, SIDEWINDER's, MAVERICK's and a host of other weapons of destruction became common parlance to the youth of the day. Inevitably, with so many eyes in the sky, we began to see - FLYING SAUCERS, but whereas all the other hardware was real enough, the SAUCERS were imaginary and it is just as well they were, considering they could out-fly anything we had at the time.

Eventually, as one would expect, some sex-starved farmers' wives claimed to have been taken on board UFOs and accosted. Then, just to confuse the issue, a herd of cattle arranged to have their reproductive organs removed. This was, however, considered a small price to pay for the impressive displays of aerobatics which the UFOs gave us in return.

Hollywood was delighted to have a brand new setting into which they could cast their heroes and heroines. The six-shooter was replaced by the laser gun and Wells Fargo became a space-freighter. Everything seemed to be progressing quite nicely, but just to make sure we did not allow our imaginations to run riot, the powers that be set up an official enquiry to deny the existence of UFOs. In the 1950's the CIA had attempted unsuccessfully to debunk them, but thousands of reports had arrived at the Air Force office responsible for gathering the material. This was classified as 'Project Blue -

Book' a somewhat unfortunate choice of colour. Using this material Prof. E. Lactic, or was it Dr E. Condon, compiled a report which was certainly a 'cover-up' job and it concluded:-

> "...that the evidence presented on Unidentified Flying Objects shows no indication that these phenomena constitute a direct physical threat to national security.
>
> We firmly believe that there is no residuum of cases which indicates phenomena which are attributable to foreign artefacts capable of hostile acts, and that there is no evidence that the phenomena indicate a need for the revision of current scientific concepts.
>
> That the continued emphasis on the reporting of these phenomena does, in these parlous times, result in a threat to the orderly functioning of the protective organs of the body politic..."

A little later, those responsible for the early warning system developed SAGE radar which operated on the exotically high frequency of 425 Mhz. Unbeknown to them, this was apparently the frequency band used by the imaginary UFOs.

Inevitably, when they switched it on, an 'imaginary' UFO crashed on the land of a 'real' farm at ROSWELL, New Mexico.

The imaginary remains of the UFO and the imaginary occupants were then removed for examination by 'real' Air Force personnel. Shortly after this, our imaginative American friends saw another strange shape in the sky, which despite all the denials became a reality in the form of the F117 Stealth Fighter-bomber. The 'one or two off' prototype then exhibited remarkable powers of reproduction and the offspring turned out in squadron strength for the 'Desert Storm' operation in the Gulf War (1990).

It would appear that the population of America has only to imagine something for a short while before it becomes a reality, a truly enviable ability. Naturally, encouraged by their previous successes they are now in the process of imagining an even more sophisticated flying machine. Probably they have not completely imagined it yet, but they have decided to imagine it is called the 'AURORA'* and by the time this book goes to press it should be making its imaginary trips to the moon.

By now the reader must be wondering where all this is leading us and how it can possibly be associated with the mystery of Rennes-le-Château. We are sure that many of you will have already seen the connection, but please be patient as there are many who are less informed. For the moment we must

---

* *The U.S.A.A.F. have recently admitted to the existence of 'AURORA'*

return to astronomy. Initially we are presented with a scenario of order and tranquillity. The predictability of the orbits of the Sun, the Moon and the planets lull one into a false sense of security. Occasionally, on a clear night, the monotonous majesty of the heavens may be broken by a meteor spectacular, safely performed at high altitude and unable to penetrate our atmospheric shield.

It would seem we have a circle seat to view a celestial continuity which will always be and always has been, since time immemorial; wrong! Behind the velvet backdrop of the night lurk demons of terrifying power. Mindless destructive serpents of such horrendous proportions as to be able to destroy our planet with a flick of their tails.

In fact, that tail can extend to some 90 million miles, almost the distance from the Earth to the Sun. Why then, can they not be easily seen? Unlike the near circular orbits of the planets, a comet circumnavigates the Sun in an elliptical orbit which takes it into deep space, far beyond the solar system with a major axis of some 50,000 times the distance from the Earth to the Sun. A long-period comet may take a million years or more to return once it has left our system. Short-period comets, on the other hand, may complete their journey in only a few years. These distances, coupled with the comparatively small size of the comet's head or nucleus are the reason they are not seen until they expel their tails. The tail of the comet is the result of the solar wind which streams out from the Sun at some 500 km/sec, pushing the tail away. It is for this reason that the head always faces the Sun.

July 1947 photo of rancher W.W. 'Mac' Brazel who first discovered the crash debris of a UFO while checking fences on his ranch at Roswell, New Mexico. (Mrs Lorraine (Brazel) Ferguson).

The composition of the head is now known to be a conglomerate of gravel or rocks bound together with ice and in the short time we have observed them and until very recently, most of their nuclei have been estimated at 2km or less in diameter. There are, however, millions of comets in orbit and we may one day be confronted with one of much larger proportions. Bearing in mind the estimated impact speed of some 50,000 mph, one is hard put to imagine the scale of such a disaster.

It is for this reason, we feel we should acquaint our readers with some of the statistics involved in a celestial mishap of this nature.

In 1883 Ignatius Donnelly published *Ragnarok -The Age of Fire and Gravel,* which suggested that a comet's tail had lashed the Earth causing wholesale destruction. The book was largely ignored by the world's astronomers as he was not considered sufficiently well-versed in the subject to have a valid opinion. It is indeed unfortunate that he was not alive at the time Walter Alvarez and his team investigated the rock structure at Gubbio in Italy. Alvarez was a professor of geology at the University of California and was analysing the excessive quantity of osmium and iridium in a band of clay between the Cretaceous and Tertiary rock formations which date back 65 million years. Continuing investigations by other scientists round the world, confirmed that his findings were not a local phenomenon, and because these elements are largely extra-terrestrial, they concluded the Earth had been subjected to an impact of massive proportions.

Eventually, in South America the search resulted in finding sites where the Cretaceous/Tertiary was clearly exposed. Examination of particles in the boundary clay showed them to be 'Tectites', tiny glass globules which can only be formed by the extremely high temperatures produced by impact.

The scientists searched for 'ground-zero' and they found it by analysing the magnetic and gravitational anomalies discovered by Glen Penfield when carrying out a survey for Pemex, the Mexican National Oil Corporation. These revealed a circular impact crater on the Yucatan Peninsular (see illustration), some 130 miles in diameter and at a depth of 2,500 feet - the signature of an immense cataclysmic explosion, only conceivably attributable to a celestial missile - the signature of the Typhon - SET.

The previously inexplicable disappearance of a large number of dinosaurs coincided with this event, and at last the world knew that planet Earth was less safe than they had previously considered. In this particular event, current opinion is divided between the fall of an asteroid and cometary impact, but whether comet or asteroid, the results would be similar. It is all a question of the amount of kinetic energy released at the time of impact, and that is the result of both the velocity and size of the body involved.

The Earth rotates and orbits the Sun at a speed of 66,660 mph and could meet a 112,000 mph comet head-on. Although comets are invariably smaller than an asteroid which is capable of reaching the Earth's surface, the degree of destruction would still be vast. In simple terms, the kinetic energy released is the result of multiplying half the mass of the body by the square of its velocity. A small high velocity comet could, therefore, achieve the same destructive force as a lower velocity large asteroid. So now we know what could happen! Some sixty five million years ago the Earth was teeming with animal and

The Yucatan Peninsula. The position which has finally been identified as the place where a massive comet struck the Earth, destroying virtually all the higher life forms at the end of the Cretaceous period.

vegetable life when quite suddenly, all but the smallest of creatures were annihilated and this mass extinction of life on Earth was the result of a celestial impact.

"Evidence is presented indicating that the extinction, at the end of the Cretaceous, of large terrestrial animals was caused by atmospheric heating during a cometary impact and that the extinction of calcareous marine plankton was a consequence of poisoning by cyanide released by the fallen comet and of a catastrophic rise in calcite-compensation depth in the oceans after the detoxification of the cyanide".

(Nature Vol. 285 22 May 1980)

It is also considered that an impact of this magnitude would result in the Earth being plunged into, what in modern terms we refer to as a nuclear winter, lasting many years. Should such an event take place today, Mankind would probably be totally destroyed. If by chance, a handful of people survived, it would be for them to begin the re-population of the Earth. Initially, generation after generation would try to preserve the legends of the past, told to them by their ancestors. Tales of great cities and of machines that flew through the skies; but could those stories survive accurately during the descent of Man through thousands of years of savage illiteracy, when his sole concern would be survival?

Slowly the ingenuity of the excessive brain of Man would overcome the animal kingdom once again, and once again subconscious memories would come back to haunt his dreams.

Are we at last beginning to see the message contained in the geometry of Rennes-le-Chateau? But if this is so, why should it have been subjected to such religious suppression in the past? Consider the principle which exists in all religious belief.

Far above the myth of the crucifixion and resurrection of an earthly Saviour lies an image of an omnipotent spirit head whose major concern, according to the teachings of the earthly potentates, is his love of Mankind. They teach us that by exercising his will, we may be guaranteed a life of serenity in the hereafter.

What if it were not so? The overwhelming evidence suggests that at any moment intelligent man could be wiped from the face of the Earth by nothing other than the mere mathematical law of probability controlling the orbit of a pile of rock and ice.

Imagine yourself promising the masses that by strict adherence to your set of rules, all will be well. Could you possibly permit it to be known that regardless of the behaviour pattern of the flock, a vicious uncaring celestial event would destroy good and bad alike? If the word Christianity is to have any meaning at all, let it be that showing love and compassion to one's fellow man is in itself sufficient reward. We should need no promises of an imaginary heaven to bribe us to commit acts of kindness which should be an integral part of our nature. Despite their intellectual superiority, our creators were foolish enough not to realise that the animal they had elevated would retain his instincts of animal love. They thought to create an inferior species, but it was one which they eventually had to admit was in many ways superior to themselves.

Should the informed reader wish to contradict us with the old axiom that 'nothing can create anything superior to itself', we would remind them, that in this case, the hybrid 'homo sapiens' was a modification, not a creation in the true sense of the word.

They probably considered the division of the sexes would weaken us, but that very division provides sensations which could now be the subject of their envy. The ultimate of intelligence may be androgynous, but without the competition of the sexes, so much is lost. One must admit that the biblical account of the instantaneous creation of Adam and Eve in the Garden of Eden goes some way to admitting to the possibility of our being a genetically created creature. It is also refreshing to see that this account accepts the presence of a superior intelligence, albeit in the guise of a serpent, but we would not argue with their choice, knowing as we do what that serpent represented.

If, however, the Church were in possession of all this information, they obviously had no alternative other than to suppress what could be revealed by a full understanding of the mystery of Rennes-le-Château. A universal knowledge of the tenuous thread by which Mankind hung on to his existence, could never be revealed, or the myth of their loving God would be exposed. Faced with the reality of the power of the TYPHON- SET, their mythical God is apparently impotent. Were those poor creatures of the Cretaceous period devil worshippers? If not, why then were they so cruelly destroyed? Why was this omnipotent God unable to save them? Surely this, together with so many other more recent disasters, casts considerable doubt on the nature of the Christian God, if not his very existence!

Rest assured we will only survive by our own devices. Having toiled from savagery to space flight, we must prepare ourselves for the impending destruction of the planet. Our creators could never have visualised the emergence of powerful organisations capable of perverting the truth to the point whereby the instrument of our destruction could be cast in the role of a demon, a Satan who must be ignored rather than investigated. It can only be by that investigation and an understanding of his destructive power that Man will survive.

In the time available, it is unlikely that we will develop space vehicles capable of destroying an incoming comet. Such an action would be to fragment a bullet into grapeshot, which would be equally or more destructive. Is there then any conceivable way to preserve intelligent life? Once again, for the sake of our readers, we must pause to take stock. Obviously, we are preparing you for the further revelations contained in the geometry of Rennes-le-Château, but before that point, we will refer to another facet of our enquiry. Being unable to ignore the warning signs laid down in the geometry, we searched for any evidence which could suggest science had progressed sufficiently to be able to preserve the seed of Mankind, should the Earth be subjected to another cataclysmic disaster. Later we will discuss certain mechanical precautions available to us, but for now we feel we should tell the reader of a rather bizarre connection which seems to have forced itself upon us.

CHAPTER 15
TIME AND TIME AGAIN

Time Portals. The Magic Talisman. Opération Orth.
Who killed Gélis? The Emma Calvé connection.
St. Germain. Dog-day mornings. Sirius rising.

THROUGHOUT our investigations of the enigma of Rennes-le-Château, the subjects of time or 'time travel' or 'time portals' kept cropping up. This was not our invention, and we felt it needed investigating.

In *GENISIS* the theme was mentioned in the contents of *Le Serpent Rouge*, with reference to the legend/fairy tale of the Sleeping Beauty by Perrault (the Peyrolles connection). It was also hinted at in the 'Fairy Tale' explanation, which was included to explain one of the possibilities of how intelligent life might have been accelerated on Earth.

However, time has moved on and what were mere suspicions have taken on sufficient substance as to warrant investigation.

GENISIS went in to some detail concerning the Egyptian legends and the inferences in them to cosmic events. In particular, we would now remind the reader of the story of the dismembering of OSIRIS by his brother SET. Some arguments exist as to how many pieces he was divided in to, but logic suggests that it was fifteen. Regardless of the specific number, ISIS, the wife of OSIRIS, attempted to recover them, but one essential piece remained missing. That piece was retrieved by a crab and possibly brought ashore. It was the phallus of OSIRIS.

This phallus is the 'Talisman of SET', and it is considered by students of the occult to be all powerful. History lost sight of the infamous talisman and the last time we read of it, it is said to have fallen in to the possession of Queen Hatshepsut of Egypt in Old Testament times. And then nothing is heard of it until French author Jean Robin writes of it in 1989 in his book *Opération Orth: Le Terrible Secret de Rennes-le-Château*. Robin's account is not, according to him, fiction, but sketched details of events which occurred in 1984 in the churchyard at Millau in the Massif Central. Robin recounts how one 'Pierre', a friend of his and a member of a secret organisation, found himself involved in 'Opération Orth'.

Opération Orth was evidently named after the pseudonym (Jean Orth), taken by Jean Salvator, brother of the late Austrian Archduke who tragically died at Mayerling in the last century. According to Jean Robin, Jean Salvator (Orth) was the same Austrian Archduke who is known to have visited Saunière at Rennes-le-Château and is also known to have opened a Swiss bank account numbered sequentially with that of Saunière.

After abdicating all rights to the throne and the Roman German Empire of the Hapsburg family, he sailed to South America, never to return.

Opération Orth consisted in locating and transporting what has been described as a 'Planetary Talisman' from the cemetery at Millau to Bear Island off the coast of Norway. It was accomplished in the dead of night, by a small group of 'commandos' who excavated a grave and retrieved a large wooden box which was then conveyed to Coustaussa, where it rested overnight before travelling via Montségur to Bear Island. This 'Planetary Talisman' was the feared Talisman of Set, whose overwhelming power, more than planetary is said to be solar.

There are one or two interesting aspects which took our attention. First Coustaussa, which lies opposite Rennes-le-Château across the valley of the Rialsesse (but which also stands on the Circle of Churches), is where Abbé Gélis was found cruelly murdered in 1897. When the crime was investigated, nothing appeared to have been stolen, but, we wonder if Gélis could have been the custodian, in those days, of the Talisman? Or perhaps he at least knew of its location?

Secondly, we have heard about a team of archaeologists from the Vatican having spent time in the Rennes valley, searching for an Egyptian talisman - could it also have been the Talisman of Set?

Lastly, although we have no absolute proof that Saunière ever visited Paris, there is a record that the famous opera singer, Emma Calvé did make a donation to the church at Rennes-le-Château. Emma Calvé, remember, enjoyed the provision of a suite of rooms at the Château de Chambord and the Comte de Chambord (one of the pretenders to the French Throne), had as two of his tutors, the Comtes de Chérisey and Blanchefort (two people who already figure in the mystery). When Emma Calvé finally retired from the opera, she bought a property at MILLAU! Of course, there are those who believe in a god of coincidence, but we were intrigued to say the least !

Cuban physicist Manuel Figueroa Herrera, who lived in the Rennes-le-Château region for more than a decade to study the enigma, states in his work *Cohomology and the Threshold of Time* :-

> "Ever since the revelations of J.Robin spread out, people living around the little village find it hard to eat or to manage to go to sleep under the impression of the coming closer of that world event that everybody here, more or less consciously, is waiting for, i.e. the arrival or materialisation of whatever has been called, cryptically and archetypically, since Saint Rémy up to our days, The Great Monarch - that, without any hesitation, I identify with

another garment of our Supreme Archetype, Our Lord Jesus Christ."

It is interesting that Herrera evaluates the Grand Monarch as Christ, for another author not altogether unfamiliar with Rennes, Michel Lamy, identifies the Grand Monarch as none other than Satan or SET. Could Charles Péguy have been right? Are the arms of Satan and the Cross of Lorraine (Christ), the same? We remind you that Mr. Herrera is a physicist.

In *Opération Orth* Jean Robin relates how 'Pierre' told him of a trip on a UFO which materialised in front of him, and his transportation by that craft to a place near Valparaiso in Chile, where deep in an underground complex in the mountains, he was introduced to members of a secret society called the 'Order of the Secret Companions of General de Gaulle'. Members of the order, according to Herrera's account from 'Pierre', moved around by levitation and were manipulating four-dimensional Space-Time -- echoes of the Tesla / von Neumann Space/Time experiments at Montauk, which will be explained later.

Lastly, Herrera's 'Pierre' character mentioned that in 1987, as part of some undercover activities, he took part with some 'army' personnel in the distribution of three specimens, described as 'psychic capacitors' in the Rennes valley.

> "The well manifested... interest of the Secret Services of some countries,of the Archduke Rudolph of Austria and even of France's President Mitterand, who has rendered a commentated visit to Rennes-le-Château - as if to certify the soundness of the strange events that endlessly whirl around this magical hill - as well as the frequent night flights of planes and helicopters, with their lights off, makes me think that very soon the world opinion will have concrete reasons to be in a spell."
>
> *(Manuel Herrera - "Cohomology and the Threshold of Time")*.

The next 'Time' reference we came across concerning Rennes was the legendary Time Traveller, the Comte de St. Germain, whose statue is inside the church at Rennes, and who has popped up over several centuries. According to the Encyclopedia Britannica, the Comte de St. Germain was born in 1710 to a Portuguese Jewish family and attained a certain level of accomplishment as a linguist in European languages, composer, violinist and chemist (of the alchemical variety).

Horace Walpole mentions St. Germain as being in London in 1743, where he was arrested as a Jacobite spy. Upon his release, he travelled to Paris where he appeared regularly at the French Court in 1748 and was employed running secret missions for Louis XV. After internecine arguments with another French courtier, the Duc de Choiseul, he moved to England for two years. Later, he turned up in St. Petersberg, where in 1762 he took part in a plot which replaced Tsar Peter III with Catherine II. Not wishing to outlive his popularity at the Russian Court, St. Germain moved on to Germany, where the Count di Cagliostro (another shadowy character), mentions in his *Mémoires Authentiques*, that he founded German Freemasonry and initiated Cagliostro in to it. After spending another four years in Paris (1770-1774), he took up residence in Schleswig Holstein where he studied the secret sciences with Charles of Hesse. Although the Encyclopedia Britannica tells of his death in Schleswig Holstein in 1784, it also records that he was seen again, five years later in 1789 when he would have been between 74 and 79 years old.

It is with a certain amount of sceptical surprise then, that we learned from a certain French lady that she had seen a signed photograph of Emma Calvé inscribed with the message:-

"To my faithful friend and tutor who read many interesting things
in my palm."

Innocent enough, except that it was addressed to the Comte de St. Germain, the ubiquitous Time Traveller. Emma Calvé at the time, was living in an apartment in the Château de Chambord. Our French lady explained that in the 1950's, she had had a strange encounter with an elegant stranger whilst on holiday in Cyprus - the Comte de St. Germain had materialised in front of her and had given her a bunch of keys, asking her to familiarise herself with the smallest key in the bunch.

 In the 1970's he reappeared to her, this time giving her the small key and instructing her to go the Persian Gulf, to visit an underground complex built of stone. There, she was to find a wooden door which the key fitted, and was to return home with whatever she found behind the door. She refused to comply, handed back the key and the count vanished in front of her eyes.

Years later, whilst visiting an antiquarian bookshop in Paris, the shop's elderly proprietor greeted her and said that he had something for her. She wondered how that could be as she had never visited the shop before. The proprietor insisted that he had a package for her. This turned out to be a hand-written manuscript by someone named Jules Bois whom she recognised as a member of an esoteric group from the Emma Calvé coterie. The manuscript fell open in her hands, and she read in it some kind of prophecy that she was to be blown up. Startled, she fled from the shop.

Another few years went by and she was visiting a bookshop in London. She was approached by a new assistant - someone she didn't recognise, who again informed her that he had a package for her. This turned out to be a 78 record of something called 'In Constanzia', written by the Comte de St. Germain. Several more years passed. It was now 1982 and she was making a second visit to

Rennes-le-Château, staying with a family in Rennes-les-Bains. During this trip, she met the authoress Elizabeth van Buren. Later in the trip, whilst changing money in a local bank, she bumped in to Elizabeth van Buren again who informed her, during their discussion, that she had obtained much of her insight from her master, the Comte de St. Germain! Our informant decided it was time to distance herself from the persistent Count. Before we left our intriguing encounter with this lady, we asked her if she knew anything about the Philadelphia Experiment.

There was no reason why we should have done so, for we had no idea whether she would even have heard of it. But what she said amazed us.

According to her, her mother had always made copious entries in her diary of events around the 12th August every year. It was on that date in 1943 when the fatal Project Rainbow/Philadelphia Experiment took place. Could there possibly be a link through the date, between Philadelphia and Rennes-le-Château? Curiously there is, and the link is through the beloved star of the Egyptians, Sothis or Sirius, the Dog Star.

The Dog Days are the period of days when the star Sirius rises heliacally at the same time as the Sun. According to the planetary position of the observer, they run from approximately July 23rd until August 11th. Is it purely coincidental that July 23rd is the day after the Saint's day of St. Mary Magdalen at Rennes-le-Château and that August 11th is the day before the Philadelphia Experiment was carried out. In other words, these two specific dates lie one day either side of the Dog Days. Could it possibly be feasible that whatever Time/Space experiments that might have been carried out at either or both locations, depended on the not quite perfect timing of the ascension of the Sun and Sirius?

Certainly it is worth further study, for the Egyptians devoted much time and effort in to arranging special channels in their temples and inside the Great Pyramid so that at one particular time of the year, the light of Sirius and of the Sun would flood through these channels in to the chambers and illuminate a crystal for secret ritualistic purposes. This is one of the profound secrets of the Mysteries of Isis as related by Robert Temple in *The Sirius Mystery*.

The contention so far as it concerns the possibility of Time/Space travel by the manipulation of the Time/Space dimension, seems, according to various sources, to place critical importance on the time of the year. We have thus identified the period known as the Dog Days, July 23rd through until August 11th as a possible candidate. There would also, according to those same sources, appear to be specific places on the surface of the Earth which might be best suited to such experimentation, and these, according to David Percy and David Myers in their book *Two Thirds*, occur at specific lines of latitude.

It would appear that the Earth's magnetic field has 'hot spots' of electromagnetic output situated at 19.5, 41, and 60 degrees above and below the equator. The physicists inform us that it is at those six lines of latitude, where, according to the tetrahedral dynamics of a sphere spinning at approximately 1,000 mph, power surges would be manifest.

In this chapter we have spoken of Time/Space travel or distortion or manipulation, and have mentioned Philadelphia, Montauk and Rennes-le-Château. It should come as no surprise then when we learn that all three of these places lie adjacent to 41 degrees north !

Another author has published information on the necessity of controlling latitude, longitude, local time and sun angle, this time in order to ensure getting the maximum explosive force from a nuclear device. The New Zealander, Bruce Cathie, has published several books on the same theme over the last few years (*Harmonic 288*, *Harmonic 695*, *Bridge to Infinity* etc.,) and has dared to suggest that the whole of the nuclear arms race might have been an unnecessary sham, because if the date, time, position and sun angle are not precise, then the maximum nuclear detonation cannot be ensured.

Now we know that one of the first effects of a nuclear detonation is the electromagnetic pulse or EMP which incapacitates electrical circuitry for hundreds of miles surrounding the explosion. So there is obviously a huge electromagnetic effect involved. Of course, Cathie must be considered quite mad - after all, why else should his book be taken off American bookshelves, - unless of course, he might be on the right track. One small feat which Bruce Cathie claims he has been able to do, is to predict precise dates and times and positions of possible future nuclear tests, something which is quite impressive, even for a so-called 'madman' !

In his book, *The Cosmic Trigger*, Robert Anton Wilson relates how Dr. Timothy Leary, his wife and two others gained a series of psychic perceptions during the Dog Days a few years ago. According to Dr. Leary, it is as though the light from Sirius is a communication channel through which the communication takes place. Dr. Leary's conclusions can be summed up in a quote from the account of his reception of the 'Starseed Transmissions' in *The Cosmic Trigger* :-

> "It is time for life on Earth to leave the planetary womb and learn
> to walk through the stars. Life was seeded on your planet billions
> of years ago by nucleotide templates which contained the
> blueprint for gradual evolution through a sequence of bio-
> mechanical stages. The goal of evolution is to produce nervous
> systems capable of communicating with and returning to the
> Galactic Network where we, your interstellar parents, await

you.Life on planet Earth has now reached this halfway point, established itself, and evolved through larval mutations and metamorphoses to the seven brain stages.

At this time, the voyage home is possible. Assemble the most intelligent, advanced, courageous of your species, divided equally between men and women . Let every race, nationality, and religion be represented.

You are about to discover the key to immortality in the chemical structure of the genetic code, within which you will find the scripture for life. The time has come for you to accept the responsibility of immortality. It is not necessary for you to die.

You will discover the key to enhanced intelligence within the chemistry of the nervous system. Certain chemicals, used wisely, will enable your nervous system to decipher the genetic code. All life on your planet is a unity. All life must come home.

Total freedom, responsibility and interspecies harmony will make the voyage possible. You must transcend larval identities of race, culture and nationality. Your only allegiance is to life. The only way you will survive is to make the voyage home. The Japanese people are the most advanced race on your planet and will give protection to the company.

We are sending a comet to your solar system as a sign that the time has come to look to the stars. When you arrive back home you will be given new instructions and powers. Your sperm ship is the flower of terrestrial life. As soon as the company is formed and the voyage begun, war, poverty, hatred, fear will disappear from your planet and the most ancient prophecies and celestial visions will be realised.

Mutate! Come home in glory."

As if this powerful message of the 'Star Seed' transmissions was not enough, we should also remember that the Wilson himself scribbled in his diary on July 23 1973 that 'Sirius is very important.'

In *The Magical Revival* by Kenneth Grant, the successor of Aleister Crowley in the OTO who has made Crowley's works approachable, we discovered :-

"Phoenix was Crowley's secret name in the Ordo Templi Orientis...
The Phoenix was also an ancient constellation in which Sothis, or
Sirius, was the chief star..."

and later Grant adds :

"Crowley identified the heart of (his magical) current with one

particular Star. In Occult Tradition, this is 'the Sun behind the Sun,'
the Hidden God, the vast star Sirius, or Sothis..."

Lastly, in this sphere we return to Robert Anton Wilson who was struck by these Grantian quotations of Crowley, when in *The Cosmic Trigger*, he comments:-

"Imagine my state of mind when I discovered that this very day,
July 23 when I had received the message 'Sirius is very important,'
is the day when, according to Egyptian tradition, the occult link
(through Hyperspace?) is most powerful between Earth and
Sirius."

Yes Robert, we know exactly how you felt!

In dealing with hyperspace, we must once again take the reader from the valley at Rennes to the Philadelphia dockyard on August 12th 1943, the day after the Dog Days ended.

CHAPTER 16.
PROJECT INVISIBILITY/PROJECT RAINBOW

Tesla and the Philadelphia Experiment. A warship disappears.
A warp in time. The Cameron brothers. Von Neumann at Montauk.
Hoagland's Face on Mars. The origin of Man. A time portal.

IN the early 1930's, research was started at the University of Chicago into the manipulation of electro magnetic fields in order to attempt to make objects invisible. By the mid-1930's, the project had grown apace and attracted the interest of the US Government, particularly the Department of the Navy whose work on the protection of ships from magnetic mines seemed to share some of the same problems and equipment as Project Invisibility. At this time, World War II was still several years away, but the US Navy already appreciated the devastating effects that German magnetic mines would have on shipping and did not want to be caught out.

In 1934, the Department of the Navy was so interested in Chicago University's Project Invisibility, that it sequestrated its research and key personnel, classified it as an ultra top-secret project, re-christened it 'Project Rainbow', and moved the whole affair to Princeton. There, under the auspices of the Bureau for Naval Research, attached to, but never part of Princeton University, the secret project gained momentum. Over the next few years before America entered the war, many experiments, ranging from table-top to real-life, continued and some were successful. And so they should have been, because the project boasted the 'crème de la crème' in its team. Later, as war became imminent, the rival factions of the US Air Army and the US Navy each backed their favourite projects. The US Air Army finally concentrated on the Manhattan Project in the west, whilst the Navy embellished their Rainbow Project in the east. Whilst the Manhattan Project utilised the brain power and skills of thousands of their top scientists, there were still enough left for the Navy to take its pick, and what a pick it was.

Nikola Tesla -.......................Inventor of A.C., mains and the
                  'Electrical Christ' of the 30's.
Albert Einstein -...................'Relatively' well known.
Norman Levinson -..............Mathematician renowned for his
                  Time Equations
Dr. John von Neumann -.....Mathematician (Inventor of the
                  electronic computer)
David Hilbert -....................Mathematician (Hilbert Space concepts
                  of multi-dimensional space).

The man in overall charge of the project was Nikola Tesla, genius and friend of Franklin Delano Roosevelt. War was coming. Money, manpower and resources were no object providing a result was forthcoming.

From the series of experiments which had already been carried out in Chicago and Princeton, the team moved on to trying to make a ship invisible. This, we believe they achieved in 1940 by placing electromagnetic field generators on board a small vessel, which was powered by cable from the dockside. The experiment was evidently a great success. So successful were they that Roosevelt offered Tesla a warship for his experiments on the understanding that if the team could make it invisible, then they could make anything invisible. And so the experiments continued through 1940 and 1941, until the first test was made on a destroyer escort vessel with people on board. Things went terribly wrong and although the ship was successfully recovered, the personnel were all adversely affected. Some never recovered and all were given mental health problems on their medical records so that no-one would ever believe them if they recounted the event. After this disaster, Tesla realised that he needed more time to work out the problems, and he requested a purpose-built ship to experiment with.

By now, the year was 1942. America was in the war and the Navy was concentrating on weapons which worked. Their line on Project Rainbow had hardened and target dates were rigorously applied. Because of the complexity of the work involved in adapting any existing warship which had already been fitted-out with the electromagnetic and power generators, and being aware of the extreme shortage of ships, it was arranged that the Rainbow team would be allowed to select an 'destroyer escort' from the drawing board. They could then change its specifications to include their own equipment, and take charge of the vessel between the time it rolled off the slipway until the time it was commissioned. In all, a period of only a few months.

Tesla realised what he was up against time-wise and knew that he could not complete the project in time for the deadline without risking the life of everybody aboard. He knew the problems lay with the personnel and the 'time-clocks' which each of them had - 'time-clocks', in the sense of there existing a unique multidimensional set of co-ordinates for every individual at the moment of conception. In other words, wherever and whenever any of us is conceived, the fertilisation of the egg takes place at a unique point in Space-Time. Tesla realised that if these unique 'signatures' were not known for each individual crew member, then if they moved physically on board the ship whilst it was dematerialised, then they might not be able to come back to exactly the same Space-Time reference which they had left. He appealed to the Navy for more time, but the Navy insisted on a 'drop dead' date. Tesla had no alternative. Rather than risk the lives of those on the vessel, he sabotaged the project and resigned, pointing out that Dr. John von Neumann was quite able to take over. He knew that although the experiment had been delayed, it would probably buy him the time needed to refine the requirements.

Von Neumann did take over and won another year. He was given a new 'drop dead' date by the Navy - August 12th 1943 - and proceeded to amend his plans accordingly. Although it is said that von Neumann and Tesla didn't exactly get on well together, von Neumann shared Tesla's view of the 'time-clock' problem and tried to solve it by adding a third shipboard generator. A small, specially trained, hand-picked team was made ready for the project and directly the new ship was available, preparations were made to meet the new deadline. On the morning of August 12th 1943, at the Naval Dockyards in Philadelphia the DE 133, USS Eldridge sailed out into the middle of the dock and at a given radio signal from the shore, started up its generators. A few minutes later, an iridescent green fog began to surround the ship and parts of it disappeared into this fog. Suddenly there was an electric blue flash and the ship was gone. It had also disappeared from the radar screens of the other ships in the bay. Strange reports later stated that two unidentified flying objects had been seen overhead shortly before the ship vanished. When the ship returned a few hours later, it was obvious that all was not right with the world. Part of the ship's transmitting radio mast had disappeared, and throughout the ship, sailors could be seen tearing at their heads as if in mortal agony. A boarding party discovered that not all the ship's crew could be accounted for, and found to their horror, that some of the men had become enmeshed in the steel decking and bulkheads of the ship. The survivors were taken ashore and given medical treatment, but nobody understood really how they could be helped. Most of the men ended up discharged from the Navy and found themselves residing in selected accommodation called Mental Institutions. In popular terms, the story became known as 'The Philadelphia Experiment' and achieved celebrated popularity when a book of the same name, by Charles Berlitz made the best-seller lists. At the time, however, with all the conditions of wartime security, the project disappeared from public view.

One sailor, nevertheless, did recover from the Eldridge and was relatively unaffected by his experience. In the film, 'The Philadelphia Experiment', two naval ratings are shown in the control room of the USS Eldridge. This was not so, for in reality, they were not ratings, but the newly commissioned lieutenants, Duncan and Edward Cameron. Both had degrees in Physics - Edward was a graduate of Princeton and Duncan, a graduate from Edinburgh.

When the USS Eldridge returned, or rematerialised, in the Philadelphia dockyard on 12th August 1943, Edward was sane and Duncan had disappeared. At his debriefing, Edward told his superiors that when the experiment started to go wrong, they were unable to shut down the generators. He claimed that both he and his brother had jumped over the side of the ship, but, instead of falling into the water, they had found themselves on dry land. He remembered being buzzed by what is now known to have been a helicopter, (helicopters only existed as prototypes in 1943). The two brothers were quickly rounded up by MP's and taken by lift to an underground complex where they were met by an elderly Dr. John von Neumann.

Several hours passed, during which the brothers were given a guided tour of the facilities and shown things like colour television and computers, cars and various pieces of technology which they knew did not exist in 1943. Von Neumann finally managed to convince them that although they had literally jumped ship in Philadelphia on August 12th 1943, they had landed in Montauk Air Force Base, Long Island, New York on August 12th 1983, and that somehow the experiment involving the manipulation of Space/Time in 1943 had become entangled with a similar experiment 40 years later. Von Neumann went on to explain that when they had tried to shut down the 1983 experiment by cutting the power to the generators and computers, they had been unable to switch the machinery off. Investigations had shown him that the reason for this inability to stop the experiment by cutting the electrical supply had been because the power was also being supplied by the generators on board the USS Eldridge, which they had become entangled with in a time warp. Evidently, there is what he described as a twenty year biorhythm for the planet. According to von Neumann, the only way in which the experiment could be stopped was if the two brothers, Edward and Duncan could be persuaded to return to the Eldridge through a 'time tunnel', and physically destroy the generator switch gear. This the brothers reluctantly agreed to do.

When the Cameron brothers cut the cables in the control room on board the USS Eldridge, the generators slowed down and the electromagnetic fields slowly collapsed. Just before they completely disappeared, Duncan Cameron once again jumped overboard, this time landing back in the Montauk Air Force Base in 1983. Edward stayed with the ship and rematerialised in the Philadelphia dock, on board the USS Eldridge in 1943. When he left the control room which by that time was a smoking ruin, he saw the fate of his fellow crew-mates, some of whom were enmeshed in the deck plating and bulkheads. One of these was his younger brother (not Duncan), who unbeknown to him, had volunteered for the mission.

When, at his debriefing, Edward Cameron explained the events on board the USS Eldridge and the disappearance of his brother Duncan, he was not believed. It was thought that the experiment had mentally deranged him as indeed it had the other crew members. This then, is the content of *The Philadelphia Project*, by Charles Berlitz as has been told and retold countless times. Except that now, there is one small difference. In 1990, there surfaced in the southern United States of America, one Al Bielek, and Al Bielek claims that he was formerly Edward Cameron, the officer who had thrown the switch that started the Project Rainbow experiment in Philadelphia, 1943. His tale is even stranger than the previous one, except that Al Bielek has been able to fill in the missing blanks from the first account and has been naming names and places and identifying the equipment used in the experiment.

According to Al Bielek, when he was finally discharged from the hospital in 1943, he was transferred to another base in the western states where he was employed to examine scientific and technical files to do with other classified projects, which he, as a physicist was able to understand. On some of them he voiced his displeasure and made his criticism well known. Shortly afterwards, he was arrested; charged with espionage; threatened with a death sentence, and given a simple choice - co-operate with the Navy, walk out on his family and accept a transfer to Montauk or face a trumped-up court martial. Al Bielek opted for New York. When he arrived at the Montauk Army Air Force Base, he was asked to stand in a circular area near to the main gate. A little while later, he found himself back in 1983. In that year, once again under the control of von Neumann, he was regressed mentally and physically to a one year old baby and inserted into a family which had just lost a one year old baby son. The year was 1927. The family was the Bielek family.

Edward Cameron now resumed life as Al Bielek, grew up for the second time around, went through college again, joined the Navy again and after the war studied electronics, subsequently going into business for himself. He retired in 1986 and happened to see the film 'The Philadelphia Experiment', which brought the memories flooding back. He tried to retrace his life and those of other people who were part of the experiment. In this, he was successful and managed to locate six others and his brother Duncan, whom he feared had died in 1943. When he managed to trace Duncan and told him that they had both been part of the experiment, Duncan evidently laughed, saying that he had realised the same thing six months beforehand and had been waiting for Edward (Al Bielek) to find him.

Duncan's story is also very strange. Evidently when he jumped ship for the second time, he wound up in Montauk, but because his 'body-clocks' had gone haywire, he had started to age very quickly - about one year every hour. The scientists soon realised that they would lose Duncan in a few days, but, by 1983, they had developed certain equipment through which they could download a person's brain capacity into Kray super computers. After they had made a complete record of his brain capacity, memories and personality, they had let him die a very old man. They then needed a surrogate body and brain into which the knowledge and life experience of Duncan could be fed.

For this, finding that Duncan's real-life father was still alive, and knowing that his father had been part of the original Rainbow Experiments, they managed to persuade the old man that it was necessary to marry again (for the fifth time) and to have his wife conceive. The resulting baby was allowed to develop unmolested until the age of ten, when the first part of the original Duncan's brain memory was instilled into the boy. Ten years later, a second session enabled them to instill the rest of the Duncan material into the young man. Duncan, as he had been christened the second time around, was then harvested by the Montauk Project at Long Island, New York.

One of the additional attributes that Duncan (II) possessed is that he had become psychic, because of the traumas he had suffered - an ability which predisposed the scientists into using him. According to Duncan, the Rainbow Project which had been closed down after the USS Eldridge episode in 1943, had been taken out of mothballs and re-evaluated in 1948. Dr. John von Neumann had again been put in charge of the project and it was later transferred to Montauk, where the Army Air Force had relinquished its base and where, operating on a 'black' budget which was untraceable, work was able to continue not only on invisibility, but also on mind control and later teleportation.

Von Neumann had evidently realised in 1943 that what the project needed for the personnel to be able to survive, was some method of keeping track of everybody involved and for calculating the multidimensional co-ordinates necessary to bring them back safely. And so to cater for this, Dr. John von Neumann had invented the electronic computer in the early 1950's. Additionally, in the 50's, strange things were going on around the world. The Russians were irradiating the US Embassy in Moscow with microwaves and the eastern European, Iron-curtain countries were inventing new methods of brain washing and mind control. Experiments were also being made into telepathy, especially of the long-range variety so as to enable bases to communicate globally with deep-sea nuclear submarines. Both East and West were running similar programmes, updating each other from the capture/defection of spies, pilots etc,. The upshot was that telepathy and mind control became a reality. A side effect that the Americans discovered, was that a 425 Megahertz radar beam, as used by their early warning 'Sage' Radar system, had a direct effect on local populations. Strange events in human and animal life were reported around Montauk town which lies nearly twenty miles from the base. However, when they investigated the cause of the strange occurrences, they found that the people had been exposed to radiation from the back-focus of the radar dish and that there was no physically detrimental effect such as the burning of tissue which had been a common fault from using the front of the array.

The work continued focusing on telepathy, using super psychic Duncan Cameron. First the 'Zenner cards' would be used locally and then the distance between sender and receiver would be increased. After much experimentation, the same experiments were successfully repeated at a distance. Later, Duncan was able to successfully 'transmit' an image to a television set. This was then improved to a point where the same thing could be done over dozens and then hundreds of miles. All it needed was the strong psychic visualisation abilities of someone like Duncan. Eventually, when the processes and machinery/computers had been refined to the nth degree, the Americans learned that they could download an entire personality from someone and reinstall the same information/mind contents into a new brain, having first wiped the receiving brain clear of useless data.

According to Duncan, it was at that time strange time-slips started occurring, and the scientists began to realise that they were displacing Time whilst engaged in the telepathy work. Duncan became invaluable and indispensable to them. The summit of Duncan's achievements occurred when he found that providing he was able to imagine a place where he wanted to travel to, a 'time-portal' could be supposedly created to it from the control room at Montauk. The problem was that this portal only lasted as long as Duncan's ability to concentrate .

Journeys were said to have been made using the 'time-portal' system, in conjunction with an electromagnetic bottle in which resided the famous Montauk chair, but they lost too many scientists in their trial and error sessions to be able to keep up the progress of the project. They needed expendable human guinea pigs - people who, if they didn't make it back from a journey in Time/Space, would not become an embarrassment to them. These they found amongst the derelicts of New York. Gradually, by trial and error, enough people started returning from their Space/Time trips for them to be able to iron out the bugs in the system.

We understand, from interviews with Duncan and Al Bielek, that by the time of the late 1970's, teleportation, and time travel had become reasonably commonplace. Specifically, they claim that since the discovery by a photographic evaluation team, (Messrs. Vincent Dipietro and Gregory Molenaar), of the 'Face on Mars', American scientists have visited the red planet several times by teleportation methods and that they have also travelled back in time to a point where the planet was inhabited - approximately 200,000 years ago (there is that date again!).

Finally, Edward and Duncan claim that the whole history of the Invisibility, Rainbow and Montauk projects have only been possible because of technology and knowledge given to Man by an alien intelligence. They state that since the first deal was done in 1934 by Roosevelt, western technology has had a helping hand or three in return for the granting of underground bases in the American deserts.

So what are we to make of this and what is its connection with Rennes-le-Château? Let us just call it keeping our minds and options open. We wouldn't have included this chapter unless we had investigated the claims and found enough verifiable facts to keep our interest. Everywhere we can check, the story seems to stand up. The illustrious names quoted, certainly worked on Project Invisibility in the 1930's and 1940's and there is a disused base at Montauk. Putting it another way, if people like Einstein, Tesla, von Neumann, Hilbert and Levinson had put their minds to making ships or aircraft invisible, with unlimited budgets, the backing of the President and the pressure of war, we would be the last to say that they could not have achieved their claims. Rather the contrary. If they hadn't achieved what they set out to achieve, we would have been most surprised.

As followers of the UFO phenomenon are well aware, the suggestion of modern science being influenced by alien technology has become almost accepted as a common-place feature of the genre. In reality, several exposés in American television documentaries have covered encounters of the fourth kind. These include abductions, sexual experimentation and cattle mutilations. This latter category has resulted from the findings throughout the United States and in some areas of Europe, Africa and Australia, of the remains of severely mutilated cattle. The animals' gastric and sexual organs have been surgically removed with such precision that it could only have been achieved by means of a 'laser- scalpel'. Unfortunately, the historical record of these laser operations has now been proved to have predated Man's invention of the instrument. Other equally obscure 'conundrums' probably exist in other disciplines and have merely not yet been brought to the attention of the general public.

One possible contact with an alien intelligence which is still being investigated, resulted from the examination of the telemetry from the Voyager spacecraft in 1976, when a huge sculpted part human/part simian face was photographed on the surface of Mars. This was the subject of a United Nations lecture and we will return to it later in this book, (see p193).

Whether this face and its mathematical correspondences to the nearby features will eventually be proved to be genuine, we cannot tell, but once more we should emphasise that the geometry of Rennes-le-Château is not on Mars, it is here and can be checked at leisure.

Thoughts of Man's possible Martian connections are of course familiar to readers of science-fiction. If such 'realities' manifest in the collective sub-conscious (as discussed previously in chapter 13), then we should not be surprised to find them so expressed, long before they become scientific concepts. When we first considered that the diagram at Rennes might be warning us of a celestial impact, we realised that thought also seemed to have come from the collective sub-conscious. Once we recognised the concept of Earth being destroyed by a comet, we looked at items which had been written about such an idea and were surprised to find the following mixture of recent fact and fiction.

Until the 1990's, the possible destruction of Earth by a comet had been ridiculed by some astronomers, but in 1979 the film 'Meteor' was released, which showed that at least Hollywood recognised the danger. As comets were considered harmless chunks of ice in those days, the script had a 'harmless' comet dislodge a very 'harmful' meteor from the asteroid belt which lies between Mars and Jupiter. The meteor threatened the destruction which we have described in this book. By the time of the film's release, the United States had already embarked on its 'Star Wars' defence program ('Hercules' in the film), and it was this system that was used to shatter the incoming meteor. Shortly after the film's release, the IRAS satellite was launched and it was this satellite, which in 1983 alarmed astro-physicists when it detected a large inbound comet heading straight for Earth. It has already been suggested that such comets might be destroyed by space-resident nuclear weapons just as in the film, but this idea has been firmly rejected by leading experts. Could the collective sub-conscious itself be acting as a unique early warning system? If so, then we would do well to heed its warnings.

Before we finish speculating about intelligent life having once existed on Mars, one other fact has recently been brought to our attention. If a human being is subjected to complete sensory deprivation in a flotation tank, then the body clocks which control all the autonomous nervous systems return to a cycle, not of 24 hours, but 24 hours and 40 minutes, the length of a Martian day, which begs the question of whether our ancestors or progenitors were Martians?

Also, in many works of literature, including some on Rennes-le-Château, there has been the suggestion that hidden in the region might be located a device which can only be described as a 'Time Portal'. The idea is certainly an interesting one, for if any people travelled to another world, they would certainly wish to remove the necessity of having to travel by spaceship at the earliest opportunity. It could only ever be regarded as unwieldy, and incredibly costly in terms of efficiency. The space travellers would surely have replaced the spaceship by some sort of 'time portal' as soon as was practicable. If they do exist, then they were probably built by the people whom we Earthlings have long regarded as 'gods'.

However, a portal is a two way thing. Not only would such a device allow us to travel to other parts of the solar system, it would also, if left open, allow creatures/entities from those other places, to come in. The *Necronomicon* gives just such a warning :-

"DO NOT OPEN THE GATE, SAVE FOR AN ESPECIAL TIME THAT THOU STATE AT THE TIME OF OPENING, AND IT MAY NOT STAY OPEN FOR A MOMENT AFTER THE PASSAGE OF THE HOUR OF TIAMAT, ELSE ALL THE ABYSS BREAK FORTH UPON THE EARTH, AND THE DEAD RISE TO EAT THE LIVING, FOR IT IS WRIT: I WILL CAUSE THE DEAD TO RISE AND DEVOUR THE LIVING, I WILL GIVE TO THE DEAD POWER OVER THE LIVING, THAT THEY MAY OUTNUMBER THE LIVING."

Later we will see a strange echo of this warning in the *Book of Revelations*. If Earth underwent catastrophe aeons ago, such as being hit by a comet, reference the destruction of the dinosaurs, then it is at least possible for that event or a more recent one to have closed the portal. Could it be that the Philadelphia Experiment opened up one of these again and that, as a result, the UFO/alien phenomena has taken hold?

One current theory is that it was the sudden appearance of electromagnetic radiation on Earth which prompted the first appearances of UFO's and one of the culprits in the latter part of the last century was none other than Nikola Tesla, who spent long periods of time in the Arizona desert, pumping millions of volts of electrical energy into the atmosphere. Perhaps it is little wonder that when he was asked where he got his strange ideas from, he replied enigmatically, "I get them from the aliens". Perhaps, he had inadvertently 'rung their bell' with his experiments. We know, after all, that Tesla built very powerful receivers and transmitters on the roof-tops of two of New York's finest hotels. We also know now from the court records that Tesla has finally been accredited with the invention of radio, which had hitherto been attributed to his assistant, Marconi. Could Tesla, the electrical genius have been telling the truth about his informants?

Messages, time-tunnel, time gates, UFOs and visitations. Are these all manifestations of the modern conspiracy syndrome or have they always been around?

> "And it came to pass, when men began to multiply on the face of the Earth, and daughters were born unto them. That the sons of God saw the daughters of men that they were fair and they took them wives of all which they chose". *(Genesis 6,v.1,2)*

> "Here is wisdom. Let him that hath understanding count the number of the beast ; for it is the number of a man ; and his number is Six hundred, threescore and six" *(Revelations 13,v.18)*

Inscribe a circle on a piece of paper. Mark its radius as 10,000 x Pi feet. Calculate its circumference. Divide the Earth's equatorial circumference in feet by the circumference of the 10,000 x Pi circle. Now, that truly is wisdom! Could it be that the legend of the 'Number of the Beast' was just another way of labelling the Earth with a number? Is it coincidental that the speed of the Earth on its orbit around the Sun is 66,600 mph.

You may, again, be wondering whether we are losing sight of Rennes-le-Château and becoming concerned as to how all these diverse subjects are connected. We will, eventually 'come down to Earth', but not until we have provided our readers with at least a working knowledge of the material we have researched. Armed with this repertoire of knowledge, the reader will be better able to judge our reasoning.

We have hinted in this chapter, at a possible means by which the 'chosen ones' could survive an Earth catastrophe. Furthermore, we have disclosed most of what we are aware is being researched 'under-cover'. Maybe the Rennes-le-Château message was found elsewhere, or has the approaching missile already be seen by the Hubble Deep Space Telescope? In fact, has the collision date already been calculated? If it has, it will certainly be a closely guarded secret. Imagine the effect of such information on the religions of the world. Consider also, the effect on the world population by knowing the date of Armageddon.

The graphic description of celestial impact, so faithfully recorded in *Revelations* would at last be read by the light of an approaching comet and the result could be a total collapse of law and order, such as the world has never experienced. Our readers must now expand their visualisation to cosmic proportions to appreciate what we will reveal.

CHAPTER 17.
THE MARTIAN LEGACY

Cratering in the Solar System. The Martian atmosphere.
Celestial events. A captured Moon. The Phobos probes.
Cydonia and the Mars mission.

BY courtesy of NASA, this generation has been privileged to see the planets of the solar system on live television. The Mariner, Viking and Voyager probes produced more and more detailed images of the planets' surfaces and their attendant moons. In the mass of information relayed back to Earth, there was one overall factor which was both obvious and unexpected by the astronomers. This was the degree of impact damage to which the whole system had been subjected.

The gas giants, Jupiter and Saturn, of course, do not maintain lasting evidence of impact any more than a pond does when a pebble is thrown into it, but the solid surfaces of Venus, Earth and Mars do retain to some degree, evidence of celestial bombardment. The dust storms of Mars have both subdued and exaggerated certain features as is the case on Venus where gale force winds lash the surface. Here on Earth we have perpetual erosion from the cyclic weather patterns of evaporation and precipitation. All the eroded features will certainly be subjected to close examination in the future, but for now we do have the advantage of seeing airless bodies which have accurately preserved their past historic record of impact. These bodies are the moons.

Study of the cratering on our Moon reveals it to be 'saturated', the term used to describe a situation where there is no place for an impact to occur without erasing or overlapping an existing one. The greater part of this cataclysmic bombardment would have occurred some four or five billion years ago, at the time the solar system was forming.

Larger bodies would have acted like vacuum cleaners sweeping up millions of tons of debris and the evidence of this process remains with remarkable clarity throughout the solar system. This alarming rate of cratering declined quite rapidly at first and then levelled out. We can find little consolation in this however, when at the same time we have discovered evidence of sudden short-lived increases in cratering due to new material being injected into the inner section of our system. This is of course, the place where we live. Although these more recent bombardments are usually attributed either to the gravitational pull of the giant planets dislodging material from the asteroid belt, or the passage of the solar system through areas of space debris, they are also caused by the return of comets from deep space. Outstanding

Mercury - This photograph by Mariner 10 clearly shows the intensive cratering on our innermost planet. The craters vary from being well defined to severely degraded, indicating continuous 'saturation'.

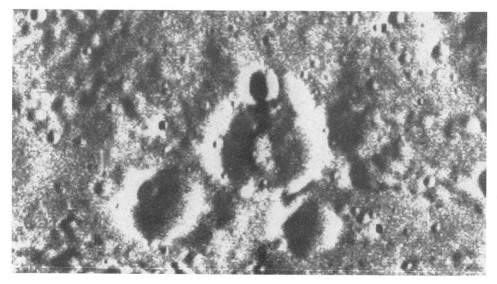

Phobos - Although the larger of the two Martian satellites it is still an extremely small target, nevertheless, as the Viking 2 photograph shows, the cratering is once again overlapping and 'saturated'.

(Photos NASA).

confirmation of the widespread nature of cratering in the inner solar system may be seen in the illustrations of the planet Mercury and the satellite Phobos.

The only protection planets have from these incoming celestial missiles is their atmosphere. As long as the meteor or falling body is not too large, the friction created by its passage through the atmosphere will cause it to burn away before it reaches the surface at a size which could cause damage. In the case of the moons there is no atmosphere, hence massive damage and from the illustration of the surface of airless Mercury, we see it too has suffered in the same way as the moons.

This brings us to the first of the Martian conundrums. In August 1976 two Viking Landers were safely deposited on the surface of Mars. Among other things, they were used to analyse what little there was of the Martian atmosphere. The atmospheric pressure on the surface was 7.5 millibars, which when compared to Earth's 1013 millibars at sea level could never be considered an effective shield against incoming celestial debris. Why then is the Martian surface not saturated with cratering? The cratering 'signature' of a planet is considered to be a good indicator of the planet's history and more than one expert has been puzzled by the Martian 'signature'. The general conclusion is that the planet had a long period of erosion and deposition that ended fairly abruptly in relatively recent Martian history. In simple terms that is saying, Mars was Earth-like not too long ago. This fact alone moves the possibility of an ancient civilisation on Mars from the realms of science-fiction to science 'feasible'. If Mars did not exist it would be nonsensical to examine any of the other planets as the possible home of our ancestors. However, it does exist and a number of other factors support the possibility of it having been the spawning ground of the brain of homo sapiens. As was discussed previously, it would appear we were designed to function in a lower gravitational field than the planet Earth and the surface gravity of Mars is only 38 per cent of that of the Earth.

Imagine the reduced strain on the human body under those conditions. Consider the advantage of all the things we have to carry, weighing less than half their weight. Admittedly, what goes up must come down, but to raise it more easily and have it fall more slowly would be in everyone's interest. Even more revealing would be to see this problem from the Martian's position. On Earth he would feel as if he were carrying another Martian on his shoulders ! Let us now take note of those other essentials to support life as we know it, air and water. When the landing sites for the Viking spacecraft were chosen, the safety of the craft was the prime consideration. The selected latitude was that of the Martian summer. The instrumentation was essentially designed to analyse the atmosphere and search for evidence of biological life in soil

Close up of the Martian surface from a Viking lander shows debris quite capable of having been the material ejected from massive volcanoes in to a low gravity environment. **(Photo NASA).**

samples. No life processes were detected, but the atmosphere, as little as it was, produced some surprises. At ground level, 95 per cent was carbon dioxide, 2.5 per cent nitrogen, 1.5 per cent oxygen and there were traces of carbon-monoxide, neon, krypton, and xenon. All that was missing was water vapour and if that had been there, we would have had the necessary ingredients required for the life processes as we know them on Earth.

The present conditions on Mars are such that water vapour would either freeze or evaporate. Blessed with the 'blanket' of higher atmospheric pressure, the heat from the Sun could be retained and the frozen water vapour could become liquid. Even so, is there enough ice on Mars to fuel the climatic cycle and 'kick-start' the conditions necessary for life? If we can find sufficient ice and then find the reason it remained frozen, we could be well on the way to our 'science-feasible' scenario of Mars having been our ancestral home. Two possibilities immediately present themselves and as different as they are, they have much in common. The first is that Mars has moved or was pushed further from the sun.In Velikovsky's, *Worlds in Collision* a number of possibilities which could result in such a movement are discussed. Although Velikovsky's conclusions have been discredited to some degree, his research into ancient references is admirable and points conclusively to celestial events.

 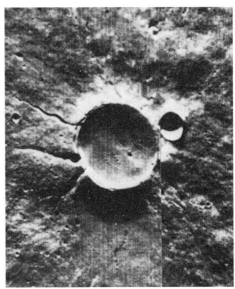

The massive volcanoes on Mars photographed by the Viking Orbiter and showing patterns which could easily be the result of lava flowing across and melting a mantle of ice. **(Photos NASA).**

Little by little we have been forced to admit to the quality of the observational records of ancient civilisations, even if they were unaware of the causes. One of the secrets of the Pythagoreans was supposedly the knowledge that a particular planet had been a comet and by various references Velikovsky deduces it to have been Venus. Considering we know it was a pentagram which served as the secret sign of the Pythagoreans, it is more than coincidental that the planet Venus traces the pentagram in its celestial movements (see *GENISIS* p108). Despite its brilliance, Venus seems not to have been noticed by the earliest astronomers which lends weight to the possibility of it having been a captured body - in effect a 'space wanderer' which was decelerated sufficiently by the gravitational pull of the sun to remain thereafter in solar orbit. An event such as this could have forced the Earth and Mars further from the sun. Possibly great heat was generated, causing massive evaporation on the two planets, which would have resulted in a deep mantle of cloud. This in turn could have insulated the lower atmosphere from the sun's rays and precipitated continuous snowfall until the mantle had sufficiently thinned down to permit sunlight to reach the surface. The surface, however, by this time would have been a sheet of ice and snow of sufficient depth to remain unaffected.

Over the major part of the planet, the sun's heat would achieve only surface melting, which through the night would re-freeze to perfect the reflecting mirror. It was indeed fortuitous in the case of our planet, that the sun was sufficiently hot in the equatorial region to generate a convecting weather pattern of wind and rain which eventually turned the tide. Slowly the ice receded to the poles and to some degree our planet recovered. Never again would it be the 'Garden of Eden', but at least it was possible to live on some parts of it. In a recently published article in *Scope* magazine, (September 26th 1993), Professor Paul Horowitz of Harvard University, asked why, in taking an area, radius 25 light years around Earth, no signs of intelligent life (by radio emissions), had been discovered. An answer was soon forthcoming from the scientists at the French Bureau des Longitudes in Paris who said that the Moon's gravitational field keeps the Earth's climate stable by moderating its axial tilt. It is highly unusual in the galaxy for an Earth sized planet to have so large a moon and to be at the right distance from its parent star (the Sun)!

Mars was less fortunate. Being that much further from the sun, the mirror of ice efficiently reflected the sun's rays and maintained the mantle of ice, thereby destroying all life and obviating the possibility of sufficient water vapour to replenish its atmosphere.

This raises the inevitable question as to why we see a planet of red deserts and not one of ice. The answer may be found in the massive volcanoes of Mars spewing out lava and volcanic dust which, because of the rarefied atmosphere and lower gravitational field, could drift for thousands of miles before settling. Eventually, the surface of ice would be covered with a layer of dust and debris as can be seen from the ground shots of the Viking Landers. The lava flows would, of course, melt the ice and cause massive ravines before they refroze and these can also be seen from the Mariner survey's of the planet. In fact, NASA stated that after examination of the Mariner 7 survey and the confirmation obtained from the Viking orbiters, Mars may indeed have had running water on its surface in the fairly recent past. Furthermore they say the evidence of the channels in the Martian desert resemble dry riverbeds and there seems to be little doubt that they were formed by a rapidly flowing liquid and the widespread agreement is that it was water. We would suggest, however, that precisely that same effect would be achieved by melting ice from a lava flow as we have indicated.

We have described a process of celestial capture and for those who find this hard to visualise, we would refer to our Moon. Its size relative to that of Earth actually denies it as being a satellite in the true sense of the word. The Earth and Moon are best described as a twin planetary system. The idea of the Moon having broken off the Earth was abandoned long ago and prior to the Apollo Moon landings some interesting data came to light concerning it origin. It was noticed that certain areas of the Moon had a higher gravitational pull than normal and the explanation suggested by Nobel prize winner, Dr. Hannes Alfren, of the University of California and Professor Gustav Arrhenius of the Oceanographic Institute of San Diego, was that they were caused by 'mascons'. These are 'mass concentrations' of dense material embedded deep in the moon's surface. Their presence is attributed to mini-moons which after impact were swallowed up by our Moon.

This was, of course, the basis of the Hoerbiger Theory (which we will return to later), which was scientifically rejected. Rock samples of the Moon have led the the astronomers to believe the Moon was a space-wanderer which was captured by our Earth. They believe the evidence shows the Earth once had anything from five to ten 'moonlets' going round it and our present Moon either 'swallowed' them or 'cannoned' them off into space. It seems that every new theory involves cataclysmic celestial events and we would be well advised to consider the possibility that others may occur in the future.

The second reason which could result in a frozen Mars is simply the impact or close passage of a large comet. The possibility of the cometary and asteroid impact has already been explained and an inevitable consequence of a serious impact is for the receiving planet to be surrounded with a mantle of dust. The obscuring of sunlight by the dust would cause a rapid fall in temperature and precipitate the same scenario as has previously been explained. With all this in mind, it is not inconceivable that the cities of the Martians are still there, buried under hundreds, of feet of ice and volcanic debris.

It would be easier for the establishment if we could leave it at that, but someone started looking through the thousands of frames transmitted to Earth by the Viking orbiter in 1976 and in the area designated THE CYDONIA REGION they saw something quite strange, which we have previously referred to.

Suddenly, we were confronted with respectable newspapers carrying the headline, 'IS THIS THE FACE OF AN ALIEN CIVILISATION THAT INVADED MARS?' As normal in these matters, the official line was 'a trick of light and shadow', 'a freak natural rock formation' and so on. Unfortunately, some persistent fellow did a little picture enhancement with his computer and the hollow socket of the eye produced an eyeball. Not content with that they looked in the rock formation's mouth and came up with a set of dentures.

All very sensational, but our most Reverend Fanthorpe probably thinks we put the face there to back up the 'Fairy Story' in *GENISIS*, where we had previously outlined this precise possibility.

It would seem the Russians took all this quite seriously and decided to make a return trip to the red planet. The first probe, Phobos I, was 'lost' two

The Daily Telegraph, Monday, November 19, 1984

Is this the face of an alien civilisation that invaded Mars?

By ADRIAN BERRY Science Correspondent

PHOTOGRAPHIC evidence of what may be the relics of a vanished civilisation on Mars is to be presented next month by a team of American scientists to President Reagan's science adviser.

This evidence includes a mile-wide rock apparently carved in the perfect semblance of a human-type face and several pyramids arranged symmetrically in what appear to be the remains of a city.

All the objects are located in the Cydonia region of Mars. The "face" is at 41 deg. N. and 9 W.

The American scientists hope to persuade their Government of the desirability of sending a joint American-Soviet mission to the planet to investigate the evidence before the Russians decide to do it alone.

Viking's photographs

The research has been expanded to include the Congressional Research Service in Washington and a group of many different fields of expertise from the University of California.

The photographs were taken in 1976 by the orbiting American Viking spacecraft, but because the craft took many thousands of pictures, until recently nobody took the trouble to examine them in detail.

The space community is strongly divided over whether

Russian moves

are planning, in addition, a manned mission to fly in orbit around Mars have been revealed recently by Dr Harrison Schmitt, a former American astronaut who has walked on the Moon and served a term in the Senate.

Dr Schmitt pointed to the existence of a huge launching rocket, nearly as big as the old American Moon rockets, seen recently at the Baikonur cosmodrome during a flight last year of the American space shuttle.

He suggested that to mark the 75th anniversary of the Bolshevik Revolution in 1992, the Russians would like to have a "space spectacular" that would have a stunning prestige effect on world opinion.

A still more ominous possibility is that the aliens, if they existed, may have left something potentially deadly on the surface of Mars.

'Library' legacy

If they created the "face" to attract attention, they might also have left a "library," a store of technological information such as would have been amassed by a star-flaring civilisation.

This, of necessity, would be of so advanced a character that it would compare with a description of our own civilisation as seen through the eyes of people of the Stone Age.

The fear is that, if the Russians were to get hold of this information before the West, they might be able to use it to conquer the solar system and dominate their rivals on Earth.

"Unusual Martian Surface Features," by Vincent DiPietro and Gregory Molenaar. Mars Research, P.O. Box 284, Glenn Dale, Maryland 20769.

"Preliminary Report of the Independent Mars Investigation Team: New Evidence of Prior Habitation?" By Richard C.

half a million years ago, when according to current theories about the history of Mars, it had a warm, wet period.

He added that the geology of the Cydonia region suggested that the objects were on the shore of an ancient lake. The face, over which the Sun would have risen directly, would have formed an island, with the pyramids on the shore beside it.

But the supposition is that if the objects really are the work of alien beings, the creatures could not have been of a species native to Mars.

All evidence from visiting spacecraft and Earth-based telescopes suggest that Mars, unlike Earth, never had a sufficiently thick atmosphere, or warmth, for a long enough period to support the evolution of an intelligent race.

The theory is that any beings who walked on its surface long ago and who left the supposed artifacts were travellers from another solar system.

The mile-wide "face" on Mars. Imaging techniques have revealed details of the side of the face that are hidden in this picture — an eyeball, an eye socket, a pupil, and a continuation of "hair" around the forehead.

months later, reportedly due to the loss of radio contact. The second probe, Phobos II, arrived in Martian orbit in January 1989. Now Mars has two small moons Deimos (terror) and Phobos (fear), named after the two sons of Mars in the Roman pantheon of gods. Both these satellites are small irregular lumps of rock - Phobos the larger, is only 23 kilometres at its widest point. Deimos is a mere 15 kilometres at most and considerably higher in orbit than Phobos. Deimos is also 'geo' or rather 'Marto-stationary' whereas Phobos orbits the planet every 7.7 hours. It was for this reason the Russians planned to have an instrument package on Phobos which would have had the capability of scanning the whole equatorial region of the planet, apart from carrying out a close investigation of Phobos itself. Some have speculated that this ground survey of Phobos may have been a forerunner of a manned space spectacular with a landing on Phobos. Using this as their base the cosmonauts would use a shuttle to explore the planet's surface.

However, as Phobos II was being aligned with its namesake something rather odd happened; all contact with the probe was lost! Any number of reasons could account for the loss, but after all the excuses were exhausted it became clear that 'something' had approached the probe from the Martian

NASA accused of wrecking £650m space probe in cover-up plot

Boffins go to war over life on Mars

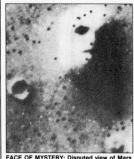

FACE OF MYSTERY: Disputed view of Mars

SPACE boffins went to war yesterday over their belief that there was once life on Mars.

They claim a face on the planet's surface was carved by intelligent beings who also built pyramids.

And they accused NASA scientists of sabotaging a £650 million space mission

From **IVOR KEY** in New York

because they wanted to cover up the truth.

A group of experts called Mars Mission claimed the Mars Observer spacecraft was deliberately disabled to stop it taking pictures of an abandoned city called Cydonia.

The satellite, which has already travelled 450 million miles, was due to start orbiting

Mars yesterday but is now feared to be lost after failing to make contact with control.

Richard Hoogland, founder of Mars Mission, has been trying for years to get NASA to investigate the face that was photographed by a Viking spacecraft in 1976.

The space control scientists in Houston, Texas, insist it is simply a mountain. But Hoagland claims it was put there by

creatures who lived on the planet.

He says they also built pyramids in a mathematical pattern that must have been the centre of the city of Cydonia.

"There is an inside group at NASA that doesn't want this pursued. Maybe they literally pulled the plug."

A NASA spokesman said last night: "We've got other things to worry about."

surface and impacted it. Under pressure to reveal all that the probe 'saw', the Russians released a number of images showing an approaching object. The final frames prior to the cessation of signals have, however, never been released. There we go again, imagining the sensational when it may have been simply bad driving on the part of the Russian scientists. Had they, in attempting to park on Phobos, rammed it? We are sure the Russians would not take too kindly to that suggestion. Was it a chance collision with space debris? Hardly likely. Whatever the reason, one more page has been added to the book of Martian mysteries.

With the Russians effectively out of the space-race, NASA have decided they will have another look at Mars and as we write, the latest Mars Observer is well on the way. The craft was scheduled to arrive in Martian orbit in August 1993 and it is equipped with the powerful Malin camera. Imagine the anticipated excitement as it sweeps down over the CYDONIA face transmitting live coverage in unprecedented detail of the first ever proof of an alien nation having inhabited Mars. But this will not happen! For the first time ever, NASA has decided not to transmit live television! Then they announced their intention that they would examine the material and decide what would be seen by the general public. We hope the Americans will strongly object to having taxpayers' money used to finance something which would be subjected to NASA censorship or censorship from an even higher level. Surely, it could never have been considered necessary to classify this material as a threat to national security, but it could certainly threaten the Christian belief that God chose this planet as his son's abode. However, when one considers the lengths to which the authorities have gone to suppress UFO incidents on this planet, it would be extremely simple for them to arrange a communication failure with the probe as it enters the Martian 'atmosphere' *. We are sure the readers are by now piecing the jigsaw together and we are doing our utmost to ensure the right pieces are at least in the box.

* (**Editor's note:-** *Precisely as the authors predicted, contact with the Martian probe was lost the day it arrived at Mars.*)

CHAPTER 18.
STONEHENGE

The year of 360 days. The Typhon at Stonehenge.
The Saros cycle. Predicting eclipses. The period of the comet.
Correspondence in the Meridian at R.l.C.

IN the previous chapters we have tried to attune the mind of the reader to the mathematical language of the geometry of Rennes-le-Château. Without wishing to over simplify the incredible ability of the designers, let us now attempt to explain, to some degree, how they decided to present it to us. Try to see it as a coarse canvas or, if you will, a grid. Only on the material of the grid can a mark be made which is significant to the solution. Any attempt to mark a point in the holes of the mesh will result in mathematical failure, but the lattice work of the grid will tolerate small variations because the mathematics carry an indecisive prediction. The indecision of the prediction is, as we will see, not to be lightly dismissed.

Try to imagine we are looking at a cross section diagram of the internal combustion engine. If the drawing was only to be used to explain the general principles it could show the pistons fitting perfectly into their cylinders and gears meshing perfectly with each other. Such an engine would, of course, never function. Without inbuilt tolerances to allow for heat expansion and so forth, it would soon seize up. An engineers drawing would, of course, be totally different. As a result of considerable research and testing, the best tolerances would have been established and they would be clearly indicated. Simply speaking, anything functional has small tolerances built in. If the reader can appreciate the necessity for these mathematical tolerances he/she is ready to receive the secret message of Rennes-le-Château.

The canvas, or grid, or mesh, upon which the secret is drawn, is the Phi/Sine 18° multiple. These ratios control the Temple walls and radii of the circles into which the ultimate message is woven.

With this information already in hand, the reader can construct the Circle, the Extended Pentagram and the Temple Rectangle. Nothing could be more convincing than to create this canvas of the designers (either on paper or in the mind) and thereby be prepared for and appreciate the mathematical genius involved in what we will subsequently reveal, is superimposed over it.

The next revelation comes when the Meridian is plotted to conform to the parameters outlined in the previous chapter where the nature of its intersections with the Temple structure were shown.

Also from this point, it is essential that the reader continuously retains in his mind all the material previously presented. To this we will now apply definitive data which will lead to an understanding of the greatest of all the mysteries. A secret which was never meant to be universally exposed for fear it would change the course of history and usurp the power of the all powerful.

For a full understanding of what is to follow we must first return, once again, to those brilliant and fearless scholars, Higgins and Whiston. Together they assembled a mass of information to support the fact that the Earth has, from time to time, suffered from the effects of celestial interference.

"Noah saw the Earth become inclined and it was shaken violently".
"The axis of the Earth may have been suddenly changed".

From the *Book of Enoch (Book IX Chapter X)*

It is Higgins' contention that the precessive wobble of the Earth was at one time greater than at present and we are witness to the effect of the diminishing consequence of an even greater eccentricity. Even more significant is Higgins' reference to the fact that Noah and others learned from 'secret science' that it was about to happen. In other words, it was mathematically predictable. He continues by suggesting that people advanced in astronomy could foresee the return of a comet which would be close enough to Earth to cause destruction. This advanced astronomical ability, according to Higgins, could have been in the hands of the 'antediluvians' and as we progress, more and more evidence comes to light of displays of intelligence which do not rest easily in the times they occurred.

From Aristotle we hear:-

"that the Pythagoreans held a comet to be one of the planets which appears after a long interval of time, and which, at the apex of its very elliptical orbit, is at as small a distance from the sun as the planet Mercury. Now the Chaldaeans held comets to be planets and the Egyptians predicted their return".

It is of considerable consequence in the understanding of the relationship between Stonehenge and Rennes-le-Château that we appreciate how convinced Higgins and Whiston were that the close passage of a comet was responsible for changing the year from 360 days to the eventual present one of 365.25. Apart from our previous references to the intercalary days of the Egyptian legends, others supported it. The walls of Babylon were supposedly built at the rate of a furlong each day and Ctesias says this perimeter was 360 furlongs. That the Persian year was 360 days is evident from the testimony of

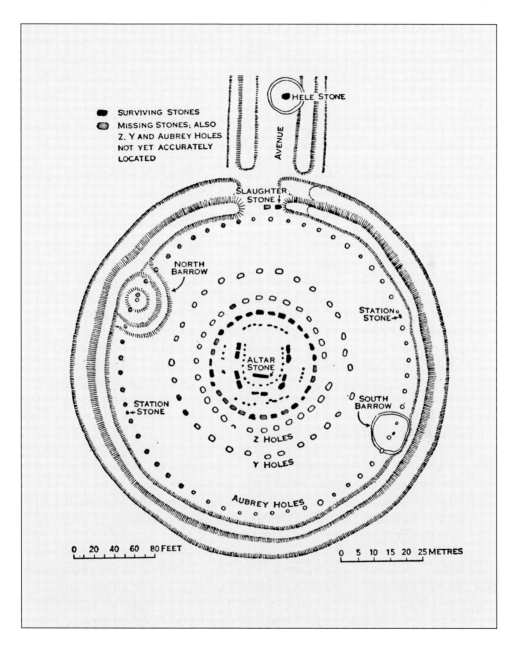

Ground plan of Stonehenge showing the 56 Aubrey holes.
(Published by The Ministry of Works)

Plutarch who affirms that more than one of the kings of that time had 360 royal concubines, implying one for each night of the year. Other examples occur where ancient nations speak of their year as either being divided into exact months of 20 or 30 days and neither of these divisions could occur, other than by a year of 360 days.

Higgins continues with page after page of proof that the orbit of the Earth round the sun was once 360 days and in this we have a mathematical harmony with the 360 degree circle, each day being one degree.

Continuing with our lateral investigation of persons well informed on matters of astronomy, it may be difficult to find scientific acceptance for the ancient year of 360 days. It is not, however, difficult to find acceptance of the cataclysmic history of our planet, even though to us, the two things may go hand in hand. In *Beyond Stonehenge* G.S. Hawkins is quite happy to quote from R.S. Newall (1959), that Diodorus speaks of a Hyperborean temple, which could be Stonehenge. He then refers to Plutarch's reference to the Typhon as being associated with the number 56 and more particularly that the Typhon was the 'demon of eclipses'. This reference is given considerable emphasis in *The Cosmic Serpent* where Clube and Napier suggest that Typhon-associated phenomena may occur at roughly 56 year intervals.

By referring to the layout of Stonehenge (see illustration), 56 markers occur in the form of holes which are arranged in a circle of approximately 290 feet in diameter and they are spread around the circumference every 16 feet. Knowing now how Phi (1.618), is used at Rennes-le-Château we have little doubt that the spacing was intended to be 16.18 feet and the inside measure of the diameter would therefore actually be 288.4 feet.

Stonehenge was, as we know, not a single construction, but the 56 Aubrey holes, so named after their discoverer, are known to have existed in the earliest layout. Stonehenge II and III are considered to be more associated with primitive ritual.

As stated by Hoyle in *On Stonehenge* :-

"One can be virtually certain that science had been displaced by ritual".

He is of the opinion that :-

"The intellectual activity of Mankind during pre-history is a vast, almost uncharted ocean".

It would appear his scholarship is leading him to similar conclusions as ours, even though they are, according to Henry Lincoln, in the realm of science fiction. Hoyle goes even further when he says that in his opinion the layout of the original Stonehenge was beyond the capability of the indigenous population and that the site was probably selected by people who must be:-

> ".... sought elsewhere, and the search is then broadened so greatly that I feel no surprise, or unease, that the forerunners are so far unknown".

Our only comment is "Well done Fred, it takes courage to make statements like that nowadays".

Hoyle's analysis of the geometry is far more detailed and accurate than that of Hawkins and we will, therefore, attend to his calculations.

Viewed from the Earth, the orbits of the Sun and the Moon are offset to each other at an angle of 5° 9' and the two intersections are clearly marked in the Stonehenge layout. These are an essential factor in the prediction of eclipses. At first 5° 9' does not seem to have any parallel in the Rennes-le-Château layout until we convert it into 309 minutes, and as we well know, this is the integer value of Sine 18° or the reciprocal of 2Ø . In seconds, it is 18,540 another close integer relationship to the radius of the Circle of Churches (185,410). This may be considered to be only weakly commensurate, but as we proceed the 'coincidences' will have more value.

Returning to the Sun and Moon orbits, although the angles of the intersections remain constant they slowly progress as shown in the diagram. The time required for them to complete the rotation is 18.61 years and is known as the Saros cycle. Remarkable as it may seem the angle of the Pentagonal Axis to the Temple walls of Rennes-le-Château is 18.61°! If we are by now generally convinced by the astronomers that one function of Stonehenge was the prediction of eclipses, we should also take heed of other events which may have also 'eclipsed' the Sun and Moon to some degree. Certainly the 'tail' of a large comet passing before them could have caused considerable darkening and, therefore, have qualified to be marked on their astronomical clock, probably with a view to predicting its recurrence. That these events could be accompanied with spectacular displays in the heavens and possibly turbulent effects on the ground would make them even more worthy of note.

This is certainly considered by Clube and Napier to be a more likely use of Stonehenge than predicting simple eclipses. They also see credibility in the possibility of the existence of those superior Hyberboreans who lived beyond Boreas (the north wind), and who Diodorus recorded as having fertile land producing every kind of crop and with such an excellent balance of climate as

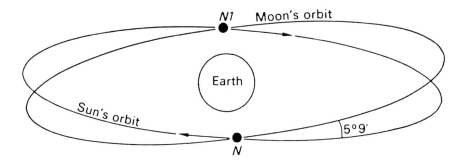

N1   Moon's orbit

Earth

Sun's orbit

N

5°9'

The paths of the Sun and Moon in the sky lie in planes which intersect at an angle of 5° 9′. The points of intersection N.N1 of the paths are the nodes of the Moon's orbit.

to produce two harvests each year. It is indeed surprising that these people of the Borealis should be so fortunate. Apparently something has moved, but as they are only mythical like the 'Aurora', they need not concern us. Before leaving this subject we must amusedly refer to the timid reference to the *Timaeus* by Clube and Napier. Naturally being men of science the word Atlantis would be taboo, but they had the temerity to say :-

"..... any link between the Platonic myth and the Cosmic Serpent is another story."

Joking aside, the work of Clube and Napier is most admirable, being not only as professional as one would expect from those gentlemen, but they also seem to be sufficiently open minded as to accept the possibility of the ancients having had advanced knowledge of celestial movements, prior to the subject being suppressed by the Church. With a comparatively brief base of observation, only short-period comets can be predicted with any certainty. This is also subject to them not having been gravitationally interfered with by the planets. A planet would certainly suffer from a close encounter, but may also only deflect or retard the comet sufficiently to interfere with its return cycle. It would be almost impossible to predict accurately under those circumstances, when precisely the Typhon would strike again, but a

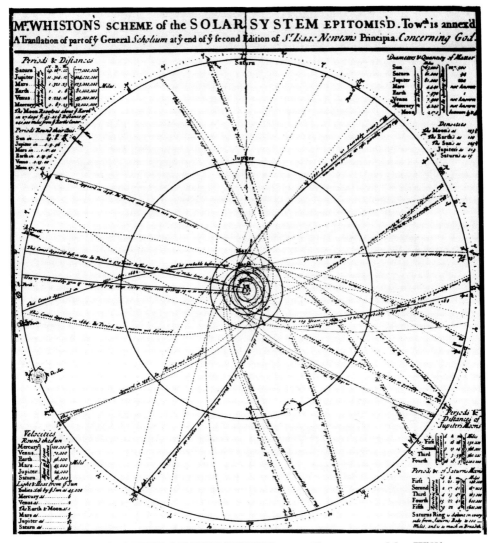

NEWTONIAN SYSTEM OF THE WORLD was diagrammed by William Whiston, who succeeded Newton as Lucasian Professor at the University of Cambridge. The diagram is from Whiston's broadside "Scheme of the Solar System Epitomis'd," published in 1724. The planets and the satellites of Jupiter and Saturn are shown orbiting the sun under the action of universal gravity. <u>Remarkably, Whiston also included the orbits of comets.</u> Newton had shown that orbits of comets are ellipses or parabolas in which a vector from the sun to the comet sweeps out equal areas in equal times.

sufficiently advanced intelligence could probably set upper and lower limits within which the comet would be likely to perform.

In attempting to use historical evidence, a number of problems arise, not the least of which is to identify whether a close cometary passage, or an asteroid impact in a distant land, was the reason for a given disaster.

Higgins and Whiston nevertheless attempt to find a correlation between disasters of one sort or another and a chronological period which could be a cometary cycle. Using the date of 2926 B.C. as the year of Noah's flood and considering it to be the 5th revolution of a comet they proceeded to carry the period forward 8 cycles until it became the comet recorded in historical times as 1680.

Simple mathematics show the period to be 575.75 years and it will shortly be shown how this figure manifests in the geometry of Rennes-le-Château.

First let us demonstrate a simple but little known mathematical code. Divide any number by a lesser whole number; next remove the resultant whole number from the answer and multiply the remainder by the original divider. A whole number will obviously always appear, and if you choose to convey that number to the recipient of your code you must have the correct combination of numbers in the first place. Let us try an example. Supposing it was a secret as to how many divisions existed in the Circle of Churches to form the extended pentagram (and it was); we could select 681, the code number in the Rennes-le-Château parchments and divide it by the pentagonal 18, the answer is 37.833 recurring. Subtract the whole number (37) and multiply the remainder by 18. The answer is, of course, the secret number of divisions, 15.

In effect, we are mathematically resolving the cyclic differences between the first two numbers. Now this is, we are told, precisely the reason for the 56 holes in the 360° circle of Stonehenge. So let us try it there. 360 divided by 56 is 6.428571429, so remove the 6 and multiply the remainder by 56, the answer is, of course, 24. We pondered on what secret could be revealed by 24. Admittedly the 15 divisions of the Circle of Churches are each 24°, but Rennes-le-Château does not have 56 markers on the circle. However, if we divide the 15 section Circle of Churches by 56 we have 0.267857142, which is the inverse Tangent of 15 degrees. This is probably co-incidental, but it is not by chance that we have 56 face stones on the Arques Tomb, on the Meridian and it certainly displays Sine 56° on its enclosed section. The Meridian is undoubtedly SET, the Typhon and that relationship has already been established by others in connection with Stonehenge. Obviously, with SET as 'God of Time' it was worth considering that 24 was meant to represent the hours of a day. Having the Circle of Churches displaying 24° so clearly in its 15 divisions we wondered whether the 24 hour time factor existed on the Meridian.

We should now recall Whiston's calculated cycle for the return of the Typhon. It was 575.75 years. We had not seen the figure represented on the Meridian, but what if we converted the Meridian inches in to hours. This you will recall as being 6 x Sine 56° or 4974225 AUs and as the reader is now aware the decimal place is of little consequence, the codes work in integers. With the length representing hours, we first divide by 24 to obtain days, (207,259). Next remembering this to be of antediluvian design we divide by the 360 days, to convert to years. The result is, to say the least, ominous for it is **575.72** years and well within such perturbations as would be encountered in the commentary cycle and the original datings of Whiston. For that matter and in the supposition of the termination of life on Earth, calculating either system by 360 or 365.25 days would be of little account, as a 365.25 day year produces 567.4. Suffice to say that there are more than enough correlations both mathematical, historical and doctrinal for us to take heed of the warning signs, so clearly placed at Rennes-le-Château. But surely Jules Verne would have known something of the dating of this threat? It had already become obvious to us that Verne had access to the hidden knowledge and being aware of the danger, the predominant question to him would have been - **When?**

Later we will see that he had indeed found an answer and he displayed it in his inimitable fashion, for all to see.

The alert reader will by now have realised an obvious omission in our deliberations on the Meridian. This is, of course the angle at which it lies, relative to the Temple Walls. In disclosing this we sincerely hope the reader will enjoy the same conviction as we did when we discovered it.

CHAPTER 19.
THE ROOT OF EVIL.

A remarkable triangle. Alvarez proves the cataclysm.
The identity of God. The Biblical 'Revelations'.
Predicted impact date of the comet. The Perseid meteors.
An imminent collision. Comet IRAS. Jules Verne again.

THE next disclosure of the geometric temple of Rennes-le-Château is unavoidably mathematical, but that is no reason to drop the book in horror. The figure we will discuss is a triangle, and nothing could be more simple; it has three straight sides and if it had any less it would not be a figure at all. Now triangles come in all shapes and sizes, but the ones we find most interesting are a special group, called 'right-angled'. This simply means that one of the three angles is 90° and as the angles of any triangle add up to 180° we are left with 90° to share out between the remaining two.

One day someone told Pythagoras that if he made a triangle with the sides of 3, 4 and 5 regardless of which particular unit of measure was used, he would finish up with an angle of 90°. This was naturally very useful, particularly to people who wanted to build things. Three pieces of wood nailed together in that ratio allowed them to build their walls square to each other and also ensure they were upright. Now these right-angled triangles became even more useful when it was realised that by knowing only two pieces of information (as long as one of them was the length of one side, everything else about the triangle could be solved. The ratios, as the reader is by now aware, have names which simply tell us which sides to use for identifying the particular ratio of an angle. The two ratios we are immediately concerned with are the Sine (opposite side divided by the hypotenuse) and the Tangent (the opposite side divided by the one adjacent to the angle).

Sometimes, in order to solve a geometric problem, it is necessary to construct an additional line to create a triangle which can then be solved. By examining the diagram (Fig. 17), the reader will see we have constructed a line from where the Meridian enters the southern wall of the Temple (A), parallel to the east wall. This line travels north and we terminate it at the north side of the square (C) which is tangential to the Circle of Churches.

It is immediately obvious that in the triangle we have marked ABC, that AC is equal to the diameter (i.e. twice the radius) of the circle (370820.4 AUs). All we need now is either length BC or one of the angles and the triangle can be completely solved. Following our established rules of analysis we wondered if we could identify any logical meaning or ratios in the lengths of the sides of

THE DIMENSIONS & FORMULÆ
OF THE MERIDIAN TRIANGLE

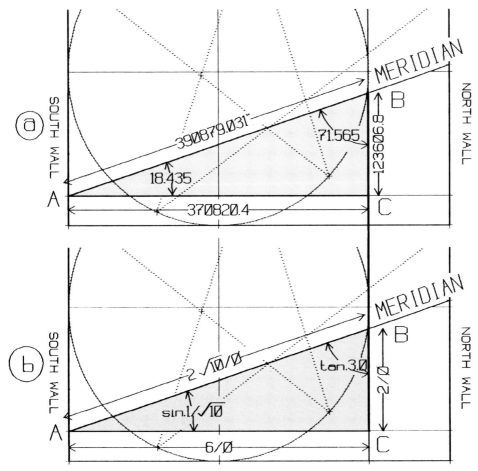

FIG. 17.   a) The **dimensions** of the Meridian Triangle.
b) The **formulæ** of the Meridian Triangle.

Together these figures display further confirmation of the Meridian plot and the orientation of the Temple walls. When one considers the unique set of values generated by the intersection of the Paris Meridian with the existing Temple layout, the correspondences are indeed remarkable. However, when taken together with the other factors of the Meridian, they are nothing short of miraculous.

the triangle. The hypotenuse (AB), which is the section of the Meridian enclosed in the tangential square was measured on the computer and found to be in the order of 390,900 AUs; a figure which meant very little to us at the time. The length of BC was, however, an old familiar face - 123,606.8, which is twice the reciprocal of Phi. Obviously, we were back in the hands of the Master Mason.

With two established sides we were now able to solve the triangle by simple trigonometry. Dividing side BC by side AC gave us the tangent of angle BAC; it was 0.333 recurring. This was certainly a unique number, but even more so, this meant that the tangent of angle ABC was exactly 3; and that was profound!

Despite this, everything we had found in the codes indicated the use of sines, not tangents, and therefore it was to those values which we turned our attention. In angular measure the two angles were 71.565051° and 18.43494881°; to say the least, we were not impressed. Their respective sine values of 0.948683298 and 0.316227765 meant nothing and left us quite depressed.

Then, once again, came that flash of insight; the last number, which was the sine value of the Meridian angle to the Temple wall seemed vaguely familiar. Indeed it is with some degree of shame that we admit to not having recognised it immediately. The number is unique; it is the only number which has exactly the same integers as its reciprocal (**0.316227765** and **3.16227765**). Furthermore, as you have no doubt realised, the latter number is the square root of 10! Immediately, we knew that the lengths of the triangle could now be formulated:-

Hypotenuse.............................390,879.0151.............$2\sqrt{10} \div \emptyset$*
Opposite Side.........................123,606.7978............**2/Ø***
Adjacent Side.........................370,820.3932............**600,000/Ø**
Meridian Angle.............Sine 18.43494882° ....$\sqrt{1/10}$
Complimentary Angle...Tan 71.56505118°............**3**

To encapsulate this, we are saying the angle of inclination of the Temple to the Meridian is **Sine** $\sqrt{1/10}$. It is almost beyond belief that this mathematical oddity should occur by chance where it does, but if it is there by design, in keeping with all the other mathematical disciplines which control the geometry, it is nothing short of miraculous. Disregarding for the moment, the 100,000 multiple required to equate the ratios to ground measure, the side AC is, as we know, the diameter of the Circle of Churches, which is **6/Ø** and using the Tangent ratio of the angle BAC, the side BC evaluates as **2/Ø**. The resultant hypotenuse of the triangle AB becomes $2\sqrt{10} \div Ø$, and it naturally follows that

* *Naturally subjected to the 100,000 multiple previously referred to.*

the remaining angle ABC has a Tangent value of exactly **3**. You must admit that for someone who collects triangles as a hobby, this is a must!

As our investigation of the Rennes-le-Château geometry progressed, we became more and more amazed that the figures being displayed are not found elsewhere. Being in the category of 'special' cases, we would not necessarily expect to find them in general school mathematics, but when one considers the number of persons examining 'Sacred Geometry' it is indeed surprising to find that none of these figures occur in their works. Where they do exist however, is marked over the French landscape and they use those very ratios which are the working tools of the sacred mathematicians, albeit interwoven with such complexity as can never have been seen before.

We should have felt a sense of triumph at each new discovery, but faced with the enormity of this prodigy, we were humbled by the realisation that we were probably the first to see it manifest in its entirety since its inception.

Poussin, Templars, Boudet, Saunière, the Priory of Sion, treasure seekers and the host of 'informed' commentators who circle like moths round the flame of Rennes-le-Château faded into obscurity. No longer was there any need to pursue the validity of the historical crumbs which had fallen from the table of these mathematical giants who had created such a feast of geometry.

Numbed by the perfection we were privileged to witness, it was hardly surprising to find the area of this amazing triangle was, within extremely close limits, to being one sixth part of the temple square. This correspondence seemed to harmonise with the body triangle of the pentagram which so closely equated the circumference of the Circle of Churches. The correspondences were exhilarating, but we could never forget that we were being witness to a mathematical perfection which may be predicting the destruction of our species.

In this respect, we will now return to the findings of the Alvarez team described previously, which put the last nail in the coffin of those who wished to believe that Planet Earth was an impregnable fortress. Suddenly, those whose heads were not firmly buried in religious sand realised we existed by nothing more than the grace of a mathematical probability and furthermore, one over which we had no control whatsoever. The manner in which the Earth's population accepts this fate, is to us, quite incredible. Certainly, unlike any other creature on Earth, Man alone knows his personal days are numbered, but surely this acceptance of the total destruction of Mankind cannot be so lightly dismissed. At what point will we begin to be concerned?

We claim to be responsible enough to care as to the state of the environment for our children's sake, but do we seriously care about the generations of children which will follow them? Apparently not! How will they view the lethargy of their forebears, when they are confronted with the Typhonic comet hurtling towards the Earth on a confirmed course of collision. Will they be forgiving and accept that we were totally unaware of the danger? How could they be, when this book had already analysed and pin-pointed the instrument of their demise.

The empiric element of the scientific academy has now been forced to accept the cataclysmic destruction of the Cretaceous dinosaurs and the inevitability of another similar disaster occuring. It is amazing to hear some argue that it was a benign event, in as much that it cleared the surface of the Earth for Man to develop and multiply. Would they now be willing to accept the destruction of homo sapiens on the presumption that it would clear the way for the eventual development of a creature far superior to ourselves?

Without wishing to detract from the efforts of Greenpeace and conceding the morals which motivate them, do they have any idea of how futile their work would appear if a celestial impact was imminent? The typical Sunday School theme is that God gave us this beautiful Earth and that we should treat it with care, but what care has he shown in the past? The pious arguments of the clergy, who claim to understand God's motives when he subjects thousands to death by natural disaster, would hardly stand up to the annihilation of our species, together with all the other noble animals of the planet. Admittedly, total annihilation of all living things is not assumed by even the most pessimistic. There will undoubtedly be survivors -- rats, fleas and flies, to name just a few, but we admit to being baffled by the good Lord's selection, unless of course he is indeed the 'King of the Rats' or 'Lord of the Flies'.

It would be more logical to consider the possibility that the God we revere is actually a super intelligence created by our own subconscious minds. In fact, a super subconscious 'group-mind'. Consider also that mass prayer, correctly directed, could produce a solution to our salvation. Is gathering together to pray, a remnant from the race memory of the gods who actually had that ability? Are we now beginning to have some insight into the true image of God; one which we have been foolish enough to personify as a dear old man in white robes, sitting on a golden throne with a bunch of girls deformed by sprouting wings, fluttering round him like moths around a flame?

We must admit to finding this imagery only slightly less offensive than that other famous Christian icon of God's supposed son nailed to a cross. There are now serious doubts as to whether this event ever took place as it is recorded in the Authorised Version, but if it did, it would hardly have been the image we would have chosen to remember his achievements. Of all the men killed in aerial combat during the war, we doubt whether any of their parents would adorn their parlour walls with a picture of the crashed aircraft, let alone their dear one's disfigured body.

As a child outgrows Father Christmas, should we not by now be willing to address historical fact. There are after all some 2,000 nails residing in churches around the world, all claiming to be 'THE NAILS'. We respectfully suggest, they be collected and relegated to the scrap-heap where they belong; wrapped if possible in the Turin Shroud.

If, on the other hand, the 'cruci-fiction' was never meant to be taken literally, we may be misjudging it. Could it be an allegory requiring interpretation? Knowing what we now do concerning the creation of Man and our planet, the Biblical *GENESIS* undoubtedly falls into that category. Read the days of creation as any time intervals you choose, it just will not work. It does, however, make good sense as the description of the planet recovering from a celestial catastrophe. Moving from the first book to the last, in *REVELATIONS* we find something which, most definitely, can be sensibly interpreted and many researchers have done so in a most professional manner.

In short, *REVELATIONS* is a collection of observations made at a time when the Earth was subjected to massive destruction due to the impact, or close passage of a comet or some other celestial body. For some researchers to have so accurately interpreted *REVELATIONS* prior to recent scientific analysis of the probable effects of such an event is, to say the least, praiseworthy. With what we now know, the message of *REVELATIONS* is all too clear.

To interpret it correctly, we must put ourselves in the position of people who had no idea whatsoever of the nature of the heavenly bodies they could see. Certainly, they could never expect violent eccentricities to occur in the canopy of lights which circled so serenely above them. To describe phenomena in the night sky which was beyond their experience, gave them no option but to liken them to objects with which their readers would be familiar.

Let us pause to consider how difficult a task it was to report on the awesome spectacle of celestial fire of such magnitude as to fill the sky above them.

> ....."I saw seven golden candlesticks; And in the mist of the seven candlesticks one like unto the Son of man, clothed with a garment down to the foot, and girt about the paps with a golden girdle. His head and his hairs were white like wool, as white as snow; and his eyes were a flame of fire;"   *(Revel I. v12-14)*

Anyone who has witnessed the re-entry of space debris from our satellite launches will have no difficulty recognising this description.

The candlesticks of ash particles illuminated in the upper atmosphere by the Sun, which has long since set, are preceded by the burning metal segments which are breaking away from the main body of the booster casing. Just as the graphic account says, in the centre of these fragments the secondary stage, achieving a far greater temperature, forms a white cone of light preceded by the fireball at the forefront of the re-entry. Even the 'hairs white like wool' is a precise description of minor particles from the head being gasified before they can display their own fire centres.

Here the parallel must cease, for as we well know, most space debris is of insufficient substance to reach the surface of the planet in a form which could cause damage. Unfortunately, such is not the case with a billion tons of rock and iron. Our protective atmosphere would rip and tear at such a missile and produce the ultimate firework display. First gravel and small rocks would be detached and burnt to ash. Temperatures in the order of 18,000° centigrade may crack the invading giant into even more horrendous serpents of fire, but try as it may, our defending atmosphere could not prevent the multiple barrage of the surface.

The Alvarez team estimated the asteroid which caused the Cretaceous destruction to be in the order of hundreds of billions of tons. The mind boggles when trying to appreciate the effect of such an event. Our ancestors had never witnessed the explosive force of nuclear devices and could, therefore, have had nothing with which to compare. However, we are slightly more aware but may still have difficulty imagining the effect of millions of Hiroshima bombs sequentially exploding across the surface of the planet.

The accurate account in *REVELATIONS* goes on to describe the atmosphere preceding the fireball being heated to incandescent blue.

> "And before the throne there was a sea of glass like unto crystal:...."
> *(Revel. IV v6)*

How better could one convey the shimmering transparent halo of pre-heated oxygen and how better the breaking up of the body, other than to say:-

> ".....and round about the throne, were four beasts full of eyes before and behind."
> *(Revel. IV v6)*

The narrator is at pains to indicate that this event has a continuing sequence and conveys this to us as 'the opening of a series of seals'. Eventually the impacts begin and the effects are recorded as Earthly disasters. God has granted his celestial assassins permission to kill and plunder the Earth.

> "....And power was given unto them over the fourth part of the earth, to kill with swords, and with hunger, and with death, and with the beasts of the earth."
> *(Revel. VI v8)*

The aftermath of this event would involve the ash and dust being suspended in the upper atmosphere, partially obliterating the light from the sun and the moon. We all know how red the setting sun and rising moon appear when their light shines edgeways through the atmospheric dust. How clearly this is described in *REVELATIONS*.

> "......and lo, there was a great earthquake; and the sun became
> black as sackcloth of hair, and the moon became as blood;"
>
> (Revel. VI v12)

Then, would you believe, this Christian book lays the blame for this inhuman act of genocide at the door of their most revered paragon of virtue - God!

> "For the great day of his wrath is come; and who shall be able to
> stand?"   (*Revel. VII v17*)

Whatever had these people done to make him be so angry? Could it perhaps have been Sunday Trading? Here we are, with morals at an all time low, designing weapons of mass destruction, chemical and nuclear, but dear old God does not turn a hair. Strangely enough, we would never accuse an omnipotent intelligence of such behaviour. Once again the Christians have demeaned their God with the human failing of jealousy, probably because some of them worshipped the wrong totem-pole.

On and on through *REVELATIONS* we find the references we seek, some direct:-

> ".... and I saw a star fall from heaven unto the earth: and to him
> was given the key of the bottomless pit".   (*Revel. IX v1*)

Other references are allegorically veiled as in the description of the inevitable tidal waves which would follow such an upheaval.

> "And I stood upon the sand of the sea, and saw a beast rise up out
> of the sea, having seven heads and ten horns, ..." (*Revel. XIII v1*)

Other nations also have legends of these dragons of the sky, the all devouring serpents and the Typhonic beast of destruction. In *REVELATIONS* XIII v18 we may have a glimmering of the estimated time of his return? Were some learned enough to attempt to estimate the cycle of destruction?

> "Let him that hath the understanding count the number of the
> beast (this being the time of his return) for it is the number of man
> (this being the date of his possible demise) and his number is 666",
> (years before he returns).

As we have previously shown, with further evidence some have arrived at a different number, namely 575.75 years and we will do our best to interpret the

Rennes-le-Château geometry as to which date is the most probable. Coincidentally, while in the process of this refinement we were pre-empted by a remarkable press announcement, to which we must now direct our attention. (See illustration).

In this article we are being invited to view the Comet Swift-Tuttle which in its next orbit is, "in line for a possible collision with the Earth, which would have 'catastrophic' effects, according to Professor Alexander Boksenberg, director of the Royal Greenwich Observatory".

The estimated date in this article is August 14th **2116** and the professor goes on to say :-

> "There is a large enough chance for us to be concerned about it. The effect of Swift-Tuttle hitting earth would be much worse than setting off every nuclear device. It would make an enormous explosion which would throw up all the water in the seas and all the dust in the atmosphere, which would blot out the light from the sun."

Other astronomers then revised the date to **2126,** and we will have reason to return to the mathematics later. Subsequent to these 'learned' estimates they agreed they had all miscalculated and the comet was no threat. Possibly our astronomical calculations are not so very accurate after all, but if that is the case how do we account for the next press announcement (see illustration) which states that "Britain will tonight be treated to the biggest celestial 'firework' display this century as the Earth is bombarded by a shower of meteors." Now these meteors are referred to as the Perseids and are caused by the Earth passing through dust grains that were ejected from the Comet Swift-Tuttle 130 years ago. Precisely on cue, the meteors appeared, so perhaps they can predict accurately after all. Admittedly this is an annual event and the basis of its calculation is refined, whereas the comet is by comparison a 'space-maverick'. We cannot help but wonder however, who told the Swift-Tuttle observers to revoke their 'collision date' calculation. Surely the 'Hubble Deep

Stargazers set for the great meteor firework show

By PAUL FULLER

But our weather could spoil the big night

BRITAIN will tonight be treated to the biggest celestial "firework" display this century as the Earth is bombarded by a shower of meteors.

Stargazers only have to step into their back gardens to enjoy a grandstand view of the greatest free show over Earth.

Thousands of shooting stars will explode across the night sky, predict astronomers, who ruled out any danger to the public.

But in the true tradition of the British summer, the weather could spoil the show. Forecasters yesterday

put a dampener on the historic event, predicting that heavy cloud and showers could blot out the display for many people in the South, the Midlands and Scotland.

Only people in the North of England and North Wales will be able to see the spectacle clearly.

The shooting star explosions, known as Perseids, will be caused by the Earth passing through dust grains that were ejected from Comet Swift-Tuttle 130 years ago.

Showers of meteors, appearing as

streaks of light in the night sky, will be visible all over the world as the comet particles enter the Earth's atmosphere.

The three-hour show should begin at around 11pm. In areas where the skies are clear, stargazers will be able to watch with the naked eye.

Experts advise that lying on a sun lounger away from bright lights is the best way to enjoy the event.

A meteor crashing to earth is believed to have triggered a nuclear winter 65 million years ago and

wiped out the dinosaurs. But astronomers have ruled out Armageddon tonight and insisted yesterday there was no risk to earth dwellers this time.

A British Astronomical Association spokesman said the Perseids were "very tiny pieces of debris which are not large enough to pass through the Earth's atmosphere".

"We don't expect to see large chunks of meteorites crashing down to Earth," he added.

"People should just go outside and

enjoy it. It should be a lot of fun." Scientists fear, however, that the millions of tiny particles from the comet's trail could disrupt the orbit of vital satellites in space.

The six-mile wide comet, travelling at 130,000 mph, was first spotted in 1862 when it missed Earth by 50 million miles. It returned last December and again missed the planet by a wide margin.

Some astronomers predicted that Doomsday was looming, with the comet destined to collide with Earth in 2126. But new calculations indicate the planet is safe for the next millennium.

Daily Express Wednesday August 11th 1993.

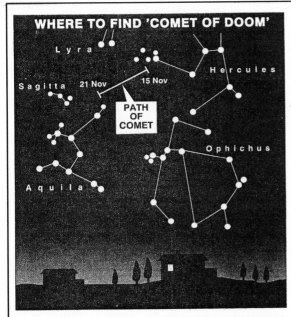

WHERE TO FIND 'COMET OF DOOM'

Lyra

Hercules

Sagitta   21 Nov   15 Nov

PATH
OF
COMET

Ophichus

Aquila

Comet orbits in a whiff of grapeshot

By Julia Llewellyn Smith

THE comet that threatens one day to wipe out life on Earth will be visible this week in the western sky at sunset and sunrise, signalled by shooting stars, according to astronomers.

Comet Swift-Tuttle was last spotted in 1862. Its next orbit in 2116 puts it in line for a possible collision with the Earth, which would have "catastrophic" effects, according to Professor Alexander Boksenberg, director of the Royal Greenwich Observatory.

The comet will appear as a fuzzy blob with a long tail, about a third the size of the moon. It will be visible to the naked eye in the countryside and in towns with a pair of binoculars, between the constellations of Hercules and the Lyre as it moves slowly across the sky. Many shooting stars, which are cometary debris, will also be visible.

Light is reflected off the comet as it approaches the sun and particles are boiled off as it heats up, to be left behind producing the effect of a tail. The comet should come closest to the sun on December 12 and will then retreat to beyond the orbit of Pluto, the most distant planet in the solar system.

Although the comet will never come closer to us than about 110 million miles in this orbit, astronomers estimate there is a one in 10,000 chance that it will hit earth on August 14, 2116.

Prof Boksenberg said: "There is a large enough chance for us to be concerned about. The effect of Swift-Tuttle hitting earth would be much worse than setting off every nuclear device. It would make an enormous explosion which would throw up all the water in the seas and all the dust in the atmosphere, which would blot out the light from the sun."

Similar collisions are thought to have set off the ice age and to have been responsible for the extinction of the dinosaurs. "Even if we blew up a dangerous comet, its particles would continue to orbit and could still hit the Earth," he said.

Space' telescope should have had something to say on the matter!

The analogy of referring to comets as 'mavericks' leads us to another 'incident'. As the reader will know, a maverick is an unbranded steer which becomes the property of the first person to mark it with their brand. Similarly, if an astronomer discovers a new comet, he informs the 'Cometary Data Center' at Harvard and it will be named after him.

When one considers the immense power of the professional telescopes, both on Earth and in space, it is surprising that new comets can still be discovered by amateur astronomers. However, this has and still does occur and the comet in question was named 'IRAS-Iraki-Alcock'.

Iraki and Alcock are the two amateur astronomers, Japanese and British respectively, whose brands, quite rightly will remain on this particular maverick, but it is to IRAS that we will now refer.

In 1992, the 'National Aeronautics and Space Administration (NASA) announced the famous background radiation 'ripples' discovered by Satellite COBE (Cosmic Background Explorer). This was undoubtedly an important step in unravelling the transition period between energy and the formation of matter, subsequent to the 'Big Bang' and it received extensive coverage by the media. Prior to this, however, in 1983 an 'Infra-Red Astronomical Satellite' (IRAS), had been launched to survey the distribution of galaxies to an

215

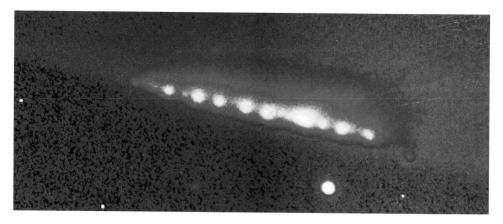

**Comet Shoemaker-Levy. Astronomers estimate that the largest of the
fragments seen here are about five kilometres across; they should
begin colliding with Jupiter on or around July 20, 1994, a far cry from
the 2km 'snowballs' of a few years ago.**

unprecedented level of scale and accuracy.The results of this survey, although
probably equally important, did not attract the attention of the media to the
same degree.

The story of IRAS,COBE and a good deal more, is now available in an
excellent book entitled *Ripples in the Cosmos*, by Michael Rowan-Robinson
who was deeply involved in the IRAS project and presently holds the Chair of
Astrophysics at London University. Although it is mentioned more as an aside
to his main work, Rowan-Robinson relates the discovery by IRAS of a comet.
Now when one considers there are probably millions of undiscovered comets,
this need not be newsworthy; but it was!

This particular comet (first seen April 26th 1983), was to pass closer to the
Earth than any other comet for two hundred years. In fact, in the early stages
of the comet's approach the IRAS scientists were not sure that the Earth was
safe from impact. In Rowan-Robinson's words :-

> "We sat round at JPL (Jet Propulsion Laboratories) digesting this
> fascinating information and debating whether we should warn the
> world's population of this worrying fact. Personally, I thought we
> should, because if the comet did hit, say, London or New York and
> we had failed to give a warning we were likely to be unpopular, to
> say the least. Typical scientific caution prevailed, however, and the
> IRAS team waited a few more days to get a better estimate of the
> orbit. The danger of a collision receded."

When the comet passed Earth at a distance of only just over four million miles, the radio-telescopes revealed the comet to have a massive nucleus with a seven mile diameter, the same size as that responsible for the destruction of the dinosaurs (so much for 'snowballs').

Rowan-Robinson then refers to Swift-Tuttle :-

> "Not only do we need to save the planet from our own damaging activities, we also need to think how we might survive this type of cosmic catastrophe which we narrowly missed in April 1983. There will be a worrying moment for our descendants in the year 2126 when comet Swift-Tuttle which was first discovered in 1862 and then crossed the Earth's orbit again in 1992, returns. On that occasion it is predicted to cross the Earth's orbit on **July 11th 2126,** while the Earth crosses the comet's orbit only one month later on **August 14th.** If the comet were delayed only one month on its **134** year orbit, a collision is possible".

Even if Earth survives this encounter, we must remember that every comet carries the signature, '**I will return**'; and so will IRAS. As the reader will see these 'missiles' are not in the domain of the 'doom-merchants,' but of serious concern to men of science; men who by the very nature of their calling are cautious. They are, however, not 'comatose', just 'Comet-aware'.

In fact, as recently as January 1993 they met in Tucson Arizona to discuss

' HAZARDS DUE TO COMETS AND ASTEROIDS'.

At that meeting it was proposed that a network of telescopes be devoted to **'SPACEGUARD'**, a system for tracking the Earth-orbit-crossing missiles.

Even more awesome is NASA's consideration to put in place hundreds of orbiting nuclear missiles, to use as a defensive shield against them.

We amateurs would seriously suggest re-directing some of the finance being used to construct the Texas Super-Collider* to repairing the Hubble Deep Space Telescope**, which when reinstated would be capable of optically imaging the threat when still at a great distance from the Earth.

The Hubble telescope is, however, presently involved in the analysis of the composition of another comet, Shoemaker-Levy. Even as this book is being written, this missile is hurtling through the solar system at approximately 134,000 miles per hour with the scientific estimation of a 95 per cent chance it will strike Jupiter on July 20th 1994. Were the impact to occur on the side of Jupiter facing us, the planet would flare to a brilliance, which some have considered would have rivalled the intensity of the light of a full moon. Unfortunately, we are told, the strike will occur on the other side of Jupiter, which indicates just how accurate our astrophysicists can be when they put their minds to it. Imagine the effect of a celestial display of this nature in the days of Galileo. Rest assured the Holy men would have turned it to their

---

* *This project has since been abandoned.*
** *Hubble was repaired Dec 1993 and fitted with a wide angle, comet seeking camera.*

advantage, probably suggesting it was a warning to those who were not toeing the ecclesiastical line.

On a more serious note, however, the study of the comet has revealed factors which are pertinent to our enquiry. During its last passage in July 1992, it missed Jupiter by a mere 60,000 odd miles and the immense gravitational field of the giant planet tore the head of the comet apart. The eight 'fragments', if one could describe them as such, are now strung out in line as can be seen in the illustration. The largest is said to be some five kilometres in diameter, which suggests the other seven range from one to three kilometres. Obviously, the once 'hallowed' theory of comet heads not exceeding two kilometres in diameter has been abandoned and in consequence the cometary, as opposed to the asteroid threat, returns as the main contender for the Cretaceous impact.

With some degree of scientific evidence available to us as to a possible date of impact, we will return to Jules Verne, supposing as we did, that he was well-informed of the approaching danger. From the moment we were aware of the Verne connection, it had been our intention to read everything he had written. Eventually it transpired that this is not as easy as it sounds. In fact it took months to find copies of some of his less popular books. One of these unobtainable works was particularly frustrating, because in its title there appeared to be a cipher which could be connected to a disaster.

The title to which we refer is *HECTOR SERVADAC*. Applying the first rule in the decipherment of Verne, we reversed **SERVADAC** which then becomes **CADAVRES**, the French equivalent of **CADAVERS**, meaning dead bodies. **HECTOR** is a simple anagram of **TORCHE** being the French for a **TORCH**. Could this title imply bodies destroyed by fire resulting from the impact of a comet or did it mean a fiery body - a reasonable description of a comet?

When we eventually read the story we were dumfounded. It was immediately obvious as to why the book was relatively unknown. So unlike Verne because the story was weak and even in his time so implausible as to probably leave his readers wondering why he had bothered to write it. To us, however, armed with our knowledge of Verne's involvement and recent astronomical findings, it was awesome! It is the story of the Earth being struck by a massive comet and his description of the event proves conclusively that he was a good deal more informed of the consequences than those amateur astronomers of 20th century television, who once labelled the comets as harmless 'snowballs'. In his chapter 'A Convulsion of Nature', his lurid description accurately describes what we now know would be the result of an impact from a large comet:-

"Whence came it that the billows raged and rose to a height hitherto unregistered in the records of science?

HECTOR SERVADAC.

50

therefore be that the earth's distance from the sun had been diminished from 91,000,000 to 66,000,000 miles. If the just equilibrium of the earth had thus been destroyed, and should this diminution of distance still continue, would there not be reason to fear that the terrestrial world would be carried onwards to actual contact with the sun, which must result in its total annihilation?

The continuance of the splendid weather afforded Servadac every facility for observing the heavens. Night after night, constellations in their beauty lay stretched before his eyes—an alphabet which, to his mortification, not to say his rage, he was unable to decipher. In the apparent dimensions of the fixed stars, in their distance, in their relative position with regard to each other, he could observe no change. Although it is established that our sun is approaching the constellation of Hercules at the rate of more than 126,000,000 miles a year, and although Arcturus is travelling through space at the rate of fifty-four miles a second—three times faster than the earth goes round the sun,—yet such is the remoteness of those stars that no appreciable change is evident to the senses. The fixed stars taught him nothing.

Far otherwise was it with the planets. The orbits of Venus and Mercury are within the orbit of the earth, Venus rotating at an average distance of 66,130,000 miles from the sun, and Mercury at that of 35,393,000. After pondering long, and as profoundly as he could, upon these figures, Captain Servadac came to the conclusion that, as the earth was now receiving about double the amount of light and heat that it had been receiving before the catastrophe, it was receiving about the same as the planet Venus; he was driven, therefore, to the estimate of the measure in which the earth must have approximated the sun, a deduction which ... him to observe Venus herself i

---

212

HECTOR SERVADAC.

treatise, exhibiting the results of all his investigations, and when, after the sudden convulsion, he found himself actually upon the surface of one of the very bodies the properties of which had engrossed so much of his interest, it was necessarily a disappointment to feel that, alone upon Formentera, he had no audience to whom he could address himself.

The treatise which Rosette had compiled had been arranged under four distinct heads:
1. The number of comets.
2. Periodic and non-periodic comets.
3. The probability of collision between a comet and the earth.
4. The consequences of such a collision.

First: with respect to the number of comets, the professor had recorded that, according to Arago, who grounded his estimate on the number that revolve between Mercury and the sun, there are at least 17,000,000 of these luminous bodies in our solar system; whilst Lambert asserts that within the orbit of Saturn, that is, within a radius of 873,135,000 miles, there are no less than 500,000,000. According to Kepler, two hundred years previously, the number of comets can only be compared to the fishes in the sea, and in following out his line from the surface of the sun angler throwing out his line from the surface of the sun could not fail to touch several of them; and now in recent times a computation has been made that their aggregate reaches a total of 74,000,000,000 distinct comets. The earth seems to be that their number really sets all calculation at defiance; so erratic, moreover, are their movements, that they sometimes pass from system to system, and whilst some, entirely escaping the influence of the sun, vanish, to find a new centre of attraction, others never before observed make their appearance upon the terrestrial

---

COMETS, OLD AND NEW.   213

parabolas or hyperbolas; and the planets, Jupiter in particular, have been observed to exercise a large disturbing action upon their paths.

Secondly: under the head of periodic and non-periodic comets, Professor Rosette had stated that as many as 500 or 600 comets have been made objects of careful astronomical investigation; those being called "periodic" of which the return at fixed intervals has been established as a certainty; those, on the other hand, being classed as "non-periodic" which recede to such immeasurable distances from the sun that it cannot be determined whether they will return or not.

Of the periodic comets there are not more than forty of which the times of their revolution have been ascertained with exact precision; but of these there are ten, generally known as the "short-period comets," the movements of which have been established with the nicest accuracy.

The short-period comets are respectively called by the names of their discoverers, and are commonly distinguished as Halley's comet, Encke's, Gambart's or Biela's, Faye's, Brörsen's, D'Arrest's, Tuttle's, Winnecke's, De Vico's, Tempel's.

Subjoined is a brief account of each of these in de Halley's comet is that which has been the ... known. It is supposed to be identical with the on was observed in the years 134 and 52 B.C., and aft in the years 400, 855, 930, 1006, 1230, 1305, 13.. 1531, 1607, 1682, 1759, and 1835 A.D. It revo.. cast to west, in a direction contrary to the plan.. intervals between its consecutive appearances va.. turbed by the attraction of Jupiter and S.. to 76 years, according as its course is such an.. sometimes influence its course to such an.. make a difference of 200 days in the period.. The last appearance of this comet was in.. John Herschel, at the Cape of Good Hope,.. able station for observation than any i.. hemisphere, was able to watch it until th..

215

HECTOR SERVADAC.

it receives 28,000 times more heat than the earth; that is, it is 2000 times hotter than molten iron.

The comet of 1744 was by far the most brilliant of the eighteenth century; it was seen on the 1st of March in full daylight, and had six tails, spread out like a fan across a large space in the heavens.

The great comet of 1811, which has caused the year of its appearance to be familiarly recognised as "the comet-year," had a nucleus 2537 miles in diameter; its head was 1,270,000 miles in diameter, and its tail 100,000,000 miles in length.

The comet of 1843, observed by Cassini, has been supposed to be identical with that of 1668, 1494, and 1317. At its perihelion it passes nearer to the sun than any other comet recorded in history, travelling at a rate of more than 40,000 miles a second. The heat that it thus receives is equal to that which 47,000 suns would communicate to the earth, and to such a degree does this prodigious temperature increase its density, that at its last appearance its tail was visible in broad daylight.

Donati's comet, which in 1858 shone with such brilliancy amongst the northern constellations, has a mass that has been estimated at '07 of that of the earth.

The comet of 1862 was adorned with luminous tufts or aigrettes, and resembled some fantastic mollusk.

The list is completed by the comet of 1868, the revolution of which occupies a period of no less than 2800 centuries, so that it may practically be considered as having vanished in infinite space.

Thirdly: the next section of the professor's dissertation was devoted to the probability of a collision between any one of these numerous comets and the earth.

As represented in plane diagrams, the orbits of planetary and cometary bodies appear continually to be intersecting one another; but in free space of three dimensions this is by no means necessarily the case; the planes of the orbits being inclined at various angles to the ecliptic, which

---

A selection of pages from *HECTOR SERVADAC* showing the level of research undertaken by Jules Verne in his determination to bring to the world's notice how serious the threat cometary impact was to Mankind.

Whence came it that the elements united in one deafening crash; that the earth groaned as though the whole framework of the globe were ruptured; that the waters roared from their innermost depths; that the air shrieked with all the fury of a cyclone?

Whence came it that a radiance, intenser than the effulgence of the Northern Lights, overspread the firmament, and momentarily dimmed the splendour of the brightest stars?

Whence came it that the Mediterranean, one instant emptied of its waters, was the next flooded with a foaming surge?

Whence came it that a new blazing spheroid, hitherto unknown to astronomy, now appeared suddenly in the firmament, though it were but to lose itself immediately behind masses of accumulated cloud?

What phenomenon was this that had produced a cataclysm so tremendous in its effects upon earth, sky, and sea?

Was it possible that a single human being could have survived the convulsion? and if so, could he explain its mystery?"

The comet Verne describes, slices off a section of the Earth and together with a few survivors, this comet and the Earth segment continue on the comet's path through the solar system.

The selected illustrations clearly show how intensely the story is connected to our enquiry. Furthermore, the pages reproduced prove convincingly that Verne was not in the slightest concerned as to whether his story was easily readable. To find page after page, devoted to astronomical data indicates that Verne was attempting something other than writing a bestseller. However, certain factors in these tedious lists, which would have been of little interest to his current readers, leapt out with startling clarity. We see references to **Whiston** and the comet of **1680** with its **575** year revolution. Equally, noticeable is the mention of the Tuttle (now called **Swift-Tuttle**) comet, which is estimated to impact the Earth either in **2116** or **2126 A.D.**

Our next task was to search the story to see if Verne had concealed a suggested date of impact. No date was given for the initial contact,but we found the evidence we needed in the only other place it could be.

As we have said, the comet continued on its elliptical orbit through the solar system and one of the survivors on board was an astronomer. He had calculated that the composite body would brush or re-impact the Earth on its return cycle, before plunging beyond the Sun into deep space.

These selected illustrations from *HECTOR SERVADAC* clearly portray Verne's determination to bring to his readers' attention the importance of what, in his day, was considered nothing but a celestial firework display.

It was therefore, to this very precise calculation that we turned our attention.

Obviously, having spent months on a rapidly rotating body our survivors could not speak in terms of Earth days, but paradoxically, the astronomer suddenly announced that he had calculated the moment of impact to be in **2** hours **47** minutes and **35.6** seconds. The sheer stupidity of this prediction was sufficient to show that Verne was waving the numbers before our eyes in the hope that they would be examined*. The seconds, particularly with their decimal point, are obviously irrelevant, as they would have changed even while the astronomer was speaking, but what of the numbers **2, 4, 7**? Were these numbers of the estimated impact time to be read in years and if so, from which starting date? It seems inevitable that one should count from the time the story was published - **1878**, and **247** years from that date is **2125 A.D.** a one year difference from one of the recently predicted Swift-Tuttle impact dates of **2126 A.D.** and a mere **132** years from now. Once again, the question arises as to why Verne would not go public and disclose his opinions openly. Was it fear of ridicule or was it something more sinister?

More and more evidence comes in from sources old and new and we will eventually show that the nature of the threat is clearly marked in the valley of Rennes-le-Château.

Before doing so, however, we feel impelled to explain why we appear to be so cynical in our dealings with Christian history. We would like to ask our readers to draw a sharp distinction between the Old and New Testament. Having studied the Bible more intently than most Christians, we accept the Old Testament as an attempt to accurately record history and for that reason, it has our respect. With sympathetic interpretation even the apparently outlandish books of *GENESIS* and *REVELATIONS* become most profound. It is of the New Testament we are critical and we will therefore, offer some of the evidence we have acquired to explain our attitude.

*Another 'Verne' way of seeing this number is 247.6. The orbital period of Pluto was reckoned to be 248 years until quite recently when a more accurate figure was given - 247.7 years. Pluto was discovered by chance when Clyde William Tombaugh of Lowell observatory was examining photographic plates of 'asteroids'. Surprisingly, the discovery was not made until February 18th 1930 whereas HECTOR SERVADAC was published in 1878 - 52 years earlier!

Is this another remarkable coincidence or does it add weight to the possibility of Verne having access to a hidden store of knowledge?

CHAPTER 20.
A TANGLED WEB

The great deception. Who was Lazarus? Another Bethany.
Discrepancies in the Scrolls. The brief Pope.

SHOULD 'a tangled web' be the motto of the Catholic Church? It may well seem to the reader that throughout this book and especially in the last chapter, that we have been attacking western religion at every opportunity. This may well be so, but it is not unjustified. Indeed, we have a lot to thank religion for and can state quite categorically that without it you would undoubtedly not be reading this or any other books at all. The reason being that the skills of reading and writing have, for all but the last two or three centuries, been part of the monopoly of knowledge held by the Church, no matter what its creed. However, this state of affairs has left the Church in the position of supreme judge of what common man can read and therefore think. If we believe (as most of us have been encouraged to do), that truth and honesty are an integral part of the teachings of the Church, then we have been cruelly deceived for, from its inception, the Church has been monopolised by the few to control the many and if that has necessitated obfuscation, omission or blatant deception, then the Church has never shrunk from using those methods of control. We fully realise that these are strong words, but wish to state that we, the authors of this book, have nothing against any religion which tells the truth. Indeed, if the Christian Church only practised what it preached as in 'I am the way, the truth and the life', then we would have little to argue about!

The means by which the Church has controlled education, thought and the expression of those thoughts has been achieved by limiting to 'club members', the opportunity to learn. Thus only those works approved of by the Church were available to the scholars. In this way, the myths and legends of the early Church were guaranteed to be disseminated to the population as a whole. Since those early days, theologians blessed with original minds, have questioned what was being served up to them, and realised the need to crosscheck other references of source material. However, as this material has mostly lain dormant in the great secret religious libraries of the world, access has been restricted to all but senior club members. The practical result of this is that for the past two millennia, very few individuals have been able to question the status quo. Throughout history the renegades who managed to voice their displeasure at the spreading of lies and half-truths, have conveniently been branded heretics and dealt with accordingly. We have no need to remind ourselves, of course, that throughout the Middle Ages the Roman Catholic Church knew exactly how to deal with such heretics - an 'examination' by the Inquisition before being burnt at the stake. Later, both Catholics and Protestants alike, dealt similarly with alleged practitioners of the 'old knowledge'....the witches.

Even today, in the latter part of the twentieth century, the honest man is not necessarily safe from the Church. The demise of Pope John Paul's predecessor, the Pope of 30 days who suddenly expired after attending a hastily arranged banquet to honour his announcement that he was going to open the secret libraries of the Vatican to the public, was not too shocking. Is it really surprising that before an autopsy could be carried out, the late Pope had been cremated? A night of the long spoons perhaps?

Less blatantly perhaps, but just as efficiently, the Church has in the past couple of centuries, tightened its grip on the world of publishing through either outright ownership or the placing of 'right-thinking' men on the boards of publishing companies. The next level of defence for the Church, has been its domination of the retail bookshop industry either by owning the bookshop, or more insidiously by owning the property in which the bookshops are situated. Although this may seem far-fetched, we experienced the power of this publishing monopoly when *GENISIS* was published. Although the book made it on to the market, promotions and agreed serialisation by a national Sunday tabloid newspaper were terminated at the eleventh hour (by which time it was too late to make alternative deals). A telephone call was received a few weeks later, expressing a complete lack of surprise that the serialisation had fallen through as the senior book reviewer was known to be a Jesuit! Phone calls were also received from Church officials who pressured the author to change his mind about any further publications. Lastly, we know of at least one major retailing chain who, having taken delivery of a stock of *GENISIS*, eventually returned them as unsold, despite the fact that their branch managers had been placing orders with the warehouse. This was exposed by our distributors receiving direct orders from the branches, having been told the book was not in the warehouse.

For publishing this last paragraph, we might be thought to be suffering from an advanced case of paranoia, but this is not so. The really hard-hitting books on religion are seldom found on retail bookshelves in England. To make this point in depth, remember the earlier chapter where we touched upon the decipherment of the Egyptian hieroglyphics by the French scholar, Champollion. The Church, over the last two millennia has managed to control reading, writing and education, but they did not know that other societies, like the Egyptians had recorded their history by incising hieroglyphs into the stone edifices of their temple buildings and monuments. Likewise, the discovery of the Sumerian clay tablets, papyri and scrolls from the Dead Sea, Qumran and Hamra Dum (See Chapter 9), left time-bombs of Truth in place, waiting to explode the myths of the false religions. Once Champollion published his decipherment of the Rosetta Stone, museum curators around the world could examine the looted Egyptian artefacts in their 'care'. What they found sent a shock wave through governments and religious centres alike, for the stories which the Egyptians had inscribed on their monuments, were the same as those claimed to be the workings and miracles of Jesus Christ as written in the New Testament by the Christian Church. In other words, large sections of the Christian Bible's New Testament were already old wives tales to the Egyptians. In modern day parlance, when a story is lifted and presented as an original work it is called plagiarism and it is considered a criminal offence!

Additionally, other scholars today, would probably argue that some of these Egyptian tales were in their turn, only watered down versions of earlier Sumerian works. The problem is, that when scholarship exposed these 'minor' faults in the western religions, the Church, aided and abetted by government, decided to put the lid back on and ignored the chance of setting the record straight. Why? Because they possibly felt vulnerable and did not consider for one moment that the population might be adult enough to accept the mistakes of misinterpretation over the years? Or, perhaps they believed that they might lose some of their power over the people? Unfortunately, their choice was not quite as simple as at first appears, because if Christian New Testament stories have Egyptian/Sumerian sun and planet worshipping origins, then the beliefs that we are asked to share today are those which could best be described as Pagan, and the greatest oppressor of Paganism, since time immemorial has been the Church!

By now, many readers may possibly feel incensed by the inferences of this chapter, but we would not have made them if we were not prepared to offer one or two of the proofs by eminent writers/philosophers who have led us to arrive at this viewpoint. If we ask ourselves where our modern day view of Christianity comes from, we would inevitably have to say the *King James Bible*. This was the first 'modern' printing, which made the work intelligible in the English language and available to the masses. This fine edition of a wonderful story book was itself culled from earlier bibles which themselves had been copied from even earlier versions by the medieval monks. These monks, in turn, were working from codices, scrolls and other sources, carefully copying, word for word in order to make more copies of the sacred books. Apart from there being a few mistakes in interpretation, the entire subject was limited by one insurmountable fact, that none of the original gospels on which the bible is partially based has been dated to within 40 years of the alleged death of the alleged Christ. This might be considered by some as a possible flaw in the foundations of the Christian religion.

Another problem which faces the independent theological scholar is that the chroniclers of the early Christian era might be said to have had a vested interest in the way the story was presented. A modern equivalent might be to have only consulted the memoirs of Hitler, Himmler, Goebels and Hess for their account of the Second World War, some forty years after it had been concluded. Would we not have expected at least some distortions and memory lapses from such an account? Of one thing we can be sure; it would be a vastly different account from one given by an allied forces commander or a concentration camp survivor. A historian would need to seek a balanced view from all the sources available to him and could never accept an obviously biased account as 'truth'. In effect, there have been few if any, 'source' accounts from the time of the alleged Christ which have so far come to light. What there are mostly come from the Christian side, and we know that these were seriously edited at the Council of Nicea in 345 A.D. when only those documents which agreed with and supported the official viewpoint of Christianity, were incorporated into the early bible. Several works which were available then, such as the Gospels according to Peter and Thomas were deliberately excluded. It is reasonable to ask why, but the situation remained thus until the decipherment of the Rosetta stone by Champollion and the discovery of various scrolls during the last 100 years.

The Dead Sea Scrolls presented a unique opportunity and danger to the orthodox Church. Once they had been discovered in caves near to Qumran in 1947 and dated to approximately the time of Christ, the Church was faced with a dilemma. Would open examination by a team of international experts confirm the accepted story of Christianity as promulgated by Rome since 345 A.D.? The pressure must have been immense, for such selected editing as had been used at Nicea could eventually come under scrutiny from the world's scholars. Rome no longer had such clear control.

By 1949, control of the scrolls had effectively fallen into the hands of the Department of Antiquities for Transjordan and Arab Palestine, under its director, Gerald Lancaster Harding and the Dominican sponsored Ecole Biblique under its director, Father Roland de Vaux. From 1947 until 1952 the site was plundered by marauding Bedouin who sold their discoveries to the highest bidder. Indeed, it was not until March 1952 that an organised search of the Qumran site was launched by de Vaux. Although this expedition was late in the day, it did produce one quality find - the Copper Scroll in cave 3. It took another three years before permission to cut open the scroll was granted, and the operation was performed in Manchester by John Allegro. When it had been translated, it turned out to be an inventory of treasure and its locations. Some think it was an inventory of the treasure of the Temple of Solomon. Further finds occurred over the next few years, but by 1959 most of the scroll fragments had been gathered together in a room known as the scrollery in the Rockefeller Museum in Jerusalem. Shortly before the Palestinian Mandate expired, the international board was set up, comprising representatives from the various archaeological schools located in Jerusalem. These consisted of the Albright Institute (USA), the Ecole Biblique, (France) and the British Palestine Exploration Society. The Rockefeller Museum and scrollery were nationalised in 1966 by the Jordanian government, but in 1967, as a result of the Six Day War, the museum fell into Israeli hands.

By 1955, several facsimile copies of the first three scrolls had been published in America and whilst Metropolitan Samuel, 'owner' of the fourth scroll refused to let it be published, an advert appeared in the Wall Street Journal, offering all four scrolls for sale. Yigael Yadin (a former Israeli military Chief of Staff, but by then a qualified archaeologist), was tipped off about the advert and using a pseudonym, purchased the scrolls for Israel for $ 250,000. The scrolls were then returned to Israel where they joined three scrolls found earlier at Qumran, in the Shrine of the Book. By the end of 1954 therefore, there were two separate teams working on the scroll material - the Israelis, working on seven scrolls in West Jerusalem and the Rockefeller Museum working on the facsimiles of the three original scrolls and various fragments of others in East Jerusalem. There was, of course, little contact between any of the eminent members of either team. The status quo was preserved until the Three Day War in 1967 when the Israelis captured the Rockefeller scrolls as a spoil of war. An additional scroll, the Temple Scroll was recovered in 1968 and published in 1977.

During an interview with David Pryce Jones about the work on the scrolls in general, Father de Vaux admitted amongst other things, that he had always refused to let any Jew examine the scrolls whilst they were under his control.

Later however, as a result of discussions between Yadin and Professor Biran (Director of the Israeli Department of Antiquities, 1961-1974), it was decided to maintain the status quo by leaving the scrolls in the charge of de Vaux, on the condition that their publication be speeded up. De Vaux was later to become Editor in Chief of the Dead Sea Scrolls and remained prominent in the field until his death in 1977. Curiously, his obituaries revealed that he had studied for the priesthood between 1925 and 1928 at St. Sulpice, Paris!

The International team appointed under the auspices of de Vaux, consisted of American Professor Frank Cross (McCormick Theological Society, Chicago and the Albright Institute), who was assigned some biblical scroll commentaries from cave 4 at Qumran; American Monsignor Patrick Skehan, (Director of the Albright Institute), similar material; Father Jean Starcky, (French, Ecole Biblique), Aramaic material; Dr. Claus-Hunno Hunzinger, (German, a papyrus expert; Father Joseph Milik, a Polish priest re-settled in France (confidant of de Vaux), to whom was assigned the Old Testament apocrypha and sectarian (Qumran) material and John M.Allegro, a Ph.D. scholar from Oxford, a philologist (and the only agnostic member of the team). His material was sectarian in nature and consisted of the psalms, sermons and exhortations of a moral and poetic character and the Copper Scroll.

Although the material was distributed to these experts according to their particular skills, there was soon a division of opinion as to what should be released to the public. Very simply, Allegro was in favour of publishing everything as it was translated, whereas the other team members were anxious that any material published should support the orthodox views of Christianity. The net result was that Allegro left the team and was replaced by John Strugnell who became a disciple of Frank Cross. Allegro went on to write *The Dead Sea Scrolls* and the infamous *The Sacred Mushroom and the Cross*, whereby he explained that he thought that several of the early religious sects, including Christianity, were based on the hallucinatory experiences of their members caused by the partaking of hallucinogenic mushrooms. Needless to say, Allegro was soon out in the academic cold. The one person in the team, with no cross to bear; the one person with an expertise in philology, the science of language, had placed himself beyond the pale.

In 1955, the distinguished American literary and cultural critic, Edmund Wilson, published a lengthy article for the New Yorker magazine, on the Dead Sea Scrolls. Although he was not an acknowledged authority on the subject, he was well-known and respected in academic circles and his reputation was solid gold. For the general public at least, his outsider's overview must have brought a breath of fresh spring air to the subject. Wilson expanded the article into a book and in 1969, added fresh material which doubled the size of the original work.

In his book, *The Scrolls from the Dead Sea*, 1969, Wilson commented on the reluctance of the international team to draw obvious conclusions from the evidence and noted their determination to distance the contents of the scrolls both from Christianity and Judaism. He commented thus:-

"One would like to see these problems discussed; and in the meantime, one cannot but ask oneself whether the scholars who have been working on the scrolls - so many of whom have taken Christian orders or have been trained in the rabbinical tradition -

may not have been somewhat inhibited in dealing with such
questions as these by their various religious commitments...one
feels a certain nervousness, a reluctance to take hold of the
subject and to place it in historical perspective."

Here, whilst being academically 'kind' to the experts, could Wilson be
hinting that they were not being objective about their task and are thus
protecting the vested interests of their religious masters?

It would seem that the background to these comments by Edmund Wilson
can be traced back to the magazine article of 1959, a time shortly prior to the
series of radio programmes in Northern England by John Allegro, the one
member of the team with no religious background. Before the broadcasts,
Allegro wrote to Professor Strugnell (Benoit's successor and the new
International team leader), that "I think we can look for fireworks" - a remark
which put the International team squarely on its guard. Apparently, at this time,
Strugnell (another British team member), was seriously considering a career in
the Church. Allegro continued in his letter:-

"I shouldn't worry about that theological job if I were you: by the
time I've finished, there won't be any Church left for you to join".

Although the first and second radio broadcasts received little attention, the
third was reported in 1956 by the New York Times.

"The origins of some Christian ritual and doctrines can be seen in
the documents of an extremist Jewish sect that existed for more
than 100 years before the birth of Jesus Christ. This is the
interpretation placed on the 'fabulous' collection of Dead Sea
Scrolls by one of an international team of seven scholars...John
Allegro said last night in a broadcast that the historical basis of the
Lord's Supper and part at least of the Lord's prayer and the New
Testament teachings of Jesus were attributable to the
Qumranians."

And so the battle was joined, with people like Allegro and Edmund Wilson
pressing for open disclosure and the members of the international team
slowing the whole process down, obfuscating the truth so skillfully that even
as recently as 1989, the world was still waiting for full publication of the
scrolls.

However, not all is lost. Throughout the last century, various finds have
been discovered in the 'Holy Land' and scholars who have studied the Egyptian
hieroglyphs in detail have published their work. We shall cite one such scholar

and one such discovery.

The American philosopher Alvin Boyd Kuhn wrote his master-work *The Lost Light* in the 1930's. It is an erudite work concerned with the comparison of tales, myths and legends of the Christians with the Egyptians. In the introduction to his book he recounts the following story of the raising of Lazarus. Now, being an erudite scholar, he offers the reader the choice of reading the story in Hebrew, Greek, Egyptian Hieroglyph or Egyptian Demotic. There are two versions. According to the Bible, Christ (the Son of God) was summoned to Bethany where Lazarus had been taken seriously ill and had subsequently died. Christ entered the chamber where Lazarus lay and resurrected him. The salient points to remember are the place, Bethany; the man, Lazarus and the man who did the raising, Jesus Christ, the Son of God. Now, unfortunately for the Christian Church, the following story had been deciphered from the Egyptian Hieroglyphs (courtesy of Champollion).

"The Lord Osiris died and was raised from the dead by Horus at a place called Beth-a-nu"

This is how Kuhn explains it. The Egyptians had an understanding of the creation of the universe. In the Beginning was the Void which was called NU. The first speck of matter which appeared in the Void was called A-NU and the place where this occurred was referred to as 'The place (house) of con-cretization'. Osiris, a familiar member of the Egyptian pantheon of gods was also known as the Lord Azar and his son was Horus.

It was usual for a god to be denoted by the prefix or suffix of the letters EL to their name by the Hebrews. So another way of referring to the Lord (God) Azar was to call him EL-AZAR. Similarly, the Greeks added the second declension (masculine) to this name which is denoted by the suffix of US. Therefore, Osiris becomes AZAR then EL-AZAR and finally EL-AZAR-US. As to the place where the miracle happened, the Hebrew for 'place' and 'house' is the same word BETH. It does not require much perspicacity to leap from 'The Place of concretization, BETH-A-NU' to the Hebrew BETHANY. As for the 'Son of God' who does the raising, it is the Horus of the Egyptians, the son of the 'Gods', Osiris and Isis and the Christ of the Christians.

Faced with the compelling evidence that the Egyptians had recorded the same miracle, using the same characters in the same place, Kuhn speculated that the New Testament version was but a repeat of a far older miracle of the Egyptians. The rest of *The Lost Light* compares countless other examples of the Christian Church lifting their stories from older versions. The story of Lazarus is one of the main miracles attributed to Jesus Christ and if, as has been shown, it was not true, then how many other deeds attributed to Jesus Christ may also be untrue, especially when we now know that the 'miracles' of the New Testament were standard work for the Egyptian priests, and that the re-enactment of particular 'miracles' was part of the diet of the Essenes, the religious sect to which Christ according to some, may have belonged?

In 1989, the academic Dead Sea Scroll community was still awaiting the publication of the scroll material, some 42 years after it had first been discovered. Another scholar who studied the material, Steve Wilson, Ph.D. Religion and Philosophy, sums it up, thus:-

> "The Dead Sea Scrolls are the records of a sect that included Jesus and James as its leaders. Internal evidence shows this clearly. The sect was established by John the Baptist as a revival of the Maccabean Zealotism with the family of Joseph as its Messiah-family. However, James, the hope of the Zealots, was killed in Jerusalem and the Zealots rose, taking the treasure of the temple into the desert when Jerusalem fell. Finally the first uprising died at Masada. But the sect continued until the death of Bar-Kochba.
>
> In the meantime, an infiltrator, Saul, had gone to Qumran,code-named Damascus,with the authority of the high priest, who had no authority whatsoever in the real Damascus. There, he began changing the message, claiming that Jesus had been somehow so special that James could not replace him. He was expelled from the Qumran community, but travelled abroad spreading a new false religion now called Christianity. With it he created a bastardised cult that was eventually to prove so useful to the Roman Empire that it was adopted as the official religion. As far as possible, all dissenting literature was suppressed, or altered when it was too well known.
>
> The discoveries at Qumran altered this. The other side of the story became known. The result is that the Catholic Church has been sitting on the true records of early Christianity with the perhaps reluctant connivance of an Israeli establishment unwilling to have Masada seen as the sacrifice not of ordinary Jews, but of the first Christians, no matter how Jewish their religion was.
>
> Now the situation is changing. Photographic records are being circulated freely by academics, and the unofficial translators are at work. It is certain that new revelations about the sect that awaited the Son of the Star, the Son of God, begotten of God, will surface soon.
>
> ...There are many great religions in the world. Those with more than a century of existence and more than ten million members

are easy enough to list. They are Christianity, Taoism, Judaism, Islam, Hinduism, Buddhism, Confucianism and Sikhism. Their founders are Jesus, Mahomet, Manu, LaoTse, Moses, Nanak, Kung Fu Tse and Gautama. Jesus sticks out like a sore thumb for two reasons. He has more followers than anyone else and yet, in spite of being from a priestly and royal background, and being familiar with all the scriptures, he never actually wrote anything himself. Or did he?"

(*Philosoforum - The Dead Sea Scrolls and the Lost Religion* by Steve Wilson.)

In a way, it is interesting to note that nothing has changed. Are the international team merely retracing the footsteps of the scholars who prepared and edited the sacred texts for the Council of Nicea? It is a point to consider. But there are chinks of light which are slowly illuminating the gloom of millennia past. Erudite and honest scholars have been picking their way through the detritus of the religious minefield. Kuhn, basing his writings on the translations and comparisons of Egyptian, Greek and Hebrew texts; John Allegro, Edmund Wilson and John Wilson and many others, accurately interpreting the scrolls. One day, perhaps the whole truth will be known.

For the full story of the discovery of the Dead Sea Scrolls and how they eventually came under the control of the international team and Rome, we recommend *The Dead Sea Scrolls* by John Allegro and *The Dead Sea Scrolls Deception* by Baigent and Leigh.

CHAPTER 21
THE SHADOW OF THE REICH

Hoerbiger, another Führer? Thule, Vril & the hollow Earth.
The search for Magic. Götterdämmerung - Twilight of the Gods.

ALTHOUGH our main concern is to place on record the undeniable mathematical design of the Temple of Rennes-le-Château, the reader will recall that we promised to include in this work, certain information that indicates there may also be material treasures connected with the mystery. To understand this, we must first know something of the motives of some at least, of the treasure hunters. In this case, they were high ranking officers of the Third Reich, who, like ourselves, would have been fascinated with the mystery of Rennes-le-Château, as it seems to concern the very origins of Man, a subject which we know so intrigued Adolf Hitler. It is to this subject we must now return.

At this time, it would be wise to sketch in some of the background of the various occult societies in Europe from the 1880's until 1939, and in particular to understand something of the idealistic scientific and occult driving forces of the Third Reich. By the end of the nineteenth century, Darwinism had already swept through the intelligentsia and had largely displaced the original biblical thoughts of divine creation. Once the religious strait-jacket had been removed, the way lay open for other, more exotic ideas to take hold. Thus, the late nineteenth century saw the rise of the Theosophists under Madame H.P. Blavatsky and secret organisations such as The Golden Dawn came into being. Each organisation inherited knowledge and rituals from the much older Rosicrucian Society, including some hermetic or alchemical practices.

For Western Europe it was a period of great unrest. The First World War and its carnage had taken a terrible toll on the populations, and this had been followed by Revolution in Russia and the Great Depression at home and in America. Defeated Germany suffered rampant inflation and in Britain, the families of the unemployed were starving to death. The civilised world's comfortable set of values had been shown to be worthless, and the nations were primed to react violently. Into this vacuum, the secret societies of the intelligentsia were swiftly drawn and left to ferment.

It is easy to ridicule societies with such backgrounds, but it is not until we consider the membership of organisations such as these that we can even imagine their potential. The Golden Dawn, created in 1887 was an offshoot of the English Rosicrucian Society, founded by Robert Wentworth Little some twenty years previously. The original movement had boasted 144 members including the famous author, Bulwer-Lytton of *The Last Days of Pompeii* fame. Most members were Freemasons. The Golden Dawn had a much smaller membership, but this membership was dedicated to the practice of ceremonial magic and the acquisition of initiatory knowledge and power. Its leading lights included Woodman, Westcott and Samuel Mathers. As a society, it kept in touch with similar organisations in Germany and Austria, including Rudolf Steiner's anthropological movement. The Ordo Templi Orientis (an offshoot of the Golden Dawn), later came under the leadership of Aleister Crowley, who promoted a theme of neo-paganism in the society, a theme which was later taken up and developed by the Nazis! At this time, the membership list of The Golden Dawn read like a scroll of honour :-

"Samuel Mathers, his successor, W.B.Yeats, the Nobel prize winning poet, Arthur Machen (author), Florence Farr (Theatre director and intimate friend of G. B. Shaw), Algernon Blackwood, Bram Stoker (author of *Dracula*), Sax Rohmer (author), Peck (Astronomer Royal of Scotland), the celebrated engineer Allan Bennett and Sir Gerald Kelly, President of the Royal Academy."

It was therefore, a time when the intellectuals of the western world, having witnessed the demise of the old world values as promulgated by the Church, oversaw the birth of a new set of sciences, some of which confirmed alchemical and hermetic ideas which had hitherto been shunned by society.

In Austria, Adolf Hitler too had been intrigued by occult matters since his youth, whilst he was a student in Vienna. He had studied the subject seriously, choosing to follow the 'left hand path', using the drug mescalin for quicker results. During his student days, he had visited the Hofburg museum and had become captivated by the Spear of Longinus, (see *The Spear of Destiny* by Trevor Ravenscroft). This spear, covered with runic inscriptions,is allegedly the spear with which the Roman centurion Longinus, had pierced the side of the crucified Christ, to put him out of his misery. The legends relate to how this spear has been possessed by all the great leaders of history, including Charlemagne, and that it only fell from their possession just before their death. On one such visit to the Hofburg, Hitler had evidently sworn to possess the spear one day. Indeed, much later, when German 'protective' forces moved into Austria, Hitler had the Spear of Destiny taken into safe keeping.

Having feasted on the hidden intrigues of the occult movements, Hitler decided to go several stages further. He planned to create a society which eschewed any idea based on Judaeo-Marxist scientific lines in favour of those founded on occult ideals. Added to this was his profound belief that Man had somehow lost his way in the development of the world, and that the ideal man was half man, half god as in the Norse legends of old. Thus started his idea of purifying humanity in general, and the German race in particular.

Although he would later approach the idea of engineering such a perfect man through genetic manipulation, Hitler started by combing the population for his ideal Aryan archetype, the blue-eyed blond. Because blue-eyed blondes are never the obvious result of the colouring of their parents, it was thought that such people were only born as an atavistic throw-back to the times when the gods were on the Earth. Before we dismiss this as a mad idea, the reference in *GENESIS* should be remembered:-

"And the Sons of the Gods looked unto the daughters of men and saw that they were fair and took them to wife."

Hitler's theory was evidently simple. Collect such blue-eyed blond specimens as you could find and encourage them to breed, thus producing a larger proportion of the 'master race' in the population than nature would normally provide. This would form the basis of the breeding stock. It must be said that Hitler was not alone in his intentions of re-creating the 'superman', at one remove from the gods.

In a previous chapter we discussed 'Mitochondrial Eves' as being the founding series of females on Earth circa 200,000 years ago, and referred to the possible genetic manipulation and creation of the 'homo sapiens sapiens' species at that time. We should be aware however, that 'Eve' would only account for half of the genetic material. The other half must have come from the super 'male' progenitor, or if we are to believe the Bible and other ancient accounts, from the gods.

As each generation was engendered, the original 'god' given genes were watered down. After thirty generations, only a minute fraction of all human sperm would represent the 'god- seed' and the odds of producing an 'avatar' or advanced being were significantly reduced with each succeeding generation. After 200,000 years and perhaps 600 generations or so, the chance would be infinitesimally small, though not impossible. Indeed, expert readings of ancient texts do hint at methods by which these odds can be improved, methods which involved the use of virgins in temples and sexual techniques now positively discouraged by the Catholic Church. Suffice to say, that if one were to succeed, then one might occasionally produce one of the super intelligent avatars mentioned in earlier chapters.

Hitler, of course, through his Aryan selections, was trying to breed out the unwanted qualities in Man and thus magnify the chance of obtaining the mutation he wanted. Later in the war, doctors under Josef Mengele began genetic experimentation in the death camps. It is thought that they succeeded in various cloning experiments but did not have sufficient time to attain their final goals.

Hitler, thus primed by being surrounded by such strange thoughts, interested himself in any scientist or philosopher who came to his notice with a half-credible but unorthodox idea based on anything except regular Judaeo-Marxist science. To such men he was predisposed to at least give them hearing. One such scientist, a fellow Austrian named Hoerbiger, did come to Hitler's attention and the resulting meeting may explain many of the subsequent actions of the little corporal.

Hoerbiger's theory was that our current moon is but the latest of a series of moons which have been captured by the Earth and that it originally was a planet called Lunar which passed on an elliptical orbit between Earth and Mars. As the orbit of Lunar gradually decayed, causing it to pass ever closer to Earth, there were a series of increasing catastrophic effects on the surface of Earth, resulting in the floods we have previously referred to. Hoerbiger also predicted that in the fullness of time, Lunar would inevitably crash into the Earth causing an even greater cataclysm. His theory also states that our solar system works on a similar principle with material first being ejected from the Sun, then cooling to form the planets, which eventually spiral back into the surface of the Sun, thus repeating the whole chain reaction. Hoerbiger also believed that the planets were basically made of ice and that the cosmic struggle between planets and Sun was really a contest between fire and ice. Although this may seem a fantastic idea, especially with the advantage of hindsight, Hitler is reported to have said:-

"We are often abused for being the enemies of the mind and spirit. Well, that is what we are, but in a far deeper sense than bourgeois science, in its idiotic pride, could ever imagine."

In 1933, one of the world's leading German rocket engineers, Dr. Willy Ley, fled to England, bringing news that apart from all the other dark forebodings which were then being experienced in Germany, a small spiritual group, based on the premises of Bulwer-Lytton's *The Coming Race*, had been founded in Germany. The ideals of this group were that there existed on Earth, a race of men far superior to common man, and that this creature was endowed with special psychic powers which made them almost godlike. At the time, this super race was thought to be hiding in caves in the centre of the Earth, biding their time for the moment when they could take over. The disciples of the German group believed that they possessed secret occult knowledge which would enable them to change the German race and become the equals of the super race. The group specialised in preparing themselves 'spiritually' for their coming time, by various meditation routines, which included staring for long periods at an apple, cut in half - a throw back to the Pythagoreans perhaps! This group styled itself as the Berlin Lodge and was otherwise known as the

Vril Society. The society was of course, associated with various Theosophical and Rosicrucian groups.

Through the founder member of the English Rosicrucian Society, Wentworth Little, contacts were forged with the German Rosicrucians and through the work *The Coming Race* by his disciple, Bulwer-Lytton. The same pre-Nazi German Rosicrucian society was enamoured of tales of mysticism, including stories of superhumans who would one day supplant Mankind and mutate into a master race. According to Dr. Achille Delmas, Adolf Hitler had been trying to create a biological mutation which would result in an exaltation of supermen and the appearance of a new race of heroes, demigods and god-men.

These references to underground super-races touch various nerves in both eastern and western ancient literature. The old records are full of them, whether they come from within the Earth or from other planets; the tales of giants and incredible beings populate the records from Tibet to the lands of the Norse. The Welsh author Arthur Machen (a leading member of the Golden Dawn), had often referred to such supermen in his writings, a theme later echoed by H. P. Lovecraft in his several books. One thing is certain. Not only did Hitler share this belief, but he also claimed to have met with such superior beings!

It is well to remind ourselves here that the founder of The Golden Dawn, Samuel Mathers, also claimed to have been in communication with these 'Unknown Supermen'. In his manifesto *Members of the Second Order*, published in 1896, he stated:-

> "As to the Secret Chiefs with whom I am in touch and from whom I have received the wisdom of the Second Order which I communicated to you, I can tell you nothing. I do not even know their Earthly names and I have very seldom seen them in their physical bodies..."

In a conversation Hitler had with Rauschning, the Governor of Danzig, about the problems of mutations in the human race, Rauschning not being aware of the Führer's strange predilections, answered as if he was referring to livestock. Hitler reportedly added that:-

> "The new man is living amongst us now! He is here. Isn't that enough for you? I will tell you a secret. I have seen the new man. He is intrepid and cruel. I was afraid of him."

> "In uttering these words," added Rauschning, "Hitler was trembling in a kind of ecstasy."

Although historians may fight shy of recognising any similarities between the Rosicrucians, Bulwer-Lytton, Little, Samuel Mathers, Aleister Crowley,

Gurdjiheff and Helena Blavatsky, history may not be so kind, for the same essence pervades them all - the occult and the 'superman'. The main difference between them is that Hitler was prepared to gamble the lives of twenty million people to prove that he was right.

The Rosicrucians, the Golden Dawn, the German Vril Society and the Thule Group (which later consisted of Haushofer, Rudolf Hess and Hitler), were all based on the Theosophical Society, which added eastern and Hindu terminology to the neo-pagan magic and occultism. René Guénon, in his study *Le Theosophism, histoire d'une pseudo-religion*, published in 1921, foresaw the pitfalls of the movement and the dangers that lurked in the shadows, when he wrote:-

> "The false Messiahs we have seen so far have only performed very inferior miracles, and their disciples were probably not very difficult to convert. But who knows what the future has in store? ...But might there not be, behind all these movements, something far more dangerous which their leaders perhaps know nothing about, being themselves in turn, the unconscious tools of a higher power? "

With Hitler therefore predisposed towards neo-paganism and shunning accepted science whilst attempting to mutate the Germanic peoples into a race of superhumans, the stage was set for two more strange theories, the frozen world and the hollow Earth. In the high summer of 1925, scientists throughout Germany and Austria received copies of the following letter:-

> "The time has come for you to choose - whether to be with us or against us. While Hitler is cleaning up politics, Hans Hoerbiger will sweep out of the way the bogus sciences. The doctrine of eternal ice will be a sign of the regeneration of the German people. Beware! Come over to our side before it is too late!"
>
> *(Hans Hoerbiger)*

Hoerbiger's expounded doctrine, 'Welteislehre' or 'eternal ice', ran completely contrary to accepted explanations of the cosmos. Yet although Hoerbiger, above all else, considered himself a scientist, he also thought that mainline science was travelling in the wrong direction. His main proposal was that science should only be practised by prophets, since as enlightened beings they had already risen to levels of higher consciousness. Hoerbiger thus prepared the way for 'enlightened' apprehension, an irrational and visionary form of knowledge. He was not alone in his views. Hitler and Himmler had found their astrologer and later named him Führer, appointing him, after they had seized power, as 'plenipotentiary of mathematics, astronomy and physics'.

Until he was thus acclaimed, however, Hoerbiger supported by almost unlimited funds from the Nazi Party, had employed thugs to break up orthodox scientific meetings, and paid people to bombard scientific institutes with leaflets carrying such warnings as :-

"When we have won, you and your like will be begging in the gutter".

Later, any business or firm engaging a new employee had to get them to sign a declaration which read:-

"I swear that I believe in the theory of eternal ice."

He later wrote to leading industrialists:-

"Either you will learn to believe in me, or you will be treated as an enemy."

To begin with, scientists at the universities protested vehemently that Hoerbiger's ideas were simply impossible, but after Hitler had taken power, few dared oppose his edicts openly. Indeed, some of Germany's leading scientists, such as Leonard (whom with Roëntgen had discovered X-Rays), and the physicists Oberth and Stark (spectroscopy), quickly embraced the 'eternal ice' theory. As a result of this, Hitler openly supported Hoerbiger and issued such statements as ;-

"Our Nordic ancestors grew strong amidst the ice and snow, and this is why a belief in a world of ice is the natural heritage of Nordic men."

(Adolf Hitler, "Wel" magazine).

The two infamous Austrians, Hitler and Hoerbiger drove out the cream of Germany's intelligentsia; Hitler, the Jewish politicians and Hoerbiger, the Jewish scientists. The Austrian amateurs had ousted the Jewish professionals and the world trembled as a result. The two men met on several occasions, Hoerbiger, being one of the very few who had told Hitler to 'shut up' and had lived to tell the tale. Hoerbiger planted the seed that Germany was being poisoned by western science and that their products, such as psychology, serology and relativity (all the products of Jewish scientists), were weapons directed against the ideals of Parzifal. However, he also added that his 'eternal ice' would provide the antidote. By destroying conventional science and astronomy, the rebirth of Magic would rise phoenix like from the ashes. Hoerbiger's closest ally in this was Rosenberg, and the two of them would enthuse on the twin subjects of National Socialism and 'eternal ice' whenever opportunity arose.

By emphasising that the history of Earth was dominated by episodes of destruction by flood, followed by great migrations that had resulted in a world dominated by giants and supermen, Hoerbiger's theories fitted in with those of

Heinrich Himmler and his ideas of a superior Aryan race. The mythologies according to Nietzsche and Wagner were also echoed here, and all supported the Magical ideals of the Nazi Party.

In all, Hoerbiger postulated that there have so far been four moons captured by Earth - the latest being Lunar - and that these match the great geological periods Primary, Secondary, Tertiary and the current Quaternary. All the periods have been marked by catastrophe, including the destruction of the dinosaurs. The gigantism which has resulted on Earth at these times, was, he postulated, the result of a weakened gravitational system caused by the capture of a moon. This, according to Hoerbiger is marked by the appearance of giant insects and grasses at the end of the Primary era and the appearance of the iguanadon, diplodocus and other creatures up to sixty feet long at the end of the Secondary period. Then, because of less gravity and the extreme height of creatures and flora, they would have received greater doses of cosmic rays causing species to mutate. This period Hoerbiger placed about fifteen million years ago as the age of the Giant. By the time the Tertiary moon had made its appearance, Hoerbiger claimed that Man had walked on to the world stage, but Man of normal stature. There were however, still giants in those days and it was they who civilised the little men and taught them agriculture, metallurgy, the arts and sciences and knowledge of the human soul. The collapse of the Tertiary moon occurred within relatively recent times and marked the extinction of Atlantis and the biblical flood of Noah, after which we enter our recorded histories.

However far-fetched Hoerbiger's theories may seem to us, the leading members of the Nazi Party accepted them as the truth and took them seriously enough to take them into consideration when working on their 'weapons of terror and destruction' programme. There was concern that a rocket might provoke a deluge on Earth if it interfered with the eternal ice which Hoerbiger had said would encircle the globe. As a result, testing at Peenemünde was delayed while checks were carried out. The hollow Earth theory was also tested when a series of Germany's top Nazi scientists travelled to the island of Ruengen in the Baltic Sea to test an infrared 'radar' system. It should be pointed out that leading Nazis believed not only that the Earth was hollow, but that its centre lay in the direction of the sky, and that the rocky crust beneath our feet was the only barrier between us and infinity. Flies caught on the inside surface of a goldfish bowl provide a good analogy. They were therefore convinced that if they pointed the equipment at 45 degrees, it would bounce off the centre (sky), and pick up an image many miles away. In one particular experiment they proposed to 'see' the fleet at Scapa Flow from the island. Needless to say, this particular experiment was somewhat less than successful, although infrared radar later served them quite well.

As to the Thule Society, this was the driving force behind the National Socialist German Workers Party. They were interested in the Nordic legends and myths as promulgated by Alfred Rosenberg in his book *The Myth of the Twentieth Century*, published in 1930. Rosenberg, through the Thule Society, rose to the offices of 'Deputy to the Führer of the National Socialist Party for the Entire Spiritual and Ideological training of the Party'. He was also 'Reichsminister for the Eastern Occupied Territories'. The Thule Society believed amongst other things that entrances to the hollow Earth lay at the poles, and several years after the war, the American Admiral Byrd claimed that he had indeed flown over a large area of almost subtropical vegetation, within a few hundred miles of the South Pole. Whatever the truth is of this claim, there are certainly records which show that many Nazi submarines, laden with various cargoes, headed for Antarctica towards the end of the war.

In the next chapter we will review certain claims which relate to the Third Reich having discovered considerable material treasure.

CHAPTER 22
OTTO RAHN

Otto goes touring. Skorzeny and Co.,- Raiders of the Found Ark?
The Quest for Parzifal. The Discovery of Montsalvat.
Templar, Cathar and Runic Graffiti. Deep-frozen treasure.

IN the last chapter we presented sufficient material to enable the reader to realise why the founders of the Third Reich were so esoterically involved with matters which unavoidably skirt the mysteries associated with the valley of Rennes-le-Château. Their interests were not however, confined to the ephemeral, for in this chapter we will see evidence of the tenacity with which they pursued the material associations of the valley.

Many assorted books on Rennes-le-Château mention that a battalion of German mining engineers made excavations in the area during World War Two. As we already had another strong link between the village and Richard Wagner, we decided to delve further. The trail led us to one Otto Rahn, a German, born in 1904 at Michelstadt, Germany. He attended university in Berlin, where he studied literature and philology (the science of language). During his youth, Otto Rahn had been attracted to studying in depth Wolfram von Eschenbach's Grail romance, *Parzifal* and the history of the Cathars. He became particularly intrigued by the mention of the Holy Grail being concealed, according to Parzifal, in the Holy mountain of Montsalvat. This was significant, especially when Rahn discovered that the Cathar stronghold of Montségur boasted a nearby gigantic cave known as Montsalvat. He was at least intrigued enough to devote much time and energy in checking out the coincidence.

Although Eschenbach could allegedly neither read nor write, the Parzifal story had been passed down through the years by the 'minnesingers', troubadours or minstrels of the medieval times. At any rate the records show that the story was first written down between 1200 and 1210, at least 33 years before the siege of Montségur.

After many deliberations over the story, it would seem that Otto Rahn reached the conclusion that the Montsalvat of the Grail poem was in reality, the Montségur of the Cathars and he decided to visit the area to continue his research.

During his travels to the region, checking out leads to the Holy Grail, German folk legends and the history of the Cathars, he came across an elderly former Austrian Army colonel, Karl Maria Wiligut-Weisthor, an expert on Germanic and pre-medieval history, runes, legends, magic and the occult.

Weisthor soon became Rahn's most trusted friend. It was to prove a historic encounter, for Wiligut (using the name Weisthor) later joined the SS in 1933 and was promoted to Brigadier General in 1936, at which point he became an advisor to Heinrich Himmler on occult matters, later becoming better known in the inner circles as Himmler's 'Rasputin'.

Into this weird maelstrom of neo-Nazi ideas strode Otto Rahn, little aware that the Cathars he was studying had already been claimed by leading National Socialists as the originators of many Nazi customs. Indeed, Hitler was so interested in the traditions and legends of the Middle Ages that he had already engaged composer Carl Orff to scour the medieval monasteries of Europe, to gather ancient chants and folk tunes. An amalgam of this material later became known as the famous Carmina Burana and was played at almost every rally. One can only imagine the response when, through his friend Weisthor's connection with Himmler, Otto Rahn announced that he was on to the location of the Holy Grail, the Treasures of the Temple of Solomon and the Ark of the Covenant - sacred relics without equal. Himmler and Co. must have been over Hoerbiger's moon!

Records show that Himmler and possibly the Thule Society agreed to finance Otto Rahn's trip to the Languedoc in 1931, where he stayed in the village of Lavelanet. On that he trip he evidently satisfied himself that Montségur was indeed the Montsalvat of the Parzifal legend. Although he had discovered various cave systems, he had not yet found any treasure. Nevertheless, he remained convinced that he was on the right trail. He had also found, deep in the cave system, drawings on the rock surface depicting Knights Templar, including one which featured a lance - possibly the lance of Longinus, the Spear of Destiny! The outcome of his early foray into Montségur was his first book *Crusade Against the Grail* published in 1933. In it, Rahn traced the story of what he had achieved so far and speculated that the evidence showed that there were two Grails - an Emerald Cup and a stone tablet. This latter artefact was supposedly inscribed with runes by a race of pre-German supermen who had attained the ultimate knowledge of the 'law of life'. They represented 'The Great Tradition' which was only valid for certain people, a theory which tied in with German legend and the beliefs of the Thule Society - that the far north was inhabited by the Hyperborean super race. Needless to say, the book found a ready made audience in Hitler, Rosenberg, Hess, Dietrich Ekhart, Himmler and other leading individuals!

In a letter written to Weisthor in September 1935, Otto Rahn informed his friend that he was at a place where he had reason to believe the Grail might be found, and that Weisthor should keep the matter secret with the exception of mentioning it to Himmler. Thus, over the next few years, Otto Rahn, historian and philologer, became inextricably involved with the hierarchy of the Nazi

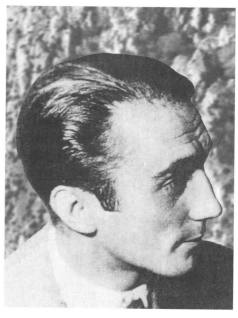

Above left: Reichsführer Heinrich Himmler was the power behind Rahn. Believing implicitly in Rahn's findings, he masterminded the expedition which supposedly found 'something'.

Above right: Otto Rahn, historical investigator achieved rapid recognition by the Nazi party for his research in the Languedoc. His conviction was that the Treasures of the Temple of Solomon were concealed in the area of Montségur.

Left: SS Colonel Otto Skorzeny - Head of Special Forces who carried out the daring mountain top rescue of Mussolini. Himmler entrusted Skorzeny with the task of removing a great treasure from Montségur in 1944.

party, meeting with Himmler, Alfred Rosenberg and Wolfram Sievers. He possibly did not realise that Adolf Hitler had been an avid student of the occult since his young days, and that the Führer's obsession would engulf his quest.

Otto Rahn returned to the area of Montségur for a short while in 1937, but by this time the ominous rumblings of an imminent war could be felt throughout Europe. Himmler, meanwhile, had encountered a Dr. Hermann Wirth, who gave him the idea of creating a unit to research German history. This was the Deutsches Ahnenerbe Society, which became totally dependent on the support of the SS. Rahn and Weisthor continued working on various projects, but having received no new assignments from Himmler for the previous four years, it was obvious that Rahn was considered untrustworthy as he was not an SS member. Rahn remedied the oversight by joining the SS Black Order as a private on March 12th 1936. As if by magic, once he had joined the SS club, doors began to open to Private Rahn. On April 20th 1936, he was promoted to sergeant without ever having been a corporal. Almost at once he received a mission to proceed to Iceland to investigate the land of Hyperborea.

Rahn's rise through the ranks was nothing short of spectacular. He made Technical Sergeant on January 30th 1937 and 2nd Lieutenant in the Black Order by April 20th 1937. His rise continued until September 11th 1938 when he was promoted 1st Lieutenant. His second book *Lucifer's Courtiers* was published in 1936 and soon became the bible of the National Socialist Party.

Meanwhile Himmler had chosen the Wewelsberg Castle in Bavaria to be the future home of the Longinus Spear, the Holy Grail and the other treasures of the Temple of Solomon of which Otto Rahn had spoken. However, it was too dangerous to move them in peace time. Better to wait for the coming war with France. Rahn's 1937 expedition to the Languedoc is therefore thought to have been just to make sure that the cache had remained undiscovered by anyone else.

On June 9th 1938, Rahn asked for and received leave of absence to write the sequel to *Lucifer's Courtiers*. From that moment on, his life took an unexpected turn for the worse. He had made his private views public - that he was opposed to the war and that instead, he thought Germany and then Europe should convert to Catharism! Opposition to the forthcoming war was tantamount to treason. On February 28th 1939, Otto Rahn wrote a letter of resignation to Gruppenführer Karl Wolff, Chief of Himmler's personal staff, telling of 'grave reasons' for his resignation which he would tell to the Reichsführer in person on his next visit to Berlin. His request was granted and his subsequent 'accidental' death was reported in the Berlin edition of the 'Volkischer Beobachter' on May 18th 1939 stating ... "that he had died tragically

in a snow storm during March 1939...signed WOLFF SS - Grüppenführer."
However the story of the Grail did not end with the death of Otto Rahn.

Although France was occupied by the Germans in June 1940, Himmler made no attempt to retrieve Otto Rahn's Grail from Montségur. Instead, excavation expeditions were dispatched by the Ahnenerbe to other territories which the Nazi forces had overrun, and one to Tibet to search for the origins of the Aryan race.

Himmler possibly thought that with the location of the treasure reasonably described, there was no reason to hurry. Why not wait until the whole of France was occupied - things would be even easier then. However, by late 1942, the Nazi forces had received several reversals of fortune including El Alamein, and in Czechoslovakia, the assassination of Heydrich. Allied forces had invaded Europe and suddenly time was running out to recover the treasure. So in June 1943, a gathering of experts appeared at Montségur and various other possible hiding places in the region of the Languedoc, including Rennes-le-Château. These experts consisted of historians, archaeologists and geologists. In the event, all of the teams came up empty handed. Himmler was left with few possibilities to consider. Had the treasure existed or not? If it did exist, then was it hidden in the area of Montségur and if that was the case, had it been located by Otto Rahn? The one thing that Himmler thought rang true was that Otto Rahn had determined the approximate location of the treasure and based on that belief, he concluded that the treasure must lie in some place that neither Otto Rahn nor his teams of experts had found.

Otto Rahn of course, could not be consulted because he had already had his 'accident' and Himmler realised that he needed a different approach to the problem and someone to tackle it laterally instead of head-on. One man came to mind - SS Colonel Otto Skorzeny. Skorzeny had a reputation for being a soldier's soldier, one who if he accepted a mission, usually never failed. Skorzeny had a unique approach to problem solving. He had been an engineer by profession and was also a gifted linguist. He leapt to fame by performing the successful, daring mountain top rescue of Mussolini at the end of the war - a feat which was considered impossible. Indeed, such was his daring that on several occasions he had met with David Stirling, founder of Britain's Special Air Service for coffee in various European cities, whilst the war was at its height.

Skorzeny also had an Intelligence background, having worked for Admiral Canaris, Chief of German Intelligence and had sometimes received his orders direct from Himmler. From April 20th 1943, he had been promoted as 'Chief of Germany's Special Troops', operating from a hunting lodge at Friendenthal in Bavaria. So it was that in February 1944, after several other missions, Skorzeny received a call from Himmler - to recover the treasure from Montségur. After making the necessary plans and briefing his men, Otto Skorzeny with a small commando force arrived in the Languedoc and set up base camp at Montségur. They spent the next several days reconnoitring the area, making several interesting discoveries, but none which revealed the treasure. Skorzeny then decided to ignore the places which Otto Rahn had reported and to concentrate on the illogical and the unlikely hiding places which would not easily present themselves. As Montségur castle sits atop a mountain peak approachable only on three sides, with a sheer drop of several thousand feet on the other, Skorzeny concentrated on the impossible precipice of the rock. After abseiling down the vertical rock face, he searched for and found, evidence of ancient tracks leading away from the foot of the mountain. By following these, he eventually discovered a walled-up cave, which, once broken open, allegedly revealed the treasure. According to *The Emerald Cup - Ark of Gold*, by Colonel Howard Buechner, Skorzeny then sent a message (probably by radio) to Himmler's headquarters in Berlin :-

"Ureka.. Signed Scar"

The reply swiftly followed:-

"Well done. Congratulations. Watch the sky
tomorrow at noon. Await our arrival.
Signed
Reichsführer - SS"

According to Buechner, Skorzeny had unwittingly discovered the treasure on the eve of the 700th anniversary of the fall of Montségur (March 16th 1244), and was surprised to come across a large gathering of Cathar descendants, heading for the castle to pay homage to their ancestors. The figure 700 was doubly important to these latter day Cathars for an ancient prophecy had foretold :-

"At the end of 700 years, the laurel will be green once more."

Whatever this strange phrase actually meant, an unusually large group had turned out for the anniversary. Although they had sought permission to go to the castle from the German Military Governor for the area, and had been refused, they nevertheless congregated at the foot of the mountain, ready for the long walk to the fortress ruins. At this moment, as luck would have it, Skorzeny and his small commando group stumbled across them. For a moment all must have seemed lost, but Skorzeny, when approached by the pilgrims for his permission, saw no reason to withhold it. Thus it was, that the group arrived at the fortress at mid-day, just at the time when Skorzeny had been told to "watch the sky".

Probably unseen by the crowd, a high-flying German aircraft, using skywriting equipment, 'painted' a huge Celtic Cross in the sky. To Skorzeny, it signalled that his mission was nearly over, but to the pilgrims in Montségur, a miracle had occurred.

The following day, an official delegation comprising of Reichsminister Alfred Rosenberg and Colonel Wolfram Sievers of the Ahnenerbe arrived to congratulate Skorzeny.

Arrangements were made for engineers to be brought to the treasure cache and for it to be taken back to the small town of Merkers, 40 miles from Berlin. And here, after it was catalogued by hand-picked members of the Ahnenerbe, most of it disappeared to various parts of the crumbling Reich. According to Colonel Howard Buechner, the catalogue of treasures included:-

"1. Thousands of gold coins...

2. Items which were believed to have come from the Temple of Solomon, which included the gold plates and fragments of wood which had once made up the Ark of Moses... a gold plated table, a candelabra with seven branches, a golden urn, a staff, a harp, a sword, innumerable golden plates and vessels, many small bells of gold and a number of precious jewels and onyx stones, some of which bore inscriptions...

3. Twelve stone tablets bearing pre-runic inscriptions which none of the experts were able to read. These items comprised the stone Grail of the Germans and of Otto Rahn.

4. A beautiful silvery Cup with an emerald-like base made of what appeared to be jasper. Three gold plaques on the Cup were inscribed with cuneiform script in an ancient language.

5. A large number of religious objects of various types... crosses from different periods which were of gold or silver and adorned with pearls and precious stones.

6. Precious stones in abundance in all shapes and sizes."

Once catalogued, many of the gold coins were melted down and turned into ingots and then the Nazis started to disperse the treasure around the world during the final days of the war. The town of Merkers fell to the 3rd US Army under General George Patton. His men soon discovered the nearby salt-mines in which the treasure had been concealed, and the amounts which they recovered may give some idea of the original size of the haul. When Generals Dwight D. Eisenhower, Omar Bradley and Patton personally inspected the mine, the official account later records:-

"...600 gold bars, 750 sacks of gold coins...many other valuables mostly in the form of paper money. The estimated worth of the treasure was $250,000,000 (by 1945 standards, when gold was selling at $ 35 per ounce)."

This of course, only represented the small portion of the treasure which had not been dispersed by the time the Americans arrived. Indeed, Buechner estimates the present day worth might be close to 60 billion dollars!

So what happened to the treasure of the millennia? According to Buechner, records show that some was dispatched to Antarctica (the Nazis' new Agharta) and other parts to South America, whilst some was buried deep beneath the Wewelsberg fortress in Bavaria and a bronze box, containing important documents was buried in a secret cave beneath the Schleigleiss Glacier near the Zillertal Mountain Pass in Bavaria. A final hoard is thought to have been hidden in the secret complex underneath Hitler's Berchtesgarden mountain retreat.

> "The last records show that the treasure of the Temple of Solomon was shipped from the Wewelsberg castle to Berchtesgarden in March 1945. It was trucked up the Obersalzberg and stored away in one or more of the many underground chambers which riddled the mountain. Here it was sealed into bunkers and placed under the continuous watchful eyes of a contingent of SS soldiers. When the bunkers were explored by troops of the US 101st., Airborne Division in the early days of May 1945 they found provisions and treasure in abundance but the Treasure of Solomon had disappeared."
>
> (*Emerald Cup - Ark of Gold* by Col.H.Buechner.)

Is this the last glimpse history will have of the Holy Grail and the treasure? Probably not, for experts have estimated that the Schleigleiss glacier is due to give up its secret by 1995, after which time, we expect the hunt to start all over again.

A word of caution. We are indebted to Col. H.Buechner for his story of Otto Rahn and the treasures of Montségur. We remain singularly impressed by the patience he has shown in waiting until 1991 to publish what must conceivably be the greatest treasure-hunt story of all time. As we write these closing chapters, history has seemingly undertaken us again, for in Time magazine, issue no. 43 dated October 25th 1993, an article by Michael Walsh has been written about the spoils of World War II and does not even mention the treasure of the Temple of Solomon. So whom should we believe, Buechner or Walsh? However, as it does not really concern us to comment on matters we cannot prove, we will return to things which we can and move from the little corporal who intended to become the King of the World, to he who really was Rex Mundi.

CHAPTER 23.
REX MUNDI (THE KING OF THE EARTH)

Another incredible find. The mark of Rex Mundi.
The cometary cycles. The Flood. The Precession. The great years.

W ITH the conviction that the geometry was a warning of the possibility of a celestial catastrophe, it was becoming increasingly urgent that we should search the geometric figure for information which would mathematically confirm both the period of the comet and its possible impact date. At first sight it would seem impossible to convey such data either geometrically or trigonometrically within the existing structure, but we had seen the designers' ingenuity at work before and were convinced that if, indeed, this was the message, we would eventually find it.

Even before the search began, we were aware that if the period were that of 575.72 years, which we had previously determined, we would still need a fixed date from which to begin the count. We were also of the conviction that further evidence would be forthcoming to associate the design with astronomical or geophysical phenomena.

Already we were being confronted with almost insurmountable evidence of a number of factors which fifty years ago, would have clashed with orthodox teaching and would also have been religiously unpalatable.

We had a complex and sophisticated geometry, apparently dating from the time of the Druids and interlaced with trigonometrical ratios in a totally unique fashion. The interactive ratios formed a mathematical matrix or canvas upon which information could be conveyed regardless of the units of measure employed by the discoverer. It will, nevertheless, be obvious to the reader that in a totally metric world the investigator would have been considerably handicapped.

The evidence produced in *GENISIS* together with the trigonometrical confirmation presented earlier in this book, leaves us in no doubt that we are dealing with a power zone of the destructive 'war-lord' SET. It would further appear that this was realised by the Roman Catholic Church in quite recent historical times and also by a number of powerful organisations including the Cathars and the Knights Templar. Even more recently, we have now established Jules Verne as one who, if not a custodian, was at least aware of the influence of the god SET and the threat he represents. Even undated, the recognition of the destruction which would result from cometary impact should be taken seriously. To ignore the warning on the grounds that 'it may not happen in my time' is irresponsible in the extreme. Parental care is a natural attribute that the greater majority share, but it is seldom extended through more than two generations. This is largely due to our brief life span which has so narrowed our concept of time. We would do well to be guided by the old adage, "He who plants an avenue of trees cannot, in the nature of things, expect to enjoy them".

During the recent Cold War when we rattled our nuclear sabres at each other, deep shelters were constructed to preserve certain elements of humanity. For very little cost, these could be moth-balled, to be re-activated when the threat appears. Thanks to the expertise of our astronomers and astrophysicists, the warning will be considerably longer than the four minutes for which we originally needed to plan.

Conditioned as we had become, by the designers of the figure, we knew that somewhere in its construction would lie their best estimate for the return of the Typhon. Furthermore, as with everything else they had shown us, we knew that once discovered it would probably be self-evident. Naturally, the most likely place to search was on the Meridian and those figures controlled by its position in the Temple layout.

The reader will recall how the length of the Meridian was established to be 600,000 Sin 56° as opposed to the more desirable 500,000 AUs which one would associate with the hypotenuse of the 3, 4, 5 Pythagorean triangle. The exact measure was therefore:- **497,422.5436**. In order to maintain the 681 Sine values of the Pythagorean triangle it is necessary to correct the sides represented by 300,000 and 400,000 to their precise length. To do this, one has only to reduce them in proportion to the hypotenuse.

The conversion factor is, of course, 0.994845087, resulting in 300,000 x 0.994845087 = 298,453.5261 and 400,000 x 0.994845087 = 397,938.0349. It is surprising, but surely only coincidental that this conversion factor (0.994845087) and its reciprocal (1.005181624) are also acceptable factors to convert Ancient Units to British Standard Inches and vice versa respectively.

Now these corrected figures **298,453.5261** and **397,938.0349** would, by the natural laws of mathematical ratio be bound to have Sin 56° as a factor and any mathematically minded person would, therefore, divide them by Sin 56° to find the other factor.

Hence **298,453.5261/Sin 56° = 360,000**, an obvious circular and pentagonal figure. The only other way to address this linear measure was to read it as an inverse-sine 0.2984535261 and the resultant angle is 17.365° which conveyed nothing to us. Applying the same reasoning to the hypotenuse or Meridian we have 600,000, an obvious time cycle and an inverse-sine of 29.83° which again was unidentifiable.

To summarise, therefore, by applying the Sine 56° factor to these two sides of the Pythagorean triangle, nothing is achieved by their anti-sine values, but both reveal the recognisable factors of 360 and 600 which are circular/pentagonal and cyclic/time respectively.

We will return to the 600 factor later but meanwhile what of the remaining side with the length of **397,938.0349**? Subjected to the Sin 56° multiple the result is 480,000, which contrary to the two previous sides is unrecognisable as having any association with the established geometry. As with the two previous tests, we then inverse-sined:-

0.397938034 with the result **23.44933816°** or **23° 27'**.

Once again David Wood's survey training came to the fore as he immediately recognised it as the 'Plane of the Ecliptic' for the Earth, which although generally referred to as 23° 30' is actually **23° 27'** precisely, as revealed in the 681 triangle of Rennes-le-Château.

A brief explanation of the discovery will convince the reader of its significance to our investigation. The Plane of the Ecliptic is the apparent path of the Sun in the celestial sphere. It is a 'great' circle and it makes an angle of 23° 27' with the celestial equator because the Earth's axis of rotation is tilted that amount from the perpendicular to the plane of the Earth's orbit round the Sun.

The illustration shows the tilt of the Earth's axis in relation to the Sun when the Earth is at those positions in its orbit which give rise to midsummer and midwinter, to an observer in the northern hemisphere.

The reason for this 'wobble' in the Earth's axis has never been fully understood, or for that matter, accurately determined, but suffice to say that it causes the axis of the Earth to describe a circle in the heavens, approximately every **26,000** years. It has been described as the effect of having 'knocked' a spinning top while it is spinning. This will cause the top to 'wobble' in the same manner as the Earth does.

Some have dared to suggest that it is the result of either a massive impact, a celestial close pass or of a polar magnetic change from which the Earth is slowly recovering. This would, of course, be supportive of all that we had found in the geometry of Rennes-le-Château, but unless the reader has already seen the closer correspondence, let us clarify the ominous connection.

The angle of the ecliptic which has the degree of 'wobble' (**23° 27'**) was exposed by the analysis of the **681** Pythagorean triangle which in turn was totally controlled by the hypotenuse of **SET**.

In simple terms the planet Earth's eccentricity is the mark of the Typhon! Little wonder he was given the title 'REX MUNDI', 'King of the Earth', by the Cathars. We should pause here to consider the genius of the designers in having used this mathematical anomaly as a way to convey so precisely the

THE ECLIPTIC

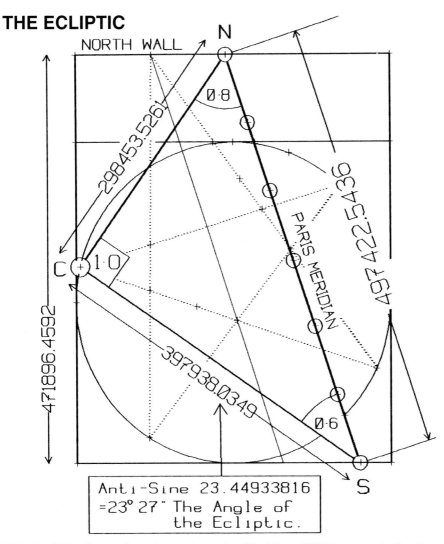

NORTH WALL

N

0·8

298453.5261

467 422.5436

PARIS MERIDIAN

C +1·0

471896.4592

397938.0349

0·6

S

Anti-Sine 23.44933816
=23° 27" The Angle of
the Ecliptic.

FIG.18. This illustration shows how the Meridian (**NS**) intersects the Temple walls in such manner as to subtend a 90 degree angle at Rennes-le-Château (**C**). In Sine values, the triangle is, therefore, .6-.8-1.0 and is extremely close to being the 300,000 - 400,000 and 500,000 unit Pythagorean Triangle. Remarkably, however, by a slight proportional reduction - due to the Meridian length of 600,000 x Sine 56 degrees the 400,000 arm is reduced to a measure - the Inverse-Sine of which is 23 degrees 27 minutes, the angle of the Ecliptic.

The Ecliptic

FIG 19. This apparent path of the Sun in the celestial sphere is called the ecliptic. It is a great circle, and it makes an angle of 23 degrees 27 minutes with the celestial equator because the Earth's axis of rotation is tilted that amount from the perpendicular to the plane of the Earth's orbit.
The figure shows the tilt of the Earth's axis in relation to the Sun when the Earth is at those positions in its orbit which give rise to midsummer and midwinter to an observer in the northern hemisphere.

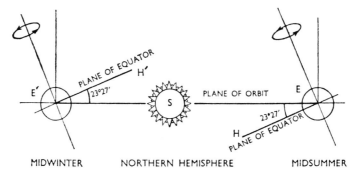

FIG 19

MIDWINTER   NORTHERN HEMISPHERE   MIDSUMMER

At the midsummer position, E, the Sun is raised above the plane of the equator by an amount equal to the tilt of the Earth's axis, which is 23 degrees 27 minutes. At the midwinter position, E1, the Sun is depressed an equal amount below the plane of the equator. The plane of the ecliptic is therefore inclined at an angle of 23 degrees 27 minutes to the plane of the equator, as shown in Fig.20.

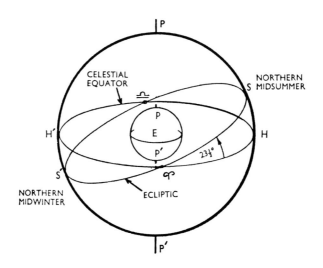

FIG 20

Earth's eccentricity. Once again we are shown, that with such accuracy, it is inconceivable for it to have occurred where it has by chance.

As the ecliptic variation of 23° 27' results in an axial eccentricity which projects a circular 'wobble', it naturally followed that we would subject it to the same analytical process we had acquired through our studies of the Rennes-le-Château system.

We are certainly not the first to examine this Precession of the Equinox as possibly resulting from celestial interference, for it receives considerable attention from Godfrey Higgins (*Anacalypsis - Vol II* p332), wherein the astronomer Dr. Keill speaks of the possible dates of a close cometary pass to Earth.

He comments as follows:-

"I think we have three well-marked floods; the last is the flood of Deucalion, or the Deus-Cali or holy Cali, and it took place **2348** years before Christ. The preceding one was really our flood of Noah and it took place, as pointed out by Mr Whiston, **2926 BC**; and the first, or the flood of Ogyges, took place **4648 BC**. This perhaps might be the flood which threw up Mont Blanc, Chimborazo etc. The last mentioned year, 4648 was the time of the entrance of the Sun into Taurus: but I think the middle flood, in **2926** was that which altered the axis of the Earth".

This is, indeed, a profound statement. It is a clear and, considering when it was said, a courageous admission that a comet, the Typhon SET so disturbed the rotation of the Earth that its effect is still here today in the precessive eccentricity of our axis, another remarkable confirmation of our findings in the Rennes-le-Château diagram.

When one considers the manner in which the eccentric axis courses through the heavens, it is little wonder that it has been so carefully observed since ancient times. Here was a 'clock' on a grand scale pointing to one constellation after another and giving the 'holy' men the ideal backcloth upon which they could predict the good and bad times ahead. There is no doubt that from the remotest times the ancient Egyptians, or their mentors, were in possession of sufficient astronomical information to align their temples with the precession of the equinoxes in mind.

In *The Dawn of Astronomy*, Sir Norman Lockyer pioneered the theory that temples oriented to the stars were redundant in two or three hundred years because Sirius, the rising star on the horizon became a little later each year. This was archaeologically confirmed by finding that temples had been reoriented to follow the precession.

Although the ancients may have thought it was not the Earth but the heavenly globe that moved, it is now accepted that this movement was known and quite accurately measured in those times. This confirmation was most gratifying and convinced us that it was not our imagination and that our diagram of great antiquity was capable of displaying the precession.

The next step was to see whether the actual period of the precession was shown in the geometry and this part of our investigation produced some remarkable figures.

First we must explain that these calculations are of time, not distance. Now as the Earth's axis describes its circle of 26,000 years it can like any other circle, be evaluated. We obviously knew that 26,000 was an approximation and we had noticed in *Anacalypis (Vol 11* p141*)*, that Higgins, quoting Whiston, gave the figure as 25,920 referring to it as **THE GREAT YEAR**. He also knew of another GREAT YEAR of antiquity, with a period of **36,000** and being unable to reconcile the two figures, he assumed the second to be based on a 360 day year. Now what Whiston did not do was to continue his reasoning by calculating the radius of this circle which is simply found as follows:-

$$\frac{25920 \times 360}{2\pi} \; = \; 1,485,107 \text{ days}$$

As we have mentioned before, numbers to us are like familiar faces and this one rang a bell. In our early work we had calculated the perimeter of the theoretical extended pentagram and the figure was **1,489,627**. With minor variations in the ground figure we had hoped that the perimeter would enlarge to the magical 1,500,000, as if confirming the 15 divisions of the circle, but it was not to be; the ground perimeter was **1,489,333**. The reader will recall that the body triangle equated the circumference of the circle which generated it, within one six thousandth of Pi. In a similar manner, we now have the Temple, or tangential square, with a perimeter of **1,483,281.6 (185,410.2 x 8)**, which varies from the perimeter of the pentagram by only one four thousandth part, an even closer correspondence to Whiston's figure. We considered the effect of using the 365.25 day per year and it failed miserably at 1,506,764 completely out of the 'ball-park'. A more accurate figure for the present year could be 365.26, but that made matters even worse. Could it be that the period of precession was wrong? We searched through several technical books, but at a late hour gave up the hunt and decided to contact the Astronomical Section of the Greenwich Observatory the next morning. Meanwhile, we reversed our formulæ to determine the necessary period of precession to reach both theoretical and numerical perfection.

$$\text{i.e. } \frac{\textbf{Precession x 365.26}}{2\pi} \; = \; 1,500,000 \text{ days}$$

This evaluates the precession at **25,803** years - apparently too short a

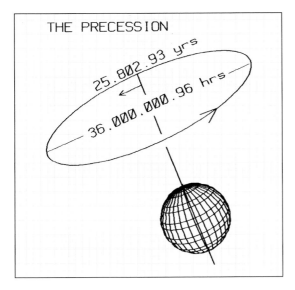

THE PRECESSION

25,802.93 yrs

36,000,000.96 hrs

Whiston believed the Earth's precession was, according to the Egyptians, related in some way to the numerical value of 36 - the holy number of femininity. Coincidentally by relating hours and years a precessive diameter of 36,000,000 hours generates a circumference of 25,802.93 years and Greenwich Observatory now gives 25,800 years as their best approximation of the great precession.

period.

The next day we called the Observatory and were put on hold while a charming lady made enquiries. Her eventual reply left us dumbfounded, "The closest estimate we can give you is **25,800** years!

Then we remembered; the Meridian calculation had been made in hours. The next move was simple, but staggering in its result! Using the Greenwich

figure:-
$$\frac{\textbf{25,800 x 365.26 x 24}}{\textbf{2}\pi} = \textbf{35,995,913.1 hours}$$

but using our figure:-
$$\frac{\textbf{25,803 x 365.26 x 24}}{\textbf{2}\pi} = \textbf{36,000,098 hours}$$

So what was the precession figure required to produce the perfect 36,000,000?

Obviously $\dfrac{\textbf{36,000,000 x 2}\pi}{\textbf{365.26 x 24}}$

and the result was **25,802.93!**

We now had a precession figure which not only was doctrinally perfect, but above all we had found the correspondence between the irreconcilable **GREAT YEARS** of precession and the previously unrelated 36 factor; they were the circumference and the radius of the same Circle of Time!

Once again this suggests that the ancients possessed a far higher degree of knowledge than we are willing to credit them with. There was, nevertheless, considerable confusion in antiquity which was brought about by their attempts to relate cycles of time which were incommensurate. Probably by considering the 'True God' as a mathematician, they sought to find whole numbers to satisfy cycles of time based on comparatively short periods of observations.

The perfection they sought was of course never there. Time intervals conjoining solar and lunar correspondences culminated in their 600 year cycle. They then attempted to make this period correspond with the Great Year of 25,920, but as it did not do so, they juggled the multiples until they found a common one (4,320,000). They certainly did not want to part with 360 x 72 which, of course, is what they had thought was the precession of 25,920 years.

Returning to our investigation, we were naturally interested in any information which would help us to identify the comet most likely to endanger our planet. As we have previously stated, comets can cause an incredible amount of damage without actually impacting the Earth. The Typhon carries a frightening arsenal of weapons; he may cause electromagnetic storms, volcanoes, earthquakes and of course floods. Some have been puzzled as to why the Typhon has such varied and apparently contradictory titles, 'God of Volcanoes', 'God of the Deep', 'God of Time' and so on, but as soon as we recognise his true identity we have solved the riddle of these ancient descriptions. It depends where on Earth you happen to be, when the 'Destroyer' or 'Serpent' passes by as to which of his attributes will affect you and thereby, how you will name him.

The reader will recall the famous Egyptian legend of the birth of the gods Osiris, Isis, Nephthys and Horus born on the intercalary days created by Thoth to accommodate them. Furthermore, Set the Typhon also tore from the womb of NUIT - the celestial orb, at the same time. Now the mist begins to clear and we may see the legend in its true light.

As the mighty Typhon tore through the inner planets, Mercury, Earth and Mars were 'sucked' from their stable axis and left 'trembling' with eccentricities of some 28°, 23° and 24° inclinations. We may wish to look again at that 'bright Morning Star', Venus and wonder why it remains so stable and rotates in the opposite direction to the other planets. The legend says that extra days were added to the Earth's year and this would seem a logical outcome of such an event. It is certainly logical that it was Thoth - The 'Lord of Measures' who should be the recorder of this incident. We are next told that he played draughts with the moon and won the 72nd part of her light. Indeed, Whiston *(Anacalypis Vol II p322)*, was of the opinion that the time of Osiris and Set was the Deluge or Typhon and that was the very name given to the flood by the Egyptians. Furthermore, he states that at this time not only did the solar year become extended, but the lunar year was equally shortened.

It is in these events and others in the history of our planet where we must search for the cycle of SET.

The Cretaceous/Tertiary destruction of the dinosaurs has shown us what could happen in the case of a collision, but that particular Typhon, or his remains, are now buried deep in the Earth and is of no further concern to us. It is to the floods we must look, for that would be the effect of a massive body passing in close proximity to our water-laden planet. The oceans would be sucked, maybe thousands of feet into the air and then released as the Typhon passed by. The collapsed tower of water would surge round the planet at hundreds of miles an hour destroying everything in its path. Possibly THE FLOOD was not quite that bad and Noah did survive it, but next time who knows? Will it be an even larger flood or will it be the nuclear fire of an Earth impact? With so little to guide us, can we possibly forecast the return of the Typhon? In fact are we even misjudging the danger by thinking of the Typhons as solitary objects?

One of the strongest arguments of the 'anti-cataclysm-club' rests on the mathematical law of probability, denying any reasonable possibility of another impact of Yucatan proportions. If one ignores the comet's tail, its ever-decreasing orbit and the gravitational factors, it could be argued that with all that space, tiny Earth and a tiny comet are unlikely to occupy the same space at the same time. However, after the success of Alvarez, the iridium search began in earnest and evidence accumulated for another five mass extinctions at more or less regular 26 to 30 million year intervals*. This, of course, stretched the mathematics of probability to breaking point, unless there was another factor which was being overlooked. Could the periodic danger be, not a single comet, but a multiple storm? Could there be something which at intervals would release such a cascade of malevolence into the solar system that collisions were inevitable? A possible answer came from one Dr. Richard A. Muller, not a crank, but a highly respected Professor of Physics at Berkely. Muller proposes that our sun has a companion star which he has named - NEMESIS and we feel sure he knew that was the name of the 'Goddess of Vengeance,' bearing the attribute, 'She whom none will escape'. Muller suggests that the periodic orbit of NEMESIS would, at intervals, dislodge masses of comets from the Oort cloud and send them crashing through the solar system. Although there seems to be a number of 'technical' objections which deny the possibility of an orbit such as that suggested by Muller, if nothing else, the publicity it received may have helped to make the population 'comet - aware'.

With the accumulation of all this recent scientific evidence, we feel sure the reader will be as shocked as we were to find that knowledge of this threat to Mankind has existed,at least for centuries, in the famous inscription on the tomb of 'Les Bergers d'Arcadie' - 'ET IN ARCADIA EGO'.

---

* *This figure has recently been revised to 15 myr intervals.*

CHAPTER 24.
THE FINAL SOLUTION

The 'ET IN ARCADIA EGO' code. THE ICE GOD.
The SEED axis and the pregnant shepherdess. The Poussin triangle.
A common origin. The Pyramid at Rennes-le-Château.
A common dating. The floods connection. Doomsday.

H AVING established the time factor of the Meridian, we turned our attention to the Seed axis, in the hope that it would reveal a starting date from which to calculate the return of the Typhon. This chapter is the result of that investigation and the unbelievable disclosures resulting from it.

The reader will recall that the line we refer to as the Seed axis is that which originates at the apex of the pentagram and passes through the North and South Seed positions. It then continues to the 'crutch' of the pentagram, but contrary to a theoretical figure it does not pass through the centre of the Circle of Churches.

Previously when we were relying on 'map-measure', we had considered that the evaluations we were finding were numerically significant. An example of this was, that by measuring from the apex of the pentagram to the North Seed position, we were very close to 125,000 AUs. Remembering that the distance between the North and South Seed was **154,508.5** AUs (5/6ths of the circle radius), and that this figure could be formulated as **250,000/Ø,** everything seemed to be going well. However, the computer CAD program rejected this figure and disclosed the distance to be **123,606** AUs, puzzling at first sight, but look again; with the 100,000 multiple applied, it is **2/Ø.**

We had moved from the pentagonal apex to the North Seed and then on to the South Seed with distances which were strictly controlled by Phi. Inevitably the distance from the apex of the pentagram to the 'crutch' responded to the same discipline; it was **100,000 x 2Ø**! (**323,606 AUs**).

In one sense this was exhilarating, for it provided further confirmation of the accuracy of our computer plot. In another way it was disappointing, for we could now see that we were witnessing another facet of the Phi canvas and not the incongruous figures for which we searched.

Finding **2Ø** at the 'crutch' of the female figure was, of course, doctrinally acceptable to us, but *GENISIS* had suffered considerable criticism for applying a sexual reading of the figure and although we are exercising more caution, we feel we should point out that we are not alone in our interpretations. As an aside, we would refer to *Journey to the Stones* by Ian Cooke, in which he states:-

> "The interlocking five pointed star or pentagram also symbolises
> the head, arms and legs of the human body, and more specifically
> the female body. One way up denotes rebirth from between the
> legs of the Goddess, while the reverse 'horned Goddess' spreads
> Her legs apart ready to entice Her male lover."

I sincerely hope the author will not be condemned for his erudite interpretation, for as the reader will recall, the fifteen division circle generates a female figure with the legs opened, thereby projecting her head outside the Circle of Churches. This is without doubt the 'Goddess Fifteen' with all her attributes (See Appendix 4).

The next move was, as we had done previously, to formulate our findings in terms of Sine values. The **123,606.7978** becomes **4 x Sine 18°** with the application of the 100,000 multiple (**0.309016994 x 4**).

The distance between the seed locations (**154,508.5**) becomes **5 x Sine 18°**. The combination of these measures (Apex to North seed and North seed to South seed) is **9 x Sin 18°** (**278,115.295 AUs**). We were reminded that the radius of the Circle of Churches could also be expressed in these terms, namely **6 x Sin 18°**. Then the thought struck us. Could these multiples have an independent meaning? It soon became clear to us that they could represent the letters of the alphabet. We had seen this previously, where the shepherd in 'Les Bergers d'Arcadie' was pointing to **'R'**, the **18th** letter of the alphabet (see page 79). Suddenly it became clear to us; the letters of the inscription 'ET IN ARCADIA EGO' could all be translated by multiplying the alphabetical position by Sine 18° in the same manner as we had been shown by the letter 'R' being the Sine of 18° which was half the reciprocal of Phi, in keeping with the half-staff clue.

Before we proceed with the full translation of the code, we would call the reader's attention to one factor which is quite surprising. As will be seen, **'O'** being the **15th** letter of the alphabet is read as 1 + 5 = 6, and then **6 x Sine 18°** = **185,410.1966 AUs** (the radius of the circle). 'O' was therefore, the obvious letter to represent both the circle and its 15 divisions. All the other values decoded were either code indicators or measures to be found on the Seed axis, except one. The **'G'** of EGO is the 7th letter of the alphabet and its translated value is therefore, **7 x Sine 18° = 216,311.8961 AUs** and that measure puzzled us for a while. When we found it we were amazed. It is the distance from the tomb near Les Pontils (as featured in Poussin's painting), to the centre of the Circle of Churches! We will now proceed to decode that famous inscription which has baffled all the investigators of the mystery of Rennes-le-Château for so long.

THE SEED AXIS

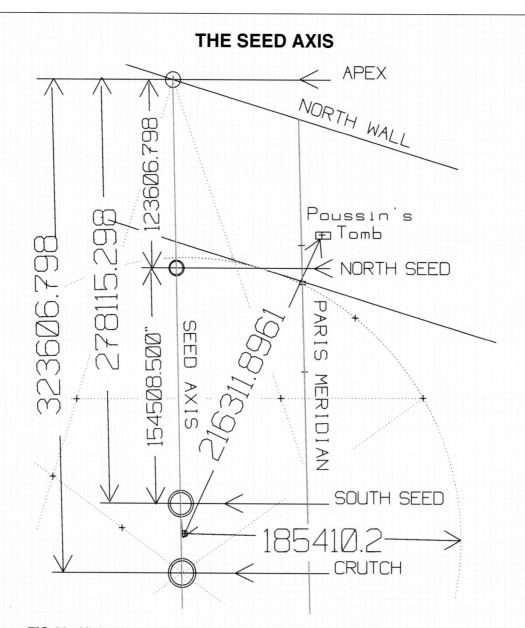

FIG.22. All the necessary measures needed to locate the seed positions - the pentagonal axis and the relationship of the Poussin Tomb to the Circle of Churches result from translating the 'ET IN ARCADIA EGO' inscription into Sine Values.

Starting with the full inscription:

ET IN ARCADIA EGO

The first part of the solution is to remove all the duplicated letters, which leaves:-

ET IN ARCD GO

Now, remembering that each letter is reduced to a single integer before being subjected to the Sine 18° multiple, we remove any letters which do no more than display Sine 18° or the reciprocal of Phi. 'T' = 20 = 2 + 0 = 2; 2 x Sine 18° = 0.618033989. Therefore 'T' is to be removed. Next as 'A' = 1; 1 x Sine 18° = 0.309016994 (1/2Ø), 'A' should also be removed. This leaves:-

E IN RCD GO

Before evaluating we will also remove the duplicated values. As 'N' = 14 = 1 + 4 = 5, we already have that value as 'E'. Also 'R' = 18 = 1 + 8 = 9 which we have as 'I'. Hence we are left with:-

E I CD GO

We will now evaluate these letters in terms of Sine 18°:-

E(5xSine 18°)   = 154,508.4972AUs....Distance between Seeds.
I(9xSine 18°)   = 278,115.295 AUs.....Distance Apex to South Seed.
C(3xSine 18°)   = 92,705.0983AUs......1/2 the Radius of the Circle.
D(4xSine 18°)   = 123,606.7978AUs....Distance Apex to North Seed.
G(7xSine 18°)   = 216,311.8961AUs....Circle Centre to Arques Tomb.
0(6xSine 18°)   = 185,410.1966AUs....Radius of Circle of Churches.

By referring to the illustration, it will be seen that these are the critical distances required to confirm the radius of the Circle of Churches, the distance from the centre of that circle to the tomb bearing the inscription and the positions of the Seeds on the pentagonal axis.

Now let us consider the sum of the values of the letters which exceeded 10. They are:-

'T'(20), 'N'(14), 'R'(18), and '0'(15), a total of 67.

Now, with these same numbers transcribed to their single integer values, we have 2, 5, 9 and 6. These added to the remaining letter values of the inscription also total 67! The reader may consider this to be purely coincidental, but now total the 67 value of 'T', 'N', 'R' and 'O' with the sum of the remaining letters:- 'E'(5), 'I'(9), 'A'(1), 'C'(3), 'A'(1), 'D'(4), 'I'(9), 'A'(1), 'E'(5) and 'G'(7). The answer, quite remarkably, is **112 (2 x 56)**, which identifies the 'halving' of the Poussin staffs with the number of SET.

If the reader is still not impressed with these numerical correspondences, let us demonstrate something which is undeniably awesome! We refer back to the final letters required to display the geometric distances. They were:-

THE ICE GOD

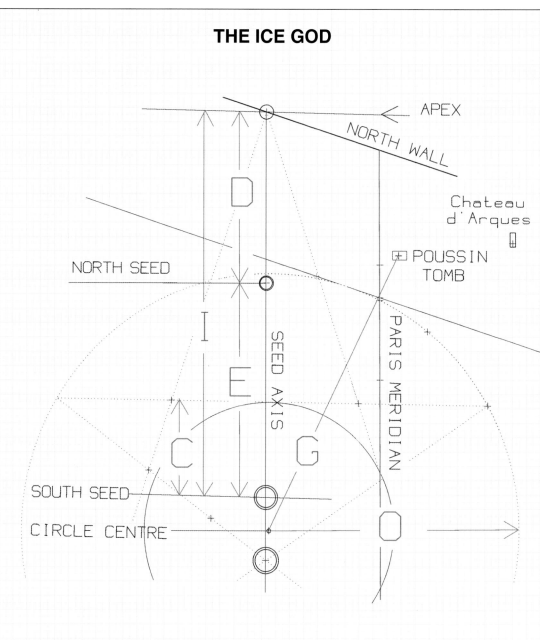

FIG.23. The self-same measures as those displayed in Fig. 22 translate to create the simple anagram - **ICE GOD**, which when re-evaluated totals **34**, the **cosine of 56**, the sigil of **SET**.

E I CD GO

The anagram is elementary: it is the **ICE GOD** - the Comet - the Typhon - SET. So the code displays his name, but what else will it show? Let us now evaluate his name:-

'E' = 5, 'I' = 9, 'C' = 3, 'D' = 4, 'G' = 7, '0'(15=1+5) = 6.

The total is **34** and the mathematically minded will immediately realise the **cosine of 34° is 0.829037572 - the SINE value of 56**, the **SIGN** of **SET**! The **ICE GOD** spells his name, which is marked by his number. Little wonder that the number of face stones on the tomb at Arques was 56 and that the Meridian was also controlled by the Sine of 56 degrees. To summarise, the 'ET IN ARCADIA EGO' inscription translates to disclose the centre of the circle, the perimeter divisions (15), the seed distances on the pentagonal axis and the distance from the centre of the circle to the place where the code was discovered. We are then shown the profound and as yet undiscovered link between the Comet and Poussin.

Furthermore, when the Poussin painting was analysed by Professor Cornford in Lincoln's Priest, Painter and Devil video, he showed the painting to be structured by an unusual combination of Golden Section and Pentagonal control (see illustration). The Pentagram superimposed on the painting is

Poussin's first version of 'Les Bergers d'Arcadie'. (Devonshire Collection)

regular and therefore the axes will intersect at one point. This intersection is on the forehead of the shepherdess, but this is also the line of the Golden Section of the length of the painting; a truly remarkable 'coincidence'. From the evidence presented in *GENISIS* and this book, the reader will, by now, be in no doubt that the pentagram represents the female body and someone should have surely noticed that the 'crutch' of the pentagram is precisely placed to correspond with the 'crutch' of the shepherdess.

Incidentally, our shepherdess is quite obviously pregnant; probably as the result of her seductive pose in the original 'Les Bergers d'Arcadie' by Poussin and now forming part of the Devonshire Collection, Chatsworth

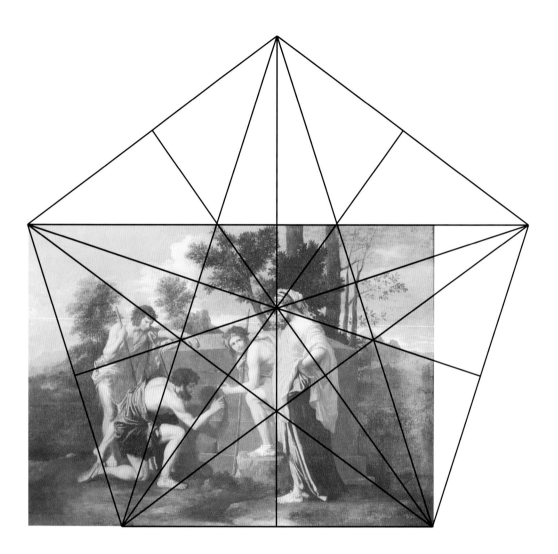

Fig.24. Here we see Professor Cornford's analysis of Poussin's 'Les Bergers d'Arcadie' as described in Lincoln's BBC Chronicle film, 'The Priest, The Painter and The Devil' where he draws our attention to the construction of the painting being a combination of the Golden Mean and Pentagonal geometry.

(Derbyshire, England). This could also be the reason she is - NO TEMPTATION! Strangely enough a stone relief of the painting exists in the grounds of Shugborough, but it has been sculptured as a mirror image of the painting. Even more strange is that the second painting which is housed in the Louvre in Paris has been copied in stone and placed as the headstone to Poussin's tomb in Rome; this is also a 'mirrored' image!

Returning to our summary, we can now see how the painting has been adjusted to reflect the geometric layout.

The Golden Section line of the painting passes from the head of the shepherdess and it is also the line to the apex of the construction pentagram. The extended pentagram of the Rennes-le-Château geometry clearly identifies the head by its extension and furthermore, the pentagonal axis is a Golden Mean intersection with the circle. The geometric axis then continues to display Golden Mean ratios through the seed positions until it intersects the 'crutch' of the pentagram. Precisely the same thing happens in the painting where the line of the Golden section, which is also the pentagonal axis, travels down the front of the shepherdess brushing her pregnant stomach wherein would lie the seed. The painting then excels itself by causing the 'crutch' of the construction pentagram to coincide with the 'crutch' of the shepherdess!

However, as we know there are two axes in the geometry, is the second axis shown in the painting? Yes, it is, and with remarkable clarity. One has only to extend the staff of the red-cloaked shepherd whom the shepherdess is touching and it perfectly intersects the apex of the construction pentagram (see illustration). One may ask how this could have been overlooked all these years, but remember we were trained by the designers of the Temple of Rennes-le-Château. Unless it is a case of extreme prudishness, we could never understand how the next factor could have been missed. The reader will recall that Professor Cornford calculated the line of the Golden Mean from the **LENGTH** of the painting and noticed it passed through the forehead of the shepherdess, but did not notice it passed through the 'crutch'. By the self-same process he could have taken the Golden Mean of the **HEIGHT** and he would have seen that it did not pass through the head of the shepherdess, but it certainly passes through her 'crutch' and also the 'crutch' of the pentagram.

Immediately, we were alerted to the fact that although the tomb was too recent to have been an integral part of the original geometry, it was nevertheless, mathematically positioned.

When we found the secret contained in its position we were further amazed. It was **100,000** AUs from the North Seed and **200,000** AUs from the South Seed. It exhibited the 'halving' process once again, but above all it reconfirmed the Seed positions!

THE POUSSIN TRIANGLE

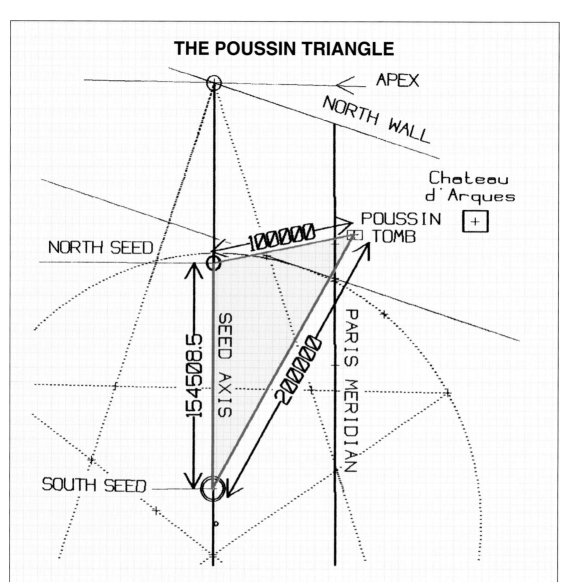

FIG.25. The tomb of Poussin's 'Les Bergers d'Arcadie' is precisely positioned at 200,000 and 100,000 AUs from the South and North Seed positions respectively, proving beyond doubt that the constructors and Poussin were fully aware of these locations. Remarkably, these measures also convert very closely to Pi and half-Pi English Miles. The position of the tomb, while in no way associated with the ancient geometry of the Temple, clearly proves their knowledge of its existence.

For readers' further amazement, **200,000** AUs are, as we know, extremely close to 200,000 British Inches. (Actually **199,000** : 200,000 x 0.995). Now Pi miles (3.1415) is **199,051** inches and the distances could, therefore, be seen as Pi and half-Pi miles. When one realises that this difference of 51 inches on the ground is two thousandths of on inch on the 1:25,000 map it is easy to see how one could be misled into believing the geometry was based on the English mile.

The truly remarkable fact is that the tomb should be placed at a distance from the South Seed which is the only distance where the 100,000 AUs multiple coincides with a mathematical axiom. In so doing, it confirms that we have the correct conversion factor for inches to AUs. Obviously, Poussin was extremely well-informed!

Although it was the 'ground' geometry with which we were mainly concerned, we could not resist the 'temptation' to reconsider 'Les Bergers d'Arcadie'. What else could Lincoln have missed? The first, and most obvious factor to examine, was the size of the original painting. If Poussin had used Golden Mean and Pentagonal geometry, he would necessarily have needed numerical data. Confronted with this, he would have immediately realised he could incorporate 'secret' measure within his geometry.

The official size of the painting is given as 85 x 121 cms but we see Professor Cornford showing the diagonal of the painting (**AG**) as a pentagonal arm. Elementary trigonometry shows this to be impossible, as the angle **DAG** would be only 35 degrees not the 36 degrees as required by a pentagram. Is, therefore Professor Cornford's analysis wrong? We do not think it is, for the Golden Sections mentioned earlier confirm it internally. The simple answer is that re-framing the painting could account for it. To produce the perfect pentagram the painting would need to be 87 x 120 cms. But as we have learnt, metric measure will achieve nothing in these matters; we need inches to solve the mysteries of Rennes-le-Château.

The height of the painting in inches is 34.288 which appears to contribute nothing until it is multiplied by the length; it then produces **1.618033989 - PHI**! So what was this magical length which could do so much?

It is **47.18964592** ins!

The reader will surely recognise these integers; they are the length of the Temple of Rennes-le-Château divided by 10,000!

The next move was inevitable; we used the unmentionable crutch point (**Y**) as the centre of a circle with the south-east corner of the painting (**G**) as its radius. As the figure shows, it performed miracles by delineating the painting at the points, **H-B-C** and **F**. Furthermore,we have now returned to an extended

LES BERGERS D'ARCADIE

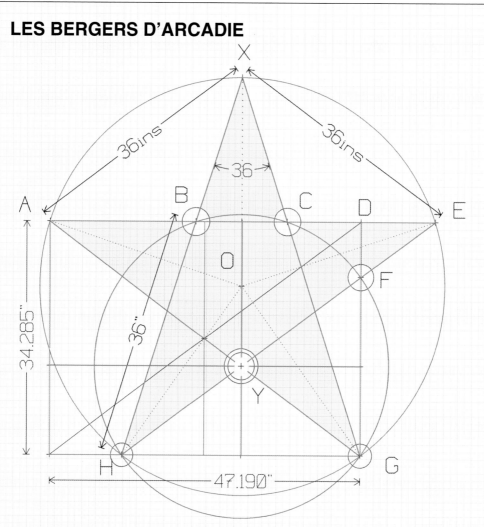

FIG.26. To produce the pentagonal diagonal claimed by Professor Cornford, the dimensions of the painting require minor modification. This immediately discloses the true ingenuity behind the interaction of the Pentagonal and Golden Mean construction. Femininity 'par excellence' is displayed in the 36 inch separation of the star-points of the pentagram together with the 36 inch body sections. Absolute confirmation of this development of the painting is obtained by constructing a circle with the crutch of the shepherdess as its centre, at which point we have three distinct correspondences; the Golden Section of the height of the painting, the geometric crutch of the pentagram and the illustrated crutch of the shepherdess.

By recognising the transference of the circle's centre from the forehead of the shepherdess to her crutch, the pentagram is transformed from being regular and internal, to being extended as discovered in the ground geometry. As can be seen, this extension through the circle is also confirmed by the fact that the extended limb is outside the painting from the common intersection of B and C. Two staffs of the Shepherds, amongst other things, can be extended to denote the circumference of the circle. Another extended staff confirmed the exterior apex in one direction and intersects with another staff, not only at the base of the painting, but also indicating the exact centre point of that base. These staffs would, therefore, always expose whether the dimensions of the work had been tampered with.

pentagram with the pentagonal limb **BXC** outside this secondary circle; numerically we see even more of the genius of Poussin in this figure. It displays the essence of femininity in the distance between each of its star points as all being **36** inches as also are the body chords of the Pentagram **BH** and **CG**.

The next action would be to orient this figure and identify the shepherds' finger positions on the ground at Rennes-le-Château. Nevertheless, out of respect for the district, we have decided to proceed no further and thereby frustrate the activities of the 'treasure hunters'. Exciting as these discoveries were, they proved conclusively that the work of Poussin and his contemporaries were recent superimpositions and not part of the original figure. In fact, it would appear they held it in sufficient reverence as to ensure their marker was never mistaken to be part of the original geometry, but, nevertheless, to indicate their awareness of the figure and the 'secret locations contained within it.

Returning to the matters in hand, we knew our search would need to be in ancient times if we were to find any correspondences which would help us on our way. We had already found valuable material in our examination of Stonehenge I, which from carbon dating led Hoyle to consider the construction date to lie between 2,500 and 3,000 BC. The reader will also recall that Hoyle boldly suggested that the construction was the work of a 'visiting' intelligence. This scenario was familiar to us in our study of ancient Egypt, where a number of Egyptologists were convinced that the knowledge of the ancient Egyptians had its origins elsewhere. There is even an ever increasing number of investigators who would contest the major pyramid to have been constructed as the tomb of Cheops, or anyone else for that matter. They consider it far more likely to have been built as a storehouse of information, and even to exhibit that information in its dimensions. With these parameters, it would certainly have a good deal in common with the geometry of Rennes-le-Château. The question arises as to whether it was designed to protect the contents from a disaster. The shape is obviously ideal to deflect falling debris and any form of precipitation. We should also bear in mind that the reason the entrance was placed so high was probably to be above an anticipated flood level. In fact, in its original condition, with polished limestone surfaces, one would be hard put to design anything more capable of deflection, regardless of the direction from which the assault came. Could it be that the pre-Egyptian settlers were the remnants of an advanced civilisation who had already suffered the loss of almost everything they possessed, except their knowledge?

Were they now determined to build something which could withstand the Typhon's destructive force? Dare we suggest these people were the

Atlanteans?

In assessing the excellence of the original construction, we can appreciate that they envisaged everything other than the vandalism of their hybrid offspring. It was probably inconceivable to them that Mankind would sink to the level of marauding savages and then destroy their inheritance so wantonly. They may have been even more shocked, had they known that one day their achievements would be classified as mere legend and their 'safety-box' attributed to the work of slaves building a tomb for a despotic pharaoh. The burning question is:- "Have we yet reached the point whereby we can be generous enough to open our minds and correct our misconceptions?" Surely the light of mathematics is sufficient to penetrate the veil.

The major pyramid of Gizeh has been a focal point for mathematicians, archaeologists and astronomers since the time of Napoleon. Countless books have been written covering all aspects of these sciences and brilliant scholars have pitted their wits against its mysteries. Slowly, but very surely, they are conceding the inevitable, which is that this edifice was probably constructed or designed by the unknown predecessors of the Egyptians. What the Greeks managed to salvage of that knowledge are mere fragments of the whole. The empiric academy preaches that an approximation of Pi was not used until 1700 BC, but we side with those who consider that the Great Pyramid discloses precise knowledge of not only Pi, but Phi and the trigonometrical ratios, even though its date of construction was at the very latest around 2,500 BC.

To save our readers from the arduous task of ploughing through the plethora of books on the Great Pyramid, we would recommend the *The Secrets of the Great Pyramid* by Peter Tompkins. This inspired work, together with its brilliant appendix by Livio Catullo Stecchini is the perfect conglomerate of all you will need to know in order to understand what follows. It is, indeed, frustrating to spend years accumulating scraps of data from innumerable sources, only to find that Peter Tompkins had already done so and in such an erudite manner.

The first snippet of information we will examine is the discovery of John Taylor - amateur astronomer and mathematician, who in the late nineteenth century found that by dividing the perimeter measure of the base of the pyramid by twice its height arrived at a figure of 3.144, so close to Pi (3.141592654), that he considered it intentional.

Due to vandalism and erosion, accurate measure of the pyramid has been, to say the least difficult, but we could accept the Encyclopedia Britannica as an unbiased approximation of the best known measures.

It gives the pyramid base perimeter as 920 metres (we hate those things), and the height as 146.59 metres. Double the height divided into the base

THE SECTION OF THE GREAT PYRAMID BY AGATHARCHIDES

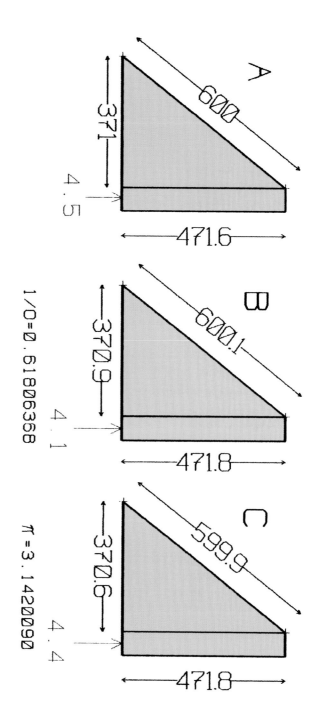

FIG. 27. Modern researchers are throwing more and more doubt on the academic dating of the Sphinx and the Great Pyramid. Early Persian records suggest they are far more ancient than have previously been accepted, and the close correspondence of Agatharchides's theoretical analysis with the ancient geometry of Rennes-le-Château indicates a relationship too close to be easily dismissed as coincidence. The mathematical truncating or beheading is a feature of the obelisk and a statue in Poussin's 'Peste d'Azoth'. It is also present in the Temple and Meridian modifications of the geometry of Rennes-le-Château.

274

perimeter gives 3.138 a reasonable approximation for Pi (3.141592654). Not as good however, as the one we had found in the geometry of Rennes-le- Château. Using the radius **185,410.2 AUs**, the perimeter of the tangential square base is **148,3281.6**. This dimension divided by the Temple length (**471,896.4592**) gives **3.143235282,** a much better figure and we did not have to double anything.

However, we must admit to being severely shaken by the next revelation. In the appendix of *The Secrets of the Great Pyramid*, Stecchini is examining the work of the second century Greek grammarian Agatharchides. One factor which has resulted in considerable debate is that of the missing tip or pyramidion of the Great Pyramid. This small tip was supposedly made from, or covered with, a precious metal and may have been some nine feet high. Its loss means that scholars may continue to argue whether the pyramid is a Pi or Phi construction for years to come. However, Agatharchides excludes the controversial tip and presents the case for the pyramid having been a compromise of both the Pi and Phi factors. These two arguments are easily understood from the illustration taken from Stecchini's article showing the pyramidion removed. Now let us compare the values (which are in feet) with the values displayed by the geometry of Rennes-le-Château. First consider the Phi argument:-

The height of the Pyramid is .... 471.8 ft.
The length of the R.L.C. Temple is ..... 471,896 AUs
The apothem of the Pyramid is .... 600.1 ft.
The diagonal of the R.L.C. Temple is.. 600,162 AUs
The half base of the Pyramid is .... 370.9 ft.
The width of the R.L.C. Temple is ...... 370,820 AUs

The Pi case shows the apothem reduced to 599.9 ft., and the reader will recall that prior to the Meridian of Set forcing the temple length away from the phi-perfect 471,690.8 AUs, the diagonal was exactly 600,000 AUs.

The inescapable conclusion is that the dimensions of the Great Pyramid are reflected in the Temple Walls of the geometry of Rennes-le-Château and at the bizarre scale of 1ft:1000 AUs.

As if that is not enough, now take note of the number shown under the baseline of the pyramid section - **375**.

The following plan view diagram explains this number, inasmuch as the irregular pyramidion is replaced to show the overall length of the pyramid's base. From West to East it is:-

370.6 + 8.8 + 370.6 = 750 ft,

THE PLAN VIEW OF THE GREAT PYRAMID BY AGATHARCHIDES

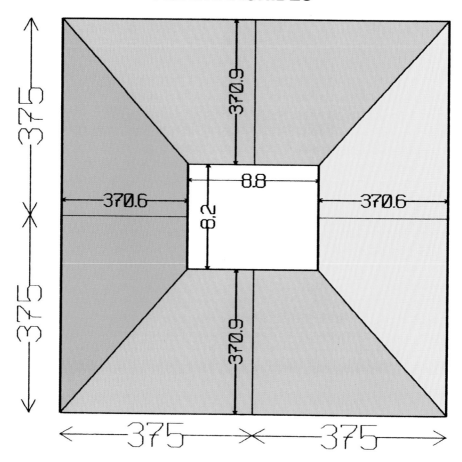

FIG. 28.

We were amused to see that this figure occurred on Page <u>375</u> of Peter Tompkin's *Secrets of the Pyramids*, but coincidental as that was, coincidence cannot be extended to explain that the Circle of Churches measures <u>375mm</u> in diameter on the 1:25,000 map of Rennes-le-Château, for it is a matter of record that the scale of 25,000 is one that was used in antiquity. Also the base perimeter of the Pyramidion is 34, the cosine of which is, as we know, 0.829037572 - the Sine of SET.

therefore the base to the central axis is 375 ft. Likewise, North to South it is:-

370.9 + 8.2 + 370.9 = 750 ft.

giving the same axis measure of **375 ft.**

By this method Agatharchides accommodates both Pi and Phi dimensions. The amusing thing about this number is that **375 MILLIMETRES** is the precise measure of the Temple width or Circle of Churches on the 1:25,000 map! These correspondences together with the multitude of Egyptian connections in the valley, may force us to return to the ancient history of Egypt and from where their ancestors came. Together with this, we will need to consider whether their homeland was irretrievably destroyed.

The only written records of the 'legendary' Atlantis are in Plato's dialogues, the *Timaeus* and *Critias* which are examined in depth in *GENISIS* (The Atlantis Connection). Many consider Atlantis was destroyed when the island broke from the tip of the mountain which supported it. This 'mushroom' configuration allowed a massive tidal surge to snap off the 'mushroom' top which slid into the depths of the Atlantic Ocean. Obviously such a surge of water was likely to have been caused by a celestial event. Assuming this event to be the close pass of a comet, we could extrapolate subsequent passages of the comet from the date of the Atlantean destruction and that date was approximately **9,250 BC.**

Although the Sun is the primary focus of a comet, we must also remember that its otherwise regular cycle can be influenced by whether it passes close to a planet during its passage through the solar system. The giants Jupiter and Saturn, could and do, drag the comets from their orbits, but the smaller bodies such as the Earth would have a far lesser effect, particularly if the comet were massive. Once the orbit of such a comet was safely inside the orbits of the giant planets, it would progressively cycle nearer and nearer to the Sun. It would then be purely a matter of chance as to where the Earth happened to be as to whether it was affected. As we have said, a large enough body would attract the surface water of the Earth in the same way that the Moon causes tides. Thereby, a close passage of a large comet causes disastrous flooding and it is the historical record of those events which we must examine. The period of the Typhon from the Meridian of Rennes-le-Château was **575.72** years. Eight passes would, therefore, take **4,605.76** years which from **9,250 BC** would bring us to **4,644.24 BC** : **4,648 BC** was the date given for the great flood of Ogyges. An error of only **4** years.

Three passes later (**1,727.16** years) brings us to **2,917.08 BC**: **2,926 BC** is the date given for the flood of Noah. An error of **9** years.

The next flood is that of Deucalion, dated as **2,348 BC** and our very next pass is **2,341.36 BC**. Here we see an error of **7** years, but now let us compare the two given dates for the floods of Noah and Deucalion; they are **2,926 BC** and **2,348 BC**, a difference of **578** years only varying our cycle by **2.28** years. The reader will see that by simply moving our cyclic dates forward by six years the correspondence is ominous.

The dating of other historical events which would assist us are insufficiently accurate to be of any use with the exception of the plagues and Exodus which certainly could be the work of the Typhon. However, moving on to the 16th cycle brings us to **38.48 BC** and Christian teaching tells us that a large comet preceded the birth of Christ. The Roman dating for this comet was **44 BC**. Another famous sighting of a large comet was **1680 AD** which **3** cycles earlier would have been **47 BC**. One cycle after **1680 AD** is **2255.72 AD**, the 20th cycle from the destruction of Atlantis and it occurs in **261.72** years time! At first sight this seems to be better news than the predicted impact of the Swift-Tuttle comet of **2116 AD** in **122** years time, but from what we know of the mighty Typhon, even a close pass from him is infinitely worse than an impact from a lesser comet.

As the reader has probably realised, we moved to the flood of Noah as a starting date because it is known more accurately than that of the Atlantean destruction. Furthermore, as we have shown, there are a number of features in the mystery which are associated with Noah and the Ark. Poussin's 'Deluge', Château d'Arques and the Pech Cardou all have flood connections, but we also have very clear mathematical and doctrinal connections with the legends and the Great Pyramid of Egypt. It is, therefore, with some regret that we feel duty bound to investigate another possible date from which to extrapolate the Typhon's return.

The dating to which we refer is that of the Exodus. Clube and Napier (*The Cosmic Serpent*) proposed that Exodus and the legendary battle of Zeus and the Typhon are one and the same. In fact, like us and most open minded investigators, they see *Revelations* as a symbolic description of that same event. However, in *Exodus (Ch.13 v 17-18)*, we find an even more accurate description of a close passing comet.

> "Yahweh went before them, by day in the form of a pillar of cloud
> to show them the way, and by night in the form of a pillar of fire to
> give them light: thus they could continue their march by day and
> by night.The pillar of cloud never failed to go before the people
> during the day, nor the pillar of fire during the night."

Clube and Napier then explain that as the tail of a comet is always away from the Sun, on passing the perihelion it would reverse, thereby becoming visible in the west, behind them. This is precisely the description given in *Exodus (Ch.14 v 18- 19)*, where it states:-

"Then the angel of God, who marched at the front of the army of Israel, changed station and moved to their rear. The pillar of cloud changed station from the front to the rear of them and remained there."

If nothing else this proves the validity of the account, for there would be no symbolic advantage in the redactor reporting such a reversal. We should also report that many others have associated the Exodus with the Zeus/Typhon conflict:-

"A terrible comet was seen by the people of Ethiopia and Egypt, to which Typhon, the King of that period, gave his name; it had a fiery appearance and was twisted like a coil and it was grim to behold: it was not really a star so much as what might be called a ball of fire"

(Pliny. Natural History)

The reason we referred to this evidence as unfortunate is because the dating for the Exodus which Clube and Napier arrived at was **1,369 BC** Moving forward six cycles of **575.72** years we arrive at **2085.32 AD**; a mere **91** years from now!

We feel we should also point out a close correspondence in the solution of the 'ET IN ARCADIA EGO' theme, which the reader may have overlooked.

We should recall that in the event of a land impact by a comet, for every three megatons of explosive energy, a million tons of fine dust particles are ejected several kilometres into the atmosphere. This together with millions of tons of smoke particles from the inevitable conflagration of all the combustible materials for miles round the ground zero, would considerably reduce the level of sunlight reaching the Earth. This in turn could possibly create a nuclear winter, the scenario of which we have been warned could happen should a large scale nuclear exchange occur.

Clube and Napier go as far as to say, that an ice age could result, and ensure the extinction of the majority of the species on the planet. With this in mind, one can appreciate that the **ICE GOD** solution of the Poussin painting is doubly true in describing not only the ice composition of the comet, but also the condition of the planet after impact.

Returning to our prediction, we hope it is only coincidental that the Meridian of Set at Rennes-le-Château displays six cycles, but his identity which is confirmed by all the evidence accumulated in this book is not coincidental; it is undeniable. Couple that with the close mathematical correspondences of this chapter and the scales swing quite heavily in favour of the **1,369 BC** starting date and the **2085 AD** return.

CHAPTER 25.
THE MISINFORMED

UFO Update. Ancient knowledge. The Holographic Future.
Locked doors. Destruction personified. Veiled archaeology.
The chosen ones. As it reaps so does it sow.

THANKFULLY there is still a minority and hopefully an increasing one, that are becoming aware they have been duped and misinformed for the major part of their lives. In olden times this manipulation was enforced by such obvious instruments as the 'Witch Finder' and the flames of the Inquisition. Gradually, the process was softened to 'Edicts' and the threat of the withdrawal of one's passport to the heavenly realms.

Inevitably, people of science, those advocates of the Devil, began making discoveries which threatened the cosy alliance which had developed in the nineteenth century between the standpoints of the academic and the religious. Archaeologists, quite often innocently, unearthed 'unearthly' artefacts which refused to fit comfortably into the previously agreed syllabus. In those days, acceptable new discoveries of any note stood a reasonable chance of being recorded in the Times and in so doing received the stamp of being also respectable. Even our finding of the geometry of Rennes-le-Château, free of interpretation, may have qualified for a column - but things are different now.

Almost unnoticeably the cloak of confidentiality has thickened, first to secret, then top secret, above top secret and eventually, 'For thine eyes only'. By now there is probably an even higher classification, 'Do not read this and if you do, shoot yourself'. No longer can we accept media reports with any confidence that what we are reading has not been cut, coloured and tailored to fit the requirements of the times. Consider the assassination of President Kennedy and the ever increasing stain of corruption to spread from it. It also seems impossible for any prominent figure of our times to avoid eventually having their names appended with the 'gate' suffix.

In most cases, including the nefarious activities of persons in high places, it has become fairly routine to set up a committee of enquiry who deliberate for a couple of years and then produce a report which nobody reads. It is, however, a totally different matter when one is confronted with a 'Saucer-gate'.

Rumours began to circulate that the three missing days in President Eisenhower's agenda were taken up in viewing a crashed UFO and the occupants. Slowly the threat of abduction by aliens, benign or otherwise is beginning to compete with 'mugging'. Sightings of UFOs, previously confined to the 'boondocks', were attributed to poor quality 'moonshine'. Then airline pilots began to see them - even a President suffered from the hallucination, but when they turned up over Washington in squadron strength, something had to be done. Obviously the time had come to talk to the little critters. Displaying that well founded human trait, 'If you can't beat them - join them', the genre slowly changed. Confirmation could never follow so closely on the heels of disinformation and so we entered the era of 'co-information'. Lovable ET appeared along with any number of productions designed to coerce the previously 'alienated' masses. Now the welter of UFO associated material is being supported by ex-NASA 'experts' who have crept from under the 'cloak' and are willing to admit they have seen 'something'. One could be surprised that they are still alive, but the fact that they are should tell us a good deal. Quite simply they are part of the plot to accustom the masses in preparation for the day when the UFO makes its official appearance and the Galactic Peace Treaty is signed on the lawns of the White House. After all, there is so much they can help us with. Our communication devices require such onerous power supplies and all that weight is counter productive to the available pay-load of a space vehicle. Think how helpful if would be if they disclosed to us the design of the low voltage ET (Electrical Transistor) circuitry. (Now that was thoughtless of us - of course they already have). On second thoughts it will be the 'ratification' of the existing treaty which President Clinton will be privileged to sign.

In all this, we are trying to do no more than present the case to those who feel they are fortunate to live in enlightened times, but may one day realise how little of the light they have been allowed to see.

People of science grapple with the mysteries of creation, determined to do their utmost to understand the 'nature of things', but also knowing that their minds, the very receivers of their findings, may be restricted to frequencies and conceptual barriers which may always prevent them from achieving their goal. It may well be that homo sapiens is not sufficiently high on the ladder of creation to ever hear the 'music of the spheres'.

How then did this brief creature, Man, begin to believe that he was any match for these great secrets? What sudden strange event took him from the savage beast, answering only to his basic instincts, to this searcher for knowledge? Why did he, of all creatures, acquire such mental capacity as to be able to move his understanding from the limited knowledge of his environment to the outer bounds of the universe? What mechanism of thought would deceive him into thinking that he could resolve the mystery of the beginning of time?

The learning graph of any creature left to its own devices is no more than a barely inclined slope; how then could we produce the exponential curve to take us from the spear to the space-shuttle in the blinking of an eye? This is not the scenario of an evolving brain; it is the process of accessing an existing storehouse of knowledge locked in the subconscious. In that great library are high shelves and rooms containing information that lies beyond the dimensions which we have been accustomed to conceive. The alert reader will probably have realised that there are certain factors associated with the Rennes-le-Château subject which would lead us to think that on one of those high shelves, we may find a book containing the geometry of the valley.

We would like to help the reader to penetrate one of those subconscious veils, with a simple analogy. Airline travel and television have caused our planet to shrink to such a degree that our concerns are now worldwide. Space probes have shrunk the solar system to an easily conceivable spiral and we can now mentally zoom in to imagine the conditions on any of our planetary neighbours. Contrast this ability with the minds of primitives who would never have left the valley in which they were born. This process is simply one whereby the mind has achieved an expanded spatial concept. Now we will attempt to do the same with Time.

Try to consider the past as a multidimensional lattice of events which are immovably written in stone. Nothing in the past can be changed or modified by virtue of the fact that Time itself is petrified, up to and including the very last second that has just ticked by. You are now in the present - an intricate matrix of the effects of every past cause and as such you have only very little freedom of movement in the seconds which are to come. Already the present and immediate future are beginning to gel. To escape from its ever-hardening clutches requires that you project your desires into the future - project them too near and the effects of the past will have already loaded the temporal disc to such a degree that it may be unable to accommodate the program you envisage. However, so powerful is the dormant mind of Man, that there probably is a way and the method would be explained in a book on a high shelf of the subconscious. More likely, however, is the possibility of a zone of the 'future' which is subconsciously pliable.

The future becomes less and less dense as it progresses away from us until it is eventually so liquid that once again it is beyond manipulation. Mark your pattern in that fluid pool and it will disappear as fast as it is drawn. If you would mould the future, nearer to your heart's desire, it must be where it is putty in your hands and capable of receiving the projections of your mind. In that state it is capable of preserving the imprint you have made, and you will be able to access it when you arrive at that present. By that time it will be sufficiently hardened for you to obtain the benefits of its design.

Unknowingly, this is precisely what we do and 'as you sow, so shall ye reap', becomes an enlightening axiom. But consider the slight change to 'what you sow and the meaning is profound, the seed is of your choice.

We live in a holographic universe of our own making. Even in science as we strive to solve a problem, time and space contrives to distort sufficiently to accept the science of our solution and, given that it can accommodate the parameters of a new theory, we eventually will reach that modified time which will provide us with the proof that we sought. But will we ever recognise that proof as being nothing but the temporal projection of our own minds on to a holographic future? The final proof of the Big Bang theory will eventually be found for no other reason than that we had conceived it in the first place, but so would any other reasonable theory have been proven in time.

This mystery is easily solved by realising that our subconscious mind is the genetic gift of the gods. A gift so complex that we still have little idea of how to use it. Were it fully integrated we would have no use for telephones; telepathic power lies dormant in all our minds together with telekinesis and a host of other attributes inherited from our creators. Evidence of the remnants of those powers existed in ancient times, but unless, like the Great Pyramid, they are too large to erase, they will be destroyed or concealed by the powers who wish to preserve the status quo.

Why did the Church of Rome go to such lengths to stem scientific progress? What did they know of the ancient history of Man that they should do so much to suffocate the archaeological evidence of Man's origin? They may well have access to records which disclose that Man has but a short while to enjoy this Earthly Paradise and like any caring parent, may not wish the child to know of its threatened termination. If this is indeed the case it would, to some degree, excuse their past behaviour; but what if the very science they chose to suppress were capable of discovering the cure? In the early centuries A.D., the Church began the monumental task of re-writing the history of Mankind and supplanting the legends, which had been so carefully preserved for aeons, with their 'authorised' account of everything from 'the Creation' to the individual's demise, when we are at last judged at the 'Golden Gate'.

Having produced their 'best-seller', the Bible, it was a gross oversight on their part that they should use the *Book of Revelations* as the ultimate chapter, when it so graphically portrays the destruction of Mankind by the very agency over which their God appears to have no control.

In the light of modern science no amount of condemnation can lie blame at the door of a celestial mass of rock and ice. To personify this threat as the ultimate evil - Satan, serves no more purpose than their personified image of God. Neither will prayer, as we know it, deflect the path of this malevolent missile. Again we must address our own psychology and decide whether knowledge of the precise date of impact would produce a 'last days of Pompeii' syndrome; an orgy of mayhem and self-indulgence with Mankind making the most of the time which is left.

Returning once again to the perplexing problem of the 'instant' origin of Man, that famous saying, 'Above all know thyself' labels a door which seems firmly locked by our educational system, otherwise our children would not still be leaving school under the impression that they evolved from apes. Furthermore, the pathway back to the knowledge of ancient civilisations is strewn with religious boulders and misleading signposts, to ensure they never cross the border into Pagan Land. George Orwell's statement, "Who controls the present controls the past", seems undoubtedly true. Even the mathematical jewels of the past are concealed. Were any of our readers taught the functions of Phi whilst still at school and can you find the pentagram in books of school geometry?

Some writers, such as Maurice Chatelain (*Our Ancestors came from Outer Space*), have gone to considerable lengths to put the record right; claiming that our remote

> "ancestors of 65,000 years ago knew as much and probably more
> than we do about the solar system".

He draws our attentions to the Cro-Magnon skull found at Del Mar near San Diego, California, by Dr. Rogers and Dr. Bada, which was dated to be between 50,000 and 65,000 years old and yet was large enough to contain a brain of 1600 cc. With considerable courage he concludes that Man was 'suddenly' elevated by "insemination and mutation" and then initiated into the knowledge of astronomy and mathematics. In the realm of archaeology, Chatelain refers to the early finds of Cuneiform tablets in the ruins of Persepolis and comments thus:-

> "Luckily no one at that time could understand these writings,
> because if the Pope had read their message and discovered it was
> the Earth that turned around the sun, or that the biblical version of
> the Flood was nothing but a pale reflection of the saga of
> Gilgamesh, or that a great part of Genesis was inspired by
> Sumerian legends, it is not difficult to imagine what would have
> happened to the old clay tablets and to the people who found or
> read them".

Chatelain also points out another door which was closed in 1549 when Diego de Landa, the bishop of **Yucatan** burned all the ancient Mayan documents, believing them to be the works of Satan. Now, Chatelain is no anti-Church fanatic - he was one of the Apollo spacecraft design scientists.

Suppression is not, however, confined to the Church of Rome. In a recent article (*Nexus, V2 No.13*), David Childress discloses that the Smithsonian Institution has 'accidentally' lost a number of important archaeological artefacts rather than being confronted with having to explain how they could have been found where they were. Simply, if something does not conform to the established pattern, then it is preferable to mislay it, rather than rock the 'academic boat'. In fact, while on the subject of boats, we could consider what happened to one which was full of these archaeological misfits.

Childress is speaking of the supposedly heretical belief that the Americas were visited by ancient civilisations many millennia before Columbus. He cites the case of a former employee of the Smithsonian having been dismissed for holding such a view. That employee, feeling obviously resentful, alleged that the Smithsonian had taken a barge full of 'unusual artefacts' out into the Atlantic and dumped them in the ocean.

Another incident to which Childress refers is that recorded as a front page story in the Phoenix Gazette, 5th April (not the 1st!), 1909. This extensive article refers to a massive underground cave system in the Grand Canyon, containing 'mysterious hieroglyphs', possibly Egyptian. The article then goes on to say that the exploration of this inaccessible site was carried out by Professor S.A. Jordan of the Smithsonian Institute. Needless to say, the Smithsonian denies all knowledge of the discovery or the exploration and, in case your are considering a visit, the area is strangely 'off- limits'.

We seem to live in an age when, whether by secret agencies, or church or dark government, we are denied access to any discoveries which may threaten established teachings. One may consider that the revelations in this book may well qualify it for attention by one or other of those organisations.

Fortunately, the geometric Temple of Rennes-le-Château, like the Great Pyramid, is not easily erased. How could our findings be lightly dismissed when there is so much supporting evidence? With the blazing spotlight of publicity focused on the subject by dozens of authors, how could this undeniable solution be denied? Piece by piece the connections have been examined and collated. The **SERPENT** of Poussin's 'Deluge' - Le **SERPENT** Rouge - The nearby village of Le **SERPENT**, all displaying the zootype of the **TYPHON - SET**, among whose titles we find the God of Time - the **MERIDIAN** - the **ICE GOD** coded in 'Les Bergers D'Arcadie' together with Plutarch's number of the TYPHON - 56 disclosed on the Arque tomb and in the MERIDIAN and in ET IN ARCADIA EGO. Works of art, construction, geography and mathematics, all saturated by the number of the TYPHON - 56. Every sign or **SINE** in the valley points in one direction and one direction only, to the **DESTROYER - THE COMET!**

All this evidence has been intrinsically woven by sine language and the

Above: The inevitable impact - tranquil Earth - a split second before the comet's impact and below, the last seconds before the comet destroys the only known intelligent species in the galaxy - Man.

transcendental ratios of Pi and Phi on to a geometric backcloth confirming the codes of the parchments and solving the function of the enigmatic 681, the supreme 'sigil' of **Pythagoras**, who is also dominating the design with his personal 'signature' - the **Pentagram**. And around and about lies the Temple of Time - the Power Zone of **SET**, impregnating the **Goddess 15** with his seed, in a manner known only to the Gods. Here we find doctrinal knowledge interwoven with trigonometrical perfection and dating from remote times, when the skills required to superimpose such a diagram over forty square miles of mountainous terrain were supposedly not known. Nevertheless, we are convinced that NASA has already recognised the seriousness of the cometary threat and is doing its utmost to define it. As early as 1978, a joint ESA and NASA spacecraft was launched which was conveniently named the International Sun-Earth Explorer - ISEE. Its mission was primarily to study the solar wind, but we could be amused by the phonetic resemblance ISEE and ICEY. Surprisingly, however, on discovering the spacecraft had far more fuel than it required for the mission, it was propelled to a trajectory which allowed it to pass through the tail of the comet Giacobini-Zinner in order to investigate its magnetic field polarity. However, it was not only redirected, but also renamed the Interplanetary Cometary Explorer (ICE). It seems the collective subconscious works in strange ways.

Even as you read these words, deep in outer space, turning slowly through their aphelions, the destroying Typhons prepare for their headlong rush to the distant Sun with his family of planets, lazily orbiting and totally unaware of the possibility of an impending disaster - the return of a Devil Star!

Already we should be preparing well provisioned shelters buried deep in the ground to protect the chosen few. Alternatively, standing-off in Earth orbiting vehicles would serve as well, if not better, and it may be that such precautions are already being planned. Possibly the time is known, if not precisely, then at least within estimated limits and that information will be very well-guarded. Should any enthusiastic astronomers be sufficiently naive as to publicise a possible date of impact in the future, they would undoubtedly be persuaded to withdraw their estimates and admit to their errors. (Well they have, haven't they?)

We have little alternative other than to rise above our animal instincts of self-preservation and be thankful that at least some of our flock may survive. Whether in deep shelters or in a space ark, it is essential for the continuance of our species that at least the chosen ones are safe.

Confronted with all this evidence of a possible holocaust, it is indeed paradoxical that the geometry of Rennes-le-Château intermixes the doctrine of destruction with that of impregnation and birth. How could the imagery of pregnancy, womb and seed be possibly connected to the destructive comet? Recent scientific discovery may, once again, provide the answer, and once again we may be forced to admit that this knowledge was in the hands of the ancients.

In a recently published article in Time (October 11, 1993 No. 41), by Madelaine Nash, we are told that the early experiments by Stanley Miller in 1953 were probably based upon a false premise. Miller, you will recall, reconstructed in a bottle the methane, ammonia, hydrogen atmosphere, which he believed were the primeval conditions prevailing on Earth prior to the evolution of a living cell. Into this mixture he fired electrical sparks to replicate the effect of lightning and in this manner produced his primordial 'soup'. Now, however, it is believed that unlike Miller's atmosphere there was an abundance of carbon dioxide present. Despite this setback, the fact remains, life did begin and it is considered that the answer may lie in the recent discovery of living cells being deposited on planet Earth from outer space. The vehicle suggested is - **THE COMET**. With this knowledge, the mystery of the cycle of life may be close to being solved. As the COMET destroys so in the aftermath it seeds the body of its victim - Mother Earth, and who are we to know whether that new seed may contain the essence of a creature which would excel Mankind? This theme is mentioned in a recently published comprehensive study of comets:-

"Recent ideas suggest comets' reputation as life-threatening, horrific missiles may have to be modified to include our indebtedness for their supplying the building blocks of life itself"   (*Comets* by D. K. Yeomans p351)

Indeed the **GENE** of **SET**, the Typhon, the comet, may well be considered to be the gene of intelligence, precisely as its zootype, the serpent, is shown to be in the Garden of Eden.

If we are to be destroyed in the not too distant future, let it be that we are 'super-seeded' by those who could re-create the Golden Age.

In closing, therefore, we would propose there could be an even more profound secret encapsulated in the design of Rennes-le-Château which is outside the scope of this book. Consider the possibility of a geometric relationship existing between Time and the human subconscious mind. Look again at the manner in which a Meridian section (Time), is projected on to the very essence of life - the Seed axis, which is an axial vibration of the spine of the Goddess. Could it imply that the mind can release itself from the capsule of the present where it is now trapped? Alternatively, could it even mean that the mind, or enough of them, could deflect the inevitable threat to Mankind?

CHAPTER 26.
THE FINALE

To whom we are indebted.....the designers. Poussin and
Jules Verne. The French Government. the Astronomers.
The search for ET and why there is no response.
Will we survive?

IN pursuing the solution of Rennes-le-Château we, like those who went before us, have been forced into diverse subjects, which at one time would have been considered to be totally unrelated to the mystery. Many investigators have wandered off into the peripheral shadows hoping to find a convincing fragment which had not yet been recognised as having a direct bearing on the known parameters of the subject.

Lincoln eventually realised that the extended pentagram, exhibited in *GENISIS* was something which could never have occurred by chance and he attempted to join the geometric club by reflecting its properties beyond its original confines. Unbeknown to him, those confines were rigid trigonometrical controls put in place by an advanced mathematical culture. In fact, as the reader has seen, those very boundaries which he chose to ignore, are an integral part of the solution, without which no solution exists. Furthermore, it is simple logic that any developing civilisation will soon begin to establish standards of weight and measure and those standards will, in the nature of things, fall within the useful limits which are determined by the size of the species and their immediate requirements. Anyone who has studied ancient metrology will be aware of the correspondences which are generated by the multiples of ancient standards of measure, much in the same way that a Vernier scale operates.

Initially units are chosen which are related to the size of the species, such as our inch, foot and yard. The primitive ant would have little use for the statute mile, nor would the elephant consider the millimetre of any value. As these creatures became more intelligent, they may well begin to establish measure based upon (for instance) the distance they could cover in a day's walk. This would eventually lead to a comparison being made between the pace of the African as opposed to that of the Indian elephant. Inevitably correspondences would occur. Unknowingly, Lincoln fell into this linear trap and claimed he had discovered a vital link between Chinese measure and the measure used in our geometric discoveries, but we are inclined to think that what he found was 'a large flat-bottomed Chinese boat'. Travel down that route and the mystery of Rennes-le-Château will go on for ever.

As the reader has now seen, the designers of the Temple of Rennes-le-Château were anticipating that the mind of the discoverer would be trigonometrically aware and that by the analysis of the sine values which they displayed, he would be forced to recognise the unit of measure they intended to convey.

They knew, and they were right, that this would in turn allow them to convey the elements of a warning. Only by mathematical analysis were we able to uncover the concealed message and so armed, we could set off into the shadows - not haphazardly - but knowing precisely what we were looking for. The evidence we have presented demonstrates with alarming clarity that Poussin was fully aware of what he was portraying and, like the geometry, it would survive the ravages of time.

As each piece of evidence appeared, the inference was always the same; the message had to be coded. At every stage it became more and more obvious that the custodians knew of a powerful suppressing influence, one which would destroy them and their record, if their work was recognised as being a component of the forbidden knowledge.

For this to have been necessary in Jules Verne's time, gives one some idea of how dangerous he must have considered the power of the suppressors. Knowing, as he would, the fate of the Cathars and Templars this is not surprising, albeit that with the passage of time the methods of suppression had become more subtle.

Now in the closing years of the 20th century physicists, mathematicians and astronomers have been able to publish their research and discoveries with comparative impunity. Without their work, the interpretation of our mathematical discoveries in the Temple of Rennes-le-Château would have remained largely guesswork. Fifty years ago comets were thought to be harmless 'snowballs' no larger than 2km in diameter, which would melt on entering the Earth's atmosphere. Now they are known to be fearsome conglomerates of rock and ice, capable of clinical annihilation and with no upper limit set as to what size they could be in the future. One thing is, however, certainly clear and that is their perpetual return, until their orbit either coincides with one of the planets, or they are consumed by the Sun.

How long the early inhabitants of planet Earth had known of this danger is a mystery, but prior to the Dark Ages there seems to be evidence of it, echoing back to the very dawn of intelligence when such knowledge could only have come from those who had cosmic awareness. Now, assisted by modern astronomical discovery, the message in the geometry is recognisable. No longer can the genius of the designers be smothered by claims of coincidence. The sophisticated interaction of mathematical axioms reduces the suggestion of chance to banality. The interlacing of the geometric components screams for the attention of logical minds.

Next we must express our gratitude to Poussin. Now, we can realise how valiantly he struggled to preserve the warning. It seems inconceivable that he would have been in possession of the trigonometrical detail revealed by the computer; but, that he knew of some of the dimensions is now certain. It is, however, abundantly clear that he knew the nature of the threat to our planet and that this knowledge "even kings would have great pains to draw from him", for that knowledge could free them from the oppressive control of the Church of Rome. Indeed, by knowing the South Seed location and what was buried there Poussin could prove his claims.

How simple it is, to now realise why the Cathars accepted the concept of REX MUNDI, and why they should have been persecuted as they were.

Our thanks must also go to that erudite master of language - Jules Verne and his posthumously published *La Chasse au Météore*. In that and other stories he established milestones which he knew would endure until we found them and recognised their significance. Nevertheless, admired as he was, until we established the connection, his knowledge of the ultimate secret of Rennes-le-Château was not known. The emphasis he placed on the Meridian had not escaped our attention and we are also indebted to the French Government for their persistence in maintaining the Paris Meridian, without which, our task would have been almost insurmountable.It is our sincerest hope that they now recognise the profound knowledge which is contained within their national boundaries and act accordingly. They, above all, should appreciate that it was their countrymen who went to such lengths to preserve the secret. It would be most fitting for them to appoint a French mathematician to verify our work, the detail of which we would make freely available to them.

How then, without electronic calculators and a CAD computer program could our predecessors have achieved the interpretation of the geometry? The answer lies in the very route we were forced to follow from the initial discovery of 'Wood's Extended Pentagram'. The solution had been written in several languages to ensure that it would survive and it was in *GENISIS* that the first of these languages was recognised. This was where the primitive inter-relationship between man, woman and her resultant pregnancy was geometrically displayed. It was a factor of which Poussin was fully aware, and he made it obvious by recasting his seductive shepherdess in his first version of 'ET IN ARCARDIA EGO' as a pregnant woman in the second.

We should also be grateful to the priest Bérenger Saunière, who by his flamboyance and bizarre taste in church decoration drew so much attention to the area in recent times. By the same token we should also probably thank the

The thousand foot antenna of the radio-radar system at the Arecibo Observatory. This and other massive and multiple devices scan the galaxy for any signal which could be recognised as other than galactic 'noise', but nothing has ever been heard!

Church of Rome, whose attention to the location in the past, gave so many investigators reason to think that something of great importance was concealed there.

Finally, we must return to the connection which Henry Lincoln finds so unpalatable - space and the search for extra-terrestrial life.

Two experts on the subject are Carl Sagan of Cornell University and Frank Drake of the University of California, who largely control the mighty Arecibo antenna in Puerto Rico. By mathematical elimination, they have attempted to deduce the possibility of life and particularly intelligent life, in the galaxy. The mechanical and chemical constituents required are, of course, the same as those which exist on Earth, or at least within narrow limits of them. This would necessarily require the planet to be located at a distance from its star where the range of temperatures would be acceptable to life forms. In short, it would not be in the sub-zero conditions at the outer limits of a system such as our distant Pluto experiences. Neither could it be so close to its star that it became a boiling cauldron like our planet Mercury. With these essential parameters in mind, planets with an abundance of hydrogen-rich gases, water and energy sources have a high probability of producing living cells which in time would evolve to life as we know it. As those conditions are common throughout the galaxy, Sagan and Drake concluded quite reasonably, that life must also be common. They then become quite philosophical by considering that those life forms could become intelligent. They reason that as we have achieved our present level of technology at the halfway mark in the life of our sun, there would be 100 billion suitable planets in the galaxy with billions of years available to them to reach intellectual status. Even if a small percentage avoided self destruction by ecological pollution or by nuclear suicide, they consider the number of potentially advanced technologies could be numbered in millions.

With this data in mind, our radio telescopes scan the heavens for that single signal which would tell us we are not alone - but we have heard **nothing!**

Could it be we are listening on the wrong frequency? This is extremely unlikely as so few frequencies are suitable. The Big Bang background radiation, together with other electromagnetic and ionised atmospheric interference would largely mask intentional intergalactic communication. There is, however, a quiet zone amongst these spurious frequencies and it exists in the 21cm. band. Nearby is the 1420 megacycle frequency which is emitted when the hydrogen electron inverts and spins in a counter-direction to the proton. As there is an abundance of hydrogen in interstellar gas, this emission is rapidly absorbed and the frequency could, therefore, on one hand be advantageous for communication, but also require considerably more power than other frequencies. Saturated as our minds had become with sine 56 degrees and its harmonic, we found it quite surprising that 10 x sine 56 (**8.29037572**) translated into centimetres was **21.058** compared to the **21.127cm**. wave length of the **1420 megahertz** frequency, but surely the influence of SET could not go that far.

Returning to our search for ET, it must be understood that our telescopes have other things to do than search for ET and the time available to listen out is limited. In fact, if the Roswell incident is true, and it might well be, why then would we bother to listen out at all? How can we reconcile countless accounts of encounters of the First, Second and even the **THIRD** kind, with spending millions of dollars trying to hear a radio transmission from beings with whom we are (according to some best-selling authors), exchanging information on a daily basis?

Having, at this time, only concentrated on a small percentage of the available stars, one may think it not surprising that we have heard nothing, but even with all the other anomalies aside, are we overlooking an obvious factor - **TIME**?

Drake and Sagan suggest that the nearest likely position of an intelligence sufficiently advanced to know how to transmit on the intergalactic network would be some 300 light years away. This rather rules out two-way conversations which would require 600 years from question to response, but that is not our immediate concern. On Earth, long before intergalactic antennas were constructed, spurious signals from Tesla, Marconi and our early broadcasting stations were leaking outward through space by default. More recently, penetrative microwaves have been used and these signals now form a sphere of emission some 20 light years in radius. Where then are the signals of those advanced technologies which predate ours by a million years?

There are none!

Consider the thousands of space freighters, ploughing between distant planets and transmitting powerful signals back to their bases, unfettered by atmospheric interference.

There are none!

Consider the signals from billions of satellite directional beacons pulsing away for thousands of years.

There are none!

Even supposing every transmission on Earth stopped at this very moment, our electromagnetic ripple would continue outward for aeons, and with advanced enhancement it would be recognisable as having an intelligent origin. Where also are the television transmissions from millions of cultures over millions of years?

There are none!

Let us reconsider the possibility of the spontaneous appearance of genetically manipulated Man. For this to be so, there must be at least one intelligence out there and with luck there may even be two, but they must be the only two who have survived the hazardous scenario we are about to describe. The burning question is, will we be the third? The reader is, at this stage, conversant with all the factors necessary for him to deduce the answer to this enigma.

For life to exist on a planet long enough to become intelligent by natural evolution, would require millions of years of comparative serenity. It would also need to be positioned in an Earth-like orbit round its parent star. Sagan and Drake make many comparisons with the mechanics of our solar system when making their assessments; why then do they totally exclude any mention of those 'vandals' of destruction of which we are now so fully aware:-

THE COMETS!

These are every bit as much a part of the solar system family as we are, so why would they not equally exist in any other system, to threaten and destroy the life bearing planets. It could surely never be that our system is the only one plagued by the Typhon.

Let us apply the mathematics of comets and asteroids to the Sagan/Drake equation and see what happens. Clube and Napier of the Royal Observatory of Edinburgh estimate the probability of celestial impact as follows:-

Cat.1	An impact with a	**30.8 km**	body every	360	million years.
Cat.2	``	``	``	**10.9 km**	``	``	58
Cat.3	``	``	``	**5 km**	``	``	14
Cat.4	``	``	``	**3.9 km**	``	``	9.2

It is now firmly established that the Cretaceous destruction of the dinosaurs was a **Category 2** impact, which means that even now, another impact is well overdue.

Are we living on borrowed time?

Furthermore, consider how long it would have taken for intelligence to have 'evolved' on Earth, had that evolution not been artificially accelerated. The simple answer is that we would have been destroyed long before we could have constructed an Arecibo aerial. Regrettably, the planetary location required to spawn intelligence happens to be the very one which would ensure its destruction before it could achieve galactic status.

That is why no signals are heard!

Our creators, or rather those who accelerated our intellectual development, were an exception. Against all the odds they survived. By the very rare chance, which must occur when the numbers are sufficiently large, their planet survived long enough for them to achieve, not only star-ship, but possibly time-ship status and in the latter category may lie the answer to the

UFO phenomenon, but we must leave that explanation for another time. Suffice to say that we have indeed stumbled across possibly the only explanation which could solve that conundrum.

However, knowing, as our creators would, how in the nature of things intelligence could never evolve in the available time of a suitably located planet, they began the process of genetically elevating animal life wherever it existed in an acceptable form. It was our good fortune, that on Earth they found a biped sufficiently close to their image to consider it worthy of intellectual advancement. It could be that they created us for no other reason than to gather the materials they required for their continuing trek of survival in this hostile galaxy. Alternatively, it may be that with the highest motives, they are doing their humble best to preserve that rare jewel or parasitic by-product of the galactic morass - INTELLIGENCE. It may be difficult for us to accept, but the galaxy is an inorganic mechanism where the interplay of immense forces produces an ever changing kaleidoscope of events so varied as to probably deny the possibility of their analysis by the mathematical criteria we have established. Life, even in its most simple form, may be nothing more than a contamination - a rare, occasional fungus on the leaves of the magnificent galactic tree. If that parasitic fungus persists long enough, it mutates into an intelligent, free moving biped - Man, which in time could become something capable of infecting the whole galaxy.

Could it be that life is the only discordant note in the 'Music of the Spheres'? If this is so, should we not in such isolation, be ashamed not to admit to our origins and our mentors? As a galactic disease, it will only be in our ability to become mobile enough to escape our dangerous locality, that there is any chance of survival. Before the 'GODS' left to continue their work elsewhere, they gave us the wherewithal to survive. If we ignore their existence and their warning,we will do so at our peril!

The intelligence we have acquired has allowed us to develop our sciences, the predominant aim of which should be to protect Mankind from the only force capable of its annihilation - celestial impact.

Will we continue to exhaust our resources and misuse our sciences pursuing meaningless religious and territorial conflicts? Will we be destroyed in our infancy for our blindness to recognise our universal threat - **THE COMET?**

ACKNOWLEDGMENTS

The authors would like to express their gratitude to the I.G.N. (Institut Géographique National) France for supplying the necessary mapping; to Autodesk whose CAD (Computer Aided Design) program provided the means to refine our calculations; to 'Scientific American' who keep the world informed of Man's scientific progress and to NASA who have opened our eyes to the universe about us.

Also to those persons who are so deeply involved in the subject with which our research deals; to Henry Lincoln who whetted our appetites at the onset; to John Michell, Peter Tompkins, Kenneth Grant and Godfrey Higgins upon whose research we have relied.

And to those dedicated astronomers whose vigilance may one day be our saving grace, in particular to Victor Clube and Bill Napier who in *The Cosmic Winter* warned Mankind of the probability of celestial impact.

Lastly to our publisher who has taught us how to punctuate a text - 'modern style' - and not forgetting poor Mollie who suffered countless hours of typing words which were completely unknown to her 'spell-checker'.

BIBLIOGRAPHY

AVAILABLE IN ENGLISH

BAIGENT, MICHAEL & LEIGH, RICHARD,
    The Temple and the Lodge,   Jonathan Cape, London, 1989,
    The Dead Sea Scrolls Deception,   Jonathan Cape, London, 1991.
BELLAMY, H.S., *The Atlantis Myth,*   Faber & Faber, London, 1948
BERLITZ, CHARLES, *The Philadelphia Experiment,*
                                    Ballantine, New York, 1979
BLAVATSKY, H.P., *Isis Unveiled,*
        Theosophical University, Pasadena, California, USA, 1976,
      The Secret Doctrine,
        Theosophical University, Pasadena, California, USA, 1976
BOSWELL, WINTHROP PALMER,
      The Gods of Egypt and the Saints of Ireland,   RILKO, London
BUECHNER, COLONEL H, *The Emerald Cup-Ark of Gold,*
           Thunderbird Press, Metairie, Louisiana, USA, 1991
CATHIE, BRUCE, *Bridge to Infinity,*
         Quark Enterprises Ltd.,Auckland, New Zealand, 1983
CHATELAIN, MAURICE, *Our Ancestors Came From Outer Space,*
                           Pan Books, London, 1980
CLUBE, VICTOR & NAPIER, BILL,
      The Cosmic Serpent,   Faber & Faber, London, 1982
      The Cosmic Winter   Basil Blackwell Ltd, Oxford, 1990
DONNELLY, IGNATIUS, *Ragnarok,*   Multimedia Publications, New York, 1971
DORESSE, JEAN, *The Secret Books of the Egyptian Gnostics,*
                         Hollis & Carter, London, 1970
DRUMMOND, PROFESSOR HENRY, *The Ascent of Man,*
                Hodder & Stoughton, London, 1894
ECO, UMBERTO, *Foucault's Pendulum,*   Picador, London, 1989
ESCHENBACH, WOLFRAM VON, *Parzifal,*   Penguin Books, London, 1982
FANTHORPE, REV. LIONEL, *Secrets of Rennes-le-Château,*
            S.Weiser, York Beach, Maine, USA, 1991
GRANT, KENNETH, *The Magical Revival,*   Frederick Muller, London, 1972,
      Nightside of Eden   Frederick Muller, London, 1973,
      Cults of the Shadows   Frederick Muller, London, 1975,
      Aleister Crowley and the Hidden God,
                Frederick Muller, London, 1973
HAWKINS, G.S., *Beyond Stonehenge,*   Arrow Books, London, 1977
HIGGINS, GODFREY, *Anacalypsis,*   Health Research, USA, 1972
HOYLE, PROFESSOR FRED, *On Stonehenge,*
      Heinemann Educational Books, Ltd., London, 1977
KUHN, ALVIN BOYD, *The Lost Light,*   Academy Press, New Jersey, 1948

LINCOLN, HENRY, BAIGENT, MICHAEL & LEIGH, RICHARD,
    The Holy Blood and the Holy Grail, Jonathan Cape, London, 1982
LINCOLN, HENRY, *The Holy Place*,   Jonathan Cape, London, 1991
McLEISH, JOHN, *Number*,   Harper/Collins, London, 1992
MICHELL, JOHN, *The New View over Atlantis*,
    Thames & Hudson, London,1983,
    The Dimensions of Paradise, Thames & Hudson, London, 1988,
    Ancient Metrology,   Pentacle Books, Bristol, 1981
MOON, PETER, *The Montauk Project*,   Sky Books, New York, 1992
RAHN, OTTO, *Crusade Against the Grail*,   Germany, 1933
    Lucifer's Courtiers,   Germany, 1936
ROWAN-ROBINSON, MICHAEL, *Ripples in the Cosmos*,
    W.H.Freeman & Co., London, 1992
SINCLAIR, ANDREW, *The Sword and the Grail*, Random House, London,1993
SUMPTION, JONATHAN, *The Albigensian Crusade*,   Faber & Faber, London,
    1978
TEMPLE, ROBERT, *The Sirius Mystery*,   Futura Publications, London, 1976
TOMPKINS, PETER, *Magic of the Obelisk*,   Harper & Row, New York, 1981
    Secrets of the Great Pyramid, Penguin Books, London, 1973
VELIKOVSKY, EMMANUEL, *Worlds in Collision*,
    Victor Gollancz, London, 1969
WILSON, ROBERT ANTON, *The Cosmic Trigger*,
    New Falcon Publications, Scottsdale, Arizona, USA, 1991
WILSON, STEVE, *The Dead Sea Scrolls and the Lost Religion*,
    The Atlantis Bookshop, London, 1993
WOOD, DAVID, *GENISIS*,   Genisis Trading, Tunbridge Wells, England, 1984

AVAILABLE IN FRENCH

BOUDET, ABBE HENRI, *La Vraie Langue Celtique et le Cromlech de Rennes-
    les-Bains*,   Belisane, Nice, 1984
FEUGERE, PIERRE, MAXENT, LOUIS SAINT & KOKER, GASTON de,
    Le Serpent Rouge,   V.R.E.S., Malakoff, 1979
LAMY, MICHEL, *Initie et Initiateur*,   Payot, Paris, 1984
LOBINEAU, HENRI, *Les Dossiers Sécret*,   Microfiche, Paris 4° Lm 249
MARIE, FRANCK, *La Résurrection du Grand Cocu*,   V.R.E.S., Malakoff, 1981
    La Surprenant message de JULES VERNE,   V.R.E.S., Bagneux, 1981
ROBIN, JEAN, *Opération Orth*,   Editions de la Maisnie, Paris, 1989
SEDE, GERARD de, *L'Or de Rennes...*,   Juillard-Tallandier, Paris, 1967
VERNE, JULES, *La Chasse au Météore*,   Hetzel, Paris, 1905
    Hector Servadac,   Hetzel, Paris, 1878
    Around the World in 80 Days,   Hetzel, Paris,
    Clovis d'Ardentor,   Hetzel, Paris,
    Journey to the Centre of the Earth,   Hetzel, Paris, 1864
    20,000 Leagues Under the Sea,   Hetzel, Paris, 1861

APPENDIX 1.

The Mathematical Principles Involved in the Solution of the Design of the Rennes-le-Château Layout.

A general knowledge of the trigonometrical ratios and a scientific calculator are all that is required to confirm the mathematics involved in the solution. There are, however, certain items which lie outside the general mathematical syllabus and to understand these at the outset is essential.

    1.   Initially it is important to realise that a unique pentagonal figure may be generated from a circle of fifteen divisions. One point of the pentagram falls outside the circle, but all the star-points are still 36 degrees. This figure has also a number of other surprising properties.

    2.   Constructing a tangential square to the circle and extending it to a rectangle, the extension can be controlled by the exterior apex of the pentagram. By rotating the rectangle, a specific point can be found whereby the dimensions of this rectangle achieve another remarkable set of properties.

    3.   On to this ground plan the designers have superimposed other special figures, also with unique properties, but furthermore synchronising with ground positions, some of the names of which correspond to their geometric function.

    4.   The designers were also aware that by the time the figure was discovered and analysed, units of measure could have changed sufficiently to largely destroy the expertise of the message they wished to convey. To avoid this, they used an ingenious combination of angular and linear measure that would survive in perpetuity. This was achieved by using the 'Sine' values of angles as their linear measure. These values subjected to a 100,000 multiple disclosed this measure as being very close to the British Inch. It would also greatly assist the reader to understand that the 3-4-5 Pythagorean triangle has Sine values of .6 - .8 and 1.0. If the triangle was, therefore, so designed as to display the values 6x, 8x and 10x corresponding to the Sine values of the angles, the 'x' value could be deduced and the intention of the designers could be immediately realised and furthermore, the particular unit of measure would be identifiable.

    5.   Lastly,it is also essential to fully appreciate the peculiarities of the ratio Phi(1.618033989) - the Golden Mean and in particular that its reciprocal(0.618033989), when halved is precisely the Sine value of 18 degrees (0.309016994).

APPENDIX 2.

THE RATIOS OF PHI AND PI.

The Phi ratio can be demonstrated in a number of ways, both geometrically and mathematically. The simplest way to understand it is to recognise that there is only one point of division on a line which will harmonise the two resultant sections with the original whole. In the following diagram if the line **AB** has been divided at the point of the Golden Section - '**C**'.

A   C   B

Then **AC : CB** is as **CB : AB**, or **AC/CB = CB/AB**, or **AC x AB = CB²**.

With AB = to 100 the Golden division would occur with: AC = 38.1966 and **CB = 61.8033989**. Now this integer value of the **Golden Section (0.618033989)**, is the reciprocal of the **Golden Mean (1.618033989)**, and these numbers perform in quite a strange way. For example:-

$$(1.618033989)^2 = 2.618033989$$

In other words to square the Golden Mean we have only to add "one". Also:-

$$1/1.618033989 = 0.618033989$$

which means, to find the reciprocal of the Golden Mean we have only to subtract one. When written as equations these attributes look quite odd:-

$$x^2 = x + 1 \text{ and } 1/x = x - 1$$

Leonardo Fibonacci (1170 - 1250), also known as Leonardo of Pisa introduced the Arabic number system to Europe and, amongst other things, he discovered the Fibonacci Series which produces the Golden Mean at infinity.

This series is produced by simply adding the last two terms together 'ad-infinitum'.

1/2/3/5/8/13/21/34/55/89/144/233/377/610/987/1597/2584/4181/6765/10946/17711/28657/etc.

If one then divides any number, by the one which precedes it, one obtains better and better approximations for the Golden Mean. By the time one divides the 22nd term by the the 21st a very accurate figure emerges:- **28657/17711 = 1.61803399** With modern calculators, however, one has only to execute:-

$$2/(\sqrt{5}-1) = 1.61803399 \quad \text{The symbol for \textbf{PHI} is Ø.}$$

PI is, of course, the very common ratio which controls all matters relating to the circle. Once again, it is an irrational number and has never been fully evaluated, even though in 1989 it was calculated to 1011 million decimal places.

For our purposes the calculator value, **3.141592654** is quite accurate enough. Simply by multiplying the diameter of a circle by this number, one obtains the circumference. Alternatively, dividing the circumference by this number gives the diameter. In the case of 'holy' constructions, dividing the perimeter by this number should give the 'holy' height or some other concealed dimension.

The symbol for **PI** is π

301

APPENDIX 3.

THE THEORETICAL PENTAGRAM.

The reader will recall that the ground pentagram at Rennes-le-Château is an almost perfect rendition of a remarkable symmetric pentagonal figure generated by a 15 division circle. Being symmetrical the figure can be easily evaluated trigonometrically. The calculated values shown below are based upon the circle having a radius of unity (1), and with the left pentagonal side placed parallel to the Temple rectangle. A close examination of these values reveals how the Phi ratio is demonstrated to perfection in some places, but is a near miss in others. As the geometry of the ground figure in this book has shown, it is slightly and obviously modified to achieve the perfect compromise which was intended by the designers. The evaluation of the theoretical pentagram is as follows:-

PQ & RS	TEMPLE WIDTH	= 2
PS & QR	TEMPLE LENGTH	= 2.538843999
AB & AC	PENTAGONAL TRIANGLE BODY SIDE	= 2.404867172
BC	" " BASE SIDE	= 1.48628965
ABC	" " PERIMETER	= 6.296023995
	(2 = 6.283185307 i.e.	= 0.006)
AM PENTAGONAL TRIANGLE PERPENDICULAR		= 2.287164593
AX	PENTAGONAL EXTENSION.	= 0.618033989(GS) or (1/Ø)
AY	BODY PERPENDICULAR EXTENDED	
	TO CIRCUMFERENCE	= 2.618033989 (Ø+1)
OM	CIRCLE CENTRE TO PENTAGONAL	
	TRIANGLE BASE	= 0.669130606
MY	EXTENSION FROM PENTAGONAL	
	BASE TO CIRCUMFERENCE	= 0.33086939
DE	PENTAGONAL ARM CHORD	= 1.732050808 (√3)
EB & DC	" UNDERARM CHORD	= 1.989043791
PQRS	TEMPLE PERIMETER	= 9.077683538
PR & SQ	" DIAGONAL	= 3.23198528
PU & QV	" EXTENSION	= 0.538841769
VS & UR DIAGONAL OF TEMPLE SQUARE		= 2 / 2√2.828427125
UQ & PV	" " COURTYARD	= 2.071316116
PQVU	PERIMETER OF COURTYARD	= 5.077683538
ABEDC	PENTAGONAL UNICURSAL LINE	= 10.51987273

OT   PERPENDICULAR FROM ARM CHORD TO CIRCLE CENTRE. = 0.5
ANGLE PSQ = 38.22962913°   (The Sin of which is 0.61814699)
Oce   OF CIRCLE = 2πR   = 6.283185307

* NB AB/BC = 1.618033989 = Ø

THE THEORETICAL FIGURE

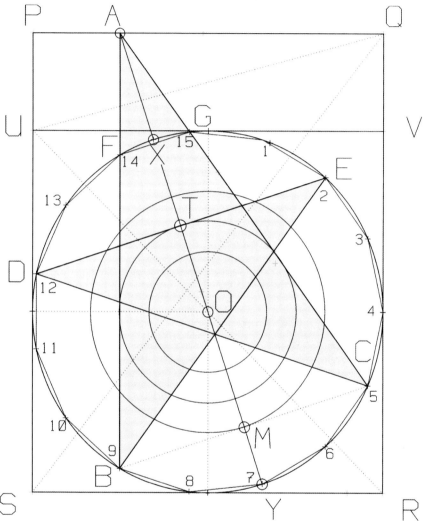

Fig. 29. The dimensions of the theoretical figure are given opposite (p302) as ratios resulting from a circle of radius 1. By multiplying any alternative radius by these figures, the Temple dimensions can be evaluated. Mathematicians will appreciate how, by using the correct radius and with the subtle movement of the pentagram described in the text, the designers caused the figure to synchronise with the Phi factors. In the theoretical figure this cannot be achieved.

The summary of these properties may be tabulated as follows:-

1. As in the regular pentagram, this figure maintains the 36-360 pentagonal and circular relationship.
2. In addition it identifies the orientation of the female body.
3. It maintains the pentagonal angles and introduces the cyclic numerals.
4. The male hexagonal chord is incorporated into the body of the female in three aspects. DE-FB-GC.
5. In the controlling divisions of the circle it expresses the doctrine of the Goddess 15.
6. By the axis of symmetry it demonstrates the thirty divisions of the Druid circle.
7. The association of the circle to the female pentagonal body is confirmed by the perimeter of the former triangle closely equating with the circumference of the circle from which it was generated.
8. The radius forming the axis of symmetry and extended to the apex of the pentagram achieves the Golden Mean at the intersection with the circumference.
9. The pentagonal legs are so divided as to form a Golden Division when related to the extended body chord.
10. The figure forms the base upon which can be constructed the Vesica Piscis and the androgenous geometry of the Star Union of pentagram and hexagram. The figure accommodates this union by either internal or external sexual geometry.

The temple diagonal alerts one to the possible presence of the Golden Mean if the figure is slightly modified.

Although it is not absolutely essential for the reader to absorb the finer points of the geometry outlined in this book, it is essential to realise that this incredible figure has never been found in any mathematical, geometrical or sacred geometrical study as yet published!

APPENDIX 4.

THE GODDESS FIFTEEN.

In the geometry of Rennes-le-Château we first saw the Circle of Churches was the 'carrier' for a pentagram of a unique type. It was based on fifteen divisions of the circle. This profound geometric image of femininity achieves a number of special properties by virtue of the fact that the legs are opened beyond the normal position found in the common pentagram of the five division circle. We are, thereby, shown that this previously undiscovered pentagram is obviously the sigil of the 'Goddess Fifteen'. Ancient texts refer to her in terms which lead us to believe the doctrine was known at the time the design of Rennes-le-Château was conceived.

In considering how mathematically advanced the designers of the Temple were, it would not be difficult to credit them, or their predecessors with knowledge of the body fluids and processes. It is indeed surprising that out present physiological knowledge appears to overlook them. To achieve a deeper understanding of the function of the Goddess Fifteen, we would refer our readers to the works of he who is the most informed on that subject - Kenneth Grant, his books are listed in the bibliography. Despite the fact that the existence of the 15 radial pentagram was not known to him when these books were written, with great foresight he predicts not only its geometric possibility, but also speaks of the close associations which we have found in our studies of the doctrinal implications at Rennes-le-Château. The following passage from his *Nightside of Eden*, typifies his deep understanding of these matters:-

> "The magical instrument ascribed to the 16th Path is the Seat, Throne, or Altar, which are curiously feminine symbols for a kala associated with the Hierophant until it is remembered that, in the New Aeon, the 'Lord initiating (i.e. the hierophant), is the god Set, who is identical with his Mother, Typhon, and therefore the continuation - as has been shown - of her kala, 15. She is in fact the Goddess 15, a name given to the Woman Fulfiled whose symbol, the full moon, occurred on the 15th day. The 16th kala was therefore her child, i.e. Set and Set-Typhon under a single image was typified by the Dog Star, Sothis. According to Wilkinson, Set-Typhon was known as 'The Giant' and this symbolism equates it with the pre-eval Nephilim."

> (Kenneth Grant *Nightside of Eden* p187)

We would now ask the reader to recall the 'triple' ring construction of the Circle of Churches (61,8033989 x 3 = 185,410.1966, the circle radius). Once again we will refer to Grant. Here he is speaking of a Triad, the Great One - Wisdom and the Seed:-

> "This Triad is the most attenuated expression of the triple ring surrounding the Goddess Fifteen in the yantra of Kali. I have interpreted this yantra in accordance with my understanding of Vama doctrine The invocation of the Goddess is therefore a direct invocation of cosmic power and an unsealing of

the Eight Directions with a consequent and reverberant opening of the Four Great Gateways of Outer Space through which the power inflows."

(Grant *Aleister Crowley and the Hidden God* p38)

It is probably only coincidental that the product of the Goddess (15), her directions (8), SET (56) and the 'method' (69,) produce a number at the 'root' of which we find the enigmatic 681

From Kuhn's *The Lost Light*, we find references which echo through the Egyptian, Biblical and geophysical factors which have surfaced in our investigations:-

"The goddess-mother Ishtar (the Hebrew Esther!) of Akkad was, like Venus and Hathor, designated "the Goddess Fifteen": being named from the date of the full moon or her productive heyday. The Egyptian goddess exclaims: "I have made the eye of Horus when it was not coming on the festival of the fifteenth day." This is perhaps a reminder that at an early day the moon revolution was more definitely known than the solar cycle, and the fourteenth was counted as the date of the full moon. Ishtar is described as ascending and descending the steps of the moon, fifteen up and down in consonance with her title of Goddess Fifteen. In *Pseudo-Matthew* (Ch.4), we learn that when the Virgin was an infant, just weaned, she ran up the fifteen steps of the temple at full speed without one looking back. In the *History of Joseph the Carpenter* Jesus says that Mary gave him birth in the fifteenth year of her age, by a mystery that no creature can understand except the Trinity. And Mary is the Egyptian Meri, who was Hathor, the Goddess Fifteen.

The *Pistis Sophia* dates the Transfiguration of Jesus on the fifteenth day of the month Tybi, the day of the full moon. The resurrection, of new birth, was always reckoned in Egypt on the full moon of this month, and as it came close after the winter solstice, about December 27 (Massey), it points to the Christmas nativity as being either ignorantly confused or knowingly identified with both the Transfiguration and the Resurrection. An address to Isis in the Ritual runs:

'I have come to see thee and thy beauties within the Utcha in thy name of Heb-enti-ses (i.e. the sixth-day festival). Thou has conquered heaven by the greatness of thy majesty in thy name of "Prince of the festival of the fifteenth day!" ... Gods and men live at sight of thee. Thou risest to us ...'

In the Ritual of the Mother is she who "gives thee water on every first and every fifteenth day of the month."

Although we would very much doubt it, if the reader needs to be further convinced and have a deeper understanding of the Goddess Fifteen, we would refer them to: *Nightside of Eden, Cults of the Shadow, Aleister Crowley and the Hidden God* ... all by Kenneth Grant, and *The Lost Light* by Alvin Boyd Kuhn

APPENDIX 5.

THE SLOTTED TEMPLET MAPPING SYSTEM.

This system, otherwise known as radial control, was a method of producing maps from aerial photographs when only a limited number of ground control positions were known. The technique was used extensively during World War II when unmapped areas needed to be overflown and mapped prior to making troop movements on the ground.

The surveying aircraft flew a straight, level line taking ground shots at regular intervals to ensure that each photograph overlapped those adjacent to it. This was then repeated with a return line overlapping the first, and so on.

Each photograph is then temporarily attached to a cardboard or acetate carrier. The geometric centre (the Nadir), and eight or more other ground positions are pricked through the photograph and recorded on the templet. The centre position is 'hole - punched' and the remaining positions form the centre of a slot, cut in such a manner as to be a radial from the centre point. Using rivet-like buttons, with holes through them, the templets are then assembled by clipping all the templets which share points of common identity. The slots allow each templet to slide within their respective radials.

Next a carrier-board is prepared with any known triangulated points marked by fixed posts. The jigsaw puzzle of templets are then laid over these posts with the commonly identified positions corresponding. To achieve this it is necessary to juggle the templets until they expand or contract to register. This establishes an average common scale throughout the structure.

Each sliding button is now fixed and by pricking through the centre holes, a comprehensive set of fixed points are transformed to the carrier.

The carrier can then be used by draughtsmen to create a map of the area. From this stage the composite base can be photographically reduced to the required scale. After this photographic plates from each colour printing are prepared which, when lithographically printed in register, produce the multi-coloured map.

INDEX